THE GREATEST

SCI-FI MOVIES

NEVER MADE

DAVID HUGHES

FOREWORD BY H.R.GIGER

AFTERWORD BY HARRY KNOWLES

a cappella

Dedication

Dedicated to all the writers, directors and producers still
looking for the green light at the end of the tunnel.

Picture Credits

Colour section:

Pages 1–3: all images copyright © H. R. Giger. All rights reserved.

For more information on H. R. Giger's art, visit www.hrgigermuseum.com

Pages 4–5: all images copyright © Neal Adams. All rights reserved.

Pages 6–7: all images copyright © Graham Humphreys. All rights reserved.

Page 8: copyright © Twentieth Century Fox Film Corporation. All rights reserved.

Cover design: Monica Baziuk

Front cover image: Tim Simmons/Getty Images

Copyright © 2001 David Hughes. All rights reserved.

Foreword copyright © 2001 H. R. Giger. All rights reserved.

Afterword copyright © 2001 Harry Knowles. All rights reserved.

Published by arrangement with Titan Publishing Group Ltd

144 Southward Street, London SE1 0UP, England

This edition published by A Cappella Books

An imprint of Chicago Review Press, Incorporated

814 North Franklin Street

Chicago, Illinois 60610

ISBN 1-55652-449-8

Printed in the United States of America

5   4   3   2   1

THE GREATEST

SCI-FI MOVIES

NEVER MADE

Contents

Foreword

I think a lot of people will be very interested in this book and its revelations, because for every film that is shot in Hollywood, there are many other fascinating projects that never make it to the screen. I've certainly had a lot of experience of working on films that never got made! Even famous directors, like Ridley Scott and James Cameron, can find that technology is not yet as advanced as their ideas, or discover that everything simply costs too much money. Science fiction films especially can prove to be very expensive compared to something like a small drama, which will have no special effects, just actors and locations.

So, what often happens to these unused stories? It seems to me that everybody helps themselves to the ideas, until there's nothing left that hasn't already found its way into other films. It's as if these unmade scripts are just there to give others inspiration; eventually there's little point in actually filming them. That's particularly true of one unrealised project I designed, *The Tourist*, as you will see from reading this book.

One of my earliest film experiences was working on *Dune*. I was surprised to learn from Alejandro Jodorowsky, the first director to take on the project, that set builders would take my artworks and then actually create them. Originally, I thought they would use my paintings as the actual background scenery — not just as the basis for the finished sets. At first, this discovery held out to me the promise of seeing my artworks faithfully translated three-dimensionally, just as I had imagined them. In fact, I should have seen it as a warning. A screenwriter or a film designer is fortunate if their film is ever made, and very lucky if they still recognize it when it is. In the case of *Dune*, when the film was finally made by David Lynch, none of my designs were used in it. Later, I worked with Bill Malone on concepts for his film *Dead Star*, which eventually came out under the name *Supernova* (and wasn't very good, I heard). I was pleased with my paintings and drawings for *Dead Star*, but everything had been changed by the time *Supernova* was released.

Based as I am in Zurich, I feel it's impossible to produce really good work for a film that's being made in another country. *Alien* was different, because I was actually at Shepperton Studios for seven months, and I modelled the alien myself — I have never had another project as satisfying as *Alien*. I did work with Ridley Scott again years later, making concept sketches for a science fiction project called *The Train*. Unfortunately, the film was never made, but I was able to use of some of those ideas in the train I later built for the dream sequence in *Species*. It is now on display in my museum, waiting to be returned to service in *The Mystery of San Gottardo*, my own film idea which I hope to see produced.

I didn't want to have my name on the last few films I've worked on, because, frankly, they were so bad. I think my movie work became more difficult when I stopped doing airbrushed artwork; now I draw. If you create a really good, finished painting with an airbrush, everything is in it, meaning film-makers can't change very much. But if you just produce a drawing, they can change *everything* — coming up with strange 'interpretations', which are usually not as good. It's always terribly stressful.

The last film I worked on was *Species II* (which, I have to admit, ended up as one of the worst films I've ever seen). I was asked too late in the development process to be properly involved with the making of the film, and the producer was constantly looking at the cost of the designs, rather than the designs themselves. Ultimately, other people's ideas were used, because, I was told, mine were too expensive. I felt bitter about that. I may have been well paid, but you also need satisfaction as an artist. Now, instead of being the designer, I would rather take a credit as a consultant.

Eventually I realised that if I'm not there in person, there's little chance of getting a good result. To get my ideas through, to get them onscreen, I have to work with the film-makers face-to-face. If you hand over your designs and then go away for two months, and they fail to do a good job, it's too late to change anything. If you just send over a drawing, and a new design is 'based' on it, your ideas get changed. In the end, the design will be more theirs than mine. That really upsets me, but it's difficult to point it out to people in Hollywood — they don't like criticism.

If I were to design another film, I would need to work here in Zurich, although that's not easy either! I tried it on *Species*, but it was hard to find really good technicians, like they have in Hollywood, to work with. So, in the end, the only satisfying film experience I've had was *Alien* — which, thankfully, *did* make it to the screen. These days, I would rather a film was not made at all, than made badly. ∎

H. R. Giger

Museum H. R. Giger, Gruyeres, Switzerland, July 2001

Destination:
Development Hell

How Alfred Bester's *The Stars My Destination* Took A Jaunt To Hollywood

"Has reached a dead end."

—Merchant Marine verdict on Gulliver Foyle AS-128/127:006,
in *The Stars My Destination* by Alfred Bester

In the early fifties, science fiction writer Alfred Bester published a four-part story entitled *Tiger! Tiger!* in the pages of *Galaxy*, the same respected magazine in which his first novel, *The Demolished Man*, had appeared serially a few years earlier. The combined impact of *The Demolished Man* and *Tiger! Tiger!* (published in novel form in 1953 and 1956 respectively) was felt throughout the genre; a shockwave which sent the science fiction community back to its typewriters in search of something that had been missing, but which Bester had in spades: style. After Bester, no longer would adolescent prose be indulged simply because the vast majority of readers were adolescents; nor would just a gripping yarn or intriguing premise be enough: the writing itself would also have to soar.

Born in 1913, Bester had begun his career in the science fiction pulp magazines of the forties, most notably *The Magazine of Fantasy & Science Fiction*, launched in 1949. Bester also wrote regularly for such comic book characters as Superman and the Green Lantern during the medium's Golden Age, and scripted radio serials, including *Charlie Chan* and *The Shadow*, before conquering yet another medium — television — with stories for *Tom Corbett: Space Cadet*. The publication of *The Demolished Man* and *Tiger! Tiger!* — the latter slightly revised and published in the US under the title *The Stars My Destination* — was both the best of times and the worst of times; although he went on writing until his death in 1987, he never produced work that was anything like as powerful as his first two novels.

Of the two books, *The Stars My Destination* was the most radically inventive, pinning its story — set in the twenty-fifth century, when humans travel short distances by teleportation or 'jaunting' — not on an intrepid space hero, but on the lowest of the low: Gulliver "Gully" Foyle AS-128/127:006, a Mechanic's Mate Third Class on the space freighter, SS *Nomad*. As Bester describes him, "Of all brutes in the world he was among the least valuable alive and most likely to survive... oiler, wiper, bunkerman; too easy for trouble, too slow for fun, too empty for friendship, too lazy for love." His official Merchant Marine personnel record damned him further: "EDUCATION: NONE. SKILLS: NONE. MERITS: NONE. RECOMMENDATIONS: NONE... A man of physical strength and intellectual potential stunted by lack of ambition. Energies at minimum. The stereotype Common Man. Some unexpected shock might possibly awaken him, but Psych cannot find the key. Not recommended for promotion. Has reached a dead end."

Yet Foyle's story is just beginning, thanks to the "unexpected shock" which Psych correctly surmises might awaken him: the virtual destruction of the *Nomad*, which leaves Foyle as the crew's sole survivor, drifting in space for almost half a year in the wrecked hulk of the ship until the prospect of rescue appears in the form of a passing vessel, the *Vorga*-T:1339. The *Vorga* passes by without slowing, however, setting Foyle on a course that will change his life and shape his destiny: revenge. "After thirty years of existence and six months of torture, Gully Foyle, the stereotype Common Man, was no more. The key turned in the lock of his soul and the door was opened. What emerged expunged the Common Man forever... The acid of fury ran through him, eating away the brute patience and sluggishness that had made a cipher of Gully Foyle, precipitating a chain of reactions that would make an infernal machine of Gully Foyle. He was dedicated. '*Vorga*, I kill you filthy.'" Foyle's sworn oath of vengeance forces the mechanic to engineer his own rescue, following which he pursues the errant *Vorga* with grim determination. Revenge is a dish Bester serves cold — it being very cold in space — with an amoral, vengeful and illiterate anti-hero unrivalled in his single-mindedness, except perhaps by Edmond Dantès, the driven hero of Alexandre Dumas's *The Count of Monte Cristo*, or Walker, the central figure of Donald E. Westlake's novel *Point Blank*. No wonder Bester's book took the science fiction community by storm.

As Neil Gaiman pointed out in his introduction to Millennium's welcome and highly successful 1999 reissue of the novel, Bester was perhaps the only science fiction writer to be revered by his contemporaries of the fifties, by the radical 'New Wave' writers of the sixties and early seventies, and by the 'cyberpunks' of the eighties, many of whom found *The Stars My Destination* to be as inspiring as it was inspired. "When I found myself in the position of having to write a whole novel all by myself," author William Gibson noted, "I remember casting back through my racial memory of SF for a work that might provide a model, a template... What did I *really* like? What, out of all that stuff, was my personal favourite? *The Stars My Destination*." Gaiman was not surprised. "[It] is, after all, the perfect cyberpunk novel," he observed. "It contains such cheerfully protocyber elements as multinational corporate intrigue; a dangerous, mysterious, hyperscientific McGuffin (PyrE); an amoral hero; a supercool thief-woman... "

Yet saying that *The Stars My Destination* was a highly influential book is to detract from the fact that it is also a rip-roaring read, which has somehow managed to date little in the five decades since it was written. Science fiction writers from across the spectrum trip over superlatives and similes when speaking of Bester in general and *The Stars My Destination* in particular: "A dazzling, dizzying, multiple-pronged assault on the senses that leaves you breathless and forever altered", James Lovegrove rhapsodised. Thomas M. Disch called it "one of the great SF novels of the fifties", while Robert Silverberg stated that it was "on everybody's list of the ten greatest SF novels." Samuel R. Delany went still further, suggesting that it might be "the greatest single SF novel", while Joe Haldeman named the book as one of "only a few works of actual genius" which the science fiction field has produced.

With such an enviable fan base, it is unsurprising that Hollywood has long considered *The Stars My Destination* to be suitable for cinematic adaptation. What *is* surprising is that the book has never been filmed. Not in the fifties during the first wave of science fiction cinema; nor in the *Star Wars* period when seemingly every genre novel and short story was optioned, with many filmed; nor during the nineties when the new wave of computer-generated special effects allowed even the most ambitious science fiction stories to be realised on screen. Not that Hollywood hasn't tried. Over the years, numerous screenwriters have been asked to turn their hands to an adaptation of the Bester book, among them Michael Backes (*Rising Sun*), writer-producer David Giler (*Aliens, Alien³*), veteran screenwriter Lorenzo Semple Jr (*The Parallax View, Three Days of the Condor, Flash Gordon*) and William Wisher (*Terminator 2: Judgment Day, Judge Dredd*).

During this interminable development period, the rights to the book were owned by Germany's Neue Constantin Films. The company hoped to secure financing for what would undoubtedly prove to be a costly picture by commissioning influential comic book artist and commercial illustrator Neal Adams to create a series of conceptual drawings for the proposed project. As Adams explains, "You can't always get someone to read a script or a novel instantly, but you can show them a picture as part of a presentation and say, 'This is what it's going to look like.'" Adams was already an admirer of *The Stars My Destination*, not least because its protagonist represented a refreshing break from the typical hero of fifties science fiction. "The heroes of science fiction novels from those days are usually tall lanky men with thinning hair, often wearing glasses, oppressed by some kind of outside corporation," he observes, "and they have to do something to overcome that. That was pretty much the standard. But the hero of *The Stars My Destination* is essentially an illiterate grunt who works in the engine room of a spaceship, who is five steps above an animal and is prone to a modest sense of rage and revenge. He is single-minded in his revenge, and if you cross him, he will eventually get you — sort of like a Charles Bronson type of character. It was one of the first times in science fiction that you presented a character that was not cut from the same mould as everybody else."

Adams also recognised that the story presented certain structural problems when considered in terms of cinematic adaptation, mostly arising from the fact that Bester had written and published it episodically. "Having re-read the story, I knew that there were some really big plot holes," he explains. "When Bester got to the middle, it didn't seem like it related to the beginning, and there is no coming back to the head of the story and resolving it, for an audience to feel a resolution." This understanding of the inherent flaws within the book meant that, when Adams met with one of the film's potential producers, he found that his story suggestions were as welcome as his visual ideas; if not more so. "A whole bunch of guys were working on the script and none of them had really nailed the structural problems in the story," he reveals. "Suddenly I give them solid advice, and they go, 'Oh, well, um, gee — I guess we are going to have to pay you for this.' They offered me $50,000 for twenty-five drawings," he adds, "and [they] didn't say twenty-five approved drawings; or twenty-five drawings in colour; or even twenty-five drawings in pen or ink — I could have done twenty-five drawings on napkins! So I think, 'Gee, that's a lot of money for some drawings...' Then the contract arrives and it had all this stuff about 'story consultation', and I go, 'Oh, I get it.' Between you, me and the fence post, I think they were not so interested in my drawings as in my story contribution."

Nevertheless, Adams was determined to give the producers their money's worth in terms of illustrations, turning out a series of large-scale drawings which defined the future setting of the film in exacting detail. "The future in the book is not very carefully described," he says, "so what I do is pick an image, and then try to do as much design as possible to describe exactly what this place is like. I set the scene and try to establish what it is all about in a way that the author of the book does not do." Among the most elaborate drawings was one of twenty-fifth century Manhattan. "It starts at ground level and goes right up into the top of the city, above St Patrick's Cathedral on Fifth Avenue," Adams explains, "with all these elevated roadways. I created a concept that I call 'spider building': as the planet becomes more populated, there's no room to build on the ground any more, so you build bridges between the upper levels of the tallest buildings, so that they are all connected by a network of bridges and walkways. And then you start putting other buildings on top of these bridges, making a spider web of buildings. And eventually you never actually need to go down to the ground any more, because all of the newest buildings are on the upper levels. So ground level becomes this terrible kind of place, where the first three storeys are like the underground."

Adams applied a similar level of engineering logic to his development of the roadways, which stretch between the maze of buildings. "I developed a technology called 'gravity pods'," he says. "The idea is that when you travel into space, you need temporary gravity in the spaceship, so they've created gravity pods that extend gravity out about three or four hundred yards from the centre of the ship. That concept, developed for interstellar travel, was grabbed by the guys who were building roads on Earth, and they put gravity pods in the elevated roadways, so they could build another road on the underside of the existing one." In this way, city planners were able to double the number of roads by having cars drive on the top of the roads and also underneath. "So you drive upside down, prevented from falling by these gravity pods, and you can look at the underworld, but you wouldn't want to go there because you could get mugged or killed." Adams was clearly satisfied with his work on the film and the producers were similarly impressed; nevertheless, the artist did not hear anything further about the project during its continuing development. "It's no big deal," he says philosophically. "They paid me a big chunk of money and they went on their way." A vision of future Manhattan coincidentally similar to Adams's did make it to the screen eventually: "If you look at the cityscapes in *The Fifth Element*, they look a lot like my designs for *The Stars My Destination*," he notes.

The closest the film ever came to production was around 1996, when British director and avowed science fiction fan Paul Anderson announced *The Stars My Destination* as the subject of his third feature, following *Shopping* and the financially successful video game adaptation *Mortal Kombat*. The script which Anderson and his producing partner Jeremy Bolt intended to film was a draft by David Giler and William Wisher, whom Anderson described to *Cinescape* as "a couple of the best screenwriters working in the States right now." Seeing it as a "classic Shakespearean tale... about a guy who was left for dead aboard a spaceship, left alone in desolation, [who] seeks revenge against those who abandoned him," Anderson was adamant that the special effects the story required would not be allowed to overshadow the characters. "If you don't care about the characters, it doesn't matter how much money you throw up there on the screen," he said, shortly after completing the character-unfriendly *Mortal Kombat* movie. "I remember seeing Han Solo in *Star Wars* and thinking, 'That guy's cool, I want to be like him.' But when I saw *Demolition Man*, I didn't care what happened to those people." Anderson, who brought in conceptual artist Trevor Goring to provide storyboards for his proposed adaptation, claimed that his priority was character development, most notably of Gully Foyle, and that one of the key relationships of the film would be the uneasy alliance between Foyle and a female con artist, Jisbella "Jiz" McQueen, with whom he has an unlikely and wary love affair.

Despite the fact that Anderson ultimately chose the science fiction/horror hybrid *Event Horizon* as his next picture, producer Jeremy Bolt remained convinced that an adaptation of Bester's story was still in their future. "*The Stars My Destination* is a $50 million science fiction epic developed by a German company, [Neue] Constantin Films," he told Graham Jones in 1996. "Paul Anderson will direct it, I will co-produce it, and I will endeavour to make sure it's shot at Pinewood or Shepperton." When *The Stars My Destination* failed to materialise as a 'go' picture, Anderson followed *Event Horizon* with *Soldier*, a futuristic epic based on an original script by *Blade Runner* and *Twelve Monkeys* screenwriter David Webb Peoples. To many observers, *Soldier* contained many of the themes which drove *The Stars My Destination*, most notably the idea of a tattooed 'grunt' who breaks ranks with the higher-ups, who see him as expendable cannon fodder, and discovers his humanity along the way.

Although Anderson's and Bolt's interest in *The Stars My Destination* presumably dissipated when *Soldier* was greenlit by Warner Bros (it ultimately became one of the studio's most expensive flops), Constantin Films continued to pursue the project under the terms of its distribution deal with Twentieth Century Fox — the studio which had, by the mid-nineties, almost single-handedly revived the science fiction genre with the double whammy of *Independence Day* and *The X-Files*. Thus, producer Bernd Eichinger commissioned the screenwriting partnership of Rudy Gaines and John Rice, who had worked in television before writing numerous celebrated but unproduced scripts, to work on an entirely new draft of *The Stars My Destination*.

"By this point, I think they'd already spent six or seven million dollars trying to get a makeable draft," says Gaines, "but they didn't give us any of the other drafts to read. Oftentimes they don't want to give you the previous drafts," he explains, "because they don't want to give you something that doesn't work — they'd rather hear your ideas. If they've got a script that they almost love, then I don't mind reading it, but generally I'd rather just let my own imagination tell the story." Gaines admits that he had not previously read *The Stars My Destination* and had never even heard of Alfred Bester. "But Bernd gave us the book and it was a great read. The thing I like about Bester's stories is that they're very character-based, even though they're big sci-fi things, and *The Stars My Destination* is basically a revenge piece about one man's journey to come from the lowest [level of society] to the highest."

Despite their enthusiasm for the book however, Gaines and Rice immediately saw areas they felt would be problematic in terms of cinema adaptation. "There were some elements of it that I thought weren't going to work on film, mainly the jaunting stuff, where they're teleporting from one place to another," Gaines explains. "They've been doing that on American television since *Bewitched* and I didn't think it was going to work very well on film, so that was one part of the story we omitted. Instead, we decided just to make it more of a straight cinematic revenge story where [Foyle] is trying to get the biggest guy, find out why his ship was destroyed and why he was left out in space.

"We also added a love story element; that there was a woman on that ship he was in love with. I believe in the book he was a mechanic's mate, so he was down in the oil and the grit of the ship's engine, and when the ship was attacked and destroyed by another ship in the very opening of the script, he was able to get to the woman who he was in love with. So they were stranded together, but then she died out there." Not only did this give the story more of an emotional punch, they felt, it also gave Foyle greater motivation for his revenge, beyond the character's sheer single-minded determination to track down and kill those who abandoned him in space. "You really need to pull for this guy, who pretty much kills everybody he comes in contact with," Gaines notes, "and somehow it's more acceptable for American audiences if our hero is seen to be hurting in some way. In the book, what essentially propels him is his own inner horror at being stuck out in space, which to me was a sort of literary conceit — you can write that on the page and get into the depths of his mind. But to me, we needed a more emotional reason for him to take his revenge."

Another potential pitfall which Gaines and Rice managed to overcome was the issue of Foyle's face, which becomes covered in tattoos at an early point in the book — hardly the most appealing character trait for any actor considering the role. As Bester tells it: "He recoiled in terror as the orderly thrust the picture of a hideous tattooed face before him. It was a Maori mask. Cheeks, chin, nose, and eyelids were decorated with stripes and swirls. Across the brow was blazoned NOMAD. Foyle stared, then cried out in agony. The picture was a mirror. The face was his own." Says Gaines, "I just loved the image of him having 'NOMAD' tattooed on his face — it's like the Maori imagery and it makes him more fearsome, so we kept that part. But then we had the tattoo taken off bit by bit by some grungy artist who takes Foyle through the very painful process of having it removed."

Gaines recalls that their draft was greeted enthusiastically by Constantin and Twentieth Century Fox. "I got a call from the head of Fox, Bill Mechanic, saying 'I love this script, we've got to make it.' They said there was no reason why they couldn't make it, but you know how Hollywood is — they found a reason. I don't know what it was, but suddenly they *weren't* making it." Nevertheless, Gaines and Rice subsequently met with Betty Thomas, the former *Hill Street Blues* actress who, as a director, has scored hits with such comedies as *The Brady Bunch Movie*, *Private Parts* and *Dr. Dolittle*. "At some point, Betty Thomas was interested," Gaines remembers. "When we sat down with her, we had all these ideas but I could just tell by being in the room that she wasn't really that attached to the script. She said a few things about what she wanted, which led me to believe that she hadn't thought about it too much."

Since then, Gaines has heard nothing about the script or even whether Constantin Films has renewed its option on the book. "I'm sure they continued to push for it, though, because they wanted it pretty badly and they'd spent a lot of money on it. I have a nice track record of not getting any sci-fi film off the ground," he adds, referring to *Silver Surfer* (see chapter 13), his script for a proposed remake of Douglas Trumbull's *Silent Running* for director Simon West (*Lara Croft: Tomb Raider*) and an unproductive meeting he took with actress-producer Talia Shire regarding another Bester adaptation, *The Demolished Man*. "The thing with these sci-fi films is that they cost so much to make, a lot of things have to fall into place," Gaines concludes. "A big actor's got to say yes; a big director's got to say yes; and the studio's got to be ready to market it. It's almost like the stars have to line up." ∎

A Difficult Childhood

The Unmanifested Destiny Of Arthur C. Clarke's Childhood's End

"It's inevitable that *Childhood's End* gets made."
—Producer Phil DeGuere

In early 1964, film-maker Stanley Kubrick, director of *Spartacus* and *Lolita*, became interested in the possibility of making what he described as "the proverbial good science fiction movie." Having been advised that British scientist and science fiction novelist Arthur C. Clarke was the world's greatest authority on the subject, Kubrick wrote to the author outlining his plans to make a film "of mythic grandeur", whose themes would be "the reasons for believing in the existence of intelligent extra-terrestrial life" and "the impact (and perhaps even lack of impact in some quarters) such discovery would have on Earth in the near future." Clarke and Kubrick, equally impressed with each other's *oeuvre*, agreed to meet in New York — appropriately enough during the 1964 World's Fair, where speculation about the planet's future and the cream of its technology would be on display. "[Kubrick] wanted to make a movie about Man's relation to the universe," Clarke later recalled, "something which had never been attempted. [He was] determined to create a work of art which would arouse the emotions of wonder, awe... even, if appropriate, terror."

Kubrick was particularly taken with the themes of Clarke's 1954 novel *Childhood's End*, in which humans discover that the evolution of mankind has been shaped by extraterrestrial, devil-like beings known as the Overlords, which return to Earth in gigantic circular ships to usher mankind towards its destiny among the stars. When it transpired that another film-maker owned the rights, Clarke suggested his 1948 short story 'Sentinel of Eternity', which dealt with the same theme in a different way: during a manned exploration of the lunar surface — at the time of writing, still two decades away — seismologists discover a mysterious structure, left behind by a higher intelligence as a kind of 'alarm' which, when triggered, will signal that mankind is ready for the stars. These themes — that Man was contacted by a higher intelligence before he was fully evolved, that we have been under the benign supervision of this alien race for millennia, and that we are 'Gods in waiting' whose destiny lies in the stars — would eventually comprise the beginning and the end of Kubrick's and Clarke's epic collaboration, *2001: A Space Odyssey*.

Childhood's End, meanwhile, continued to attract interest in Hollywood, although its grand themes and even grander scope made it a seemingly impossible challenge for the special effects available during the sixties and seventies. The project, the option on which had been continually renewed by Universal Pictures, briefly emerged as a possible feature film in 1975, when veteran writer-producer Gene Kearney (TV's *Night Gallery*) tabled the idea. Yet, two years before *Star Wars* proved that the idea of a populist science fiction film — virtually absent from the screen since *Planet of the Apes* and *2001* were released in the same year, 1968 — was commercially viable, Kearney was unable to get the project off the ground, and when he left Universal in 1977, the challenge of bringing the novel to the screen fell to Philip DeGuere, whose credits included the TV series *Alias Smith and Jones*. "The power of *Childhood's End* remains undiminished as the years go by," DeGuere told *Starlog* in 1981. "The real reason for making the picture is that the story is worth telling to a large number of people. It fills you with a sense of wonder and enlightenment." DeGuere knew that *Childhood's End* was one of the few science fiction novels that even those who did not regularly read the genre could enjoy. "But, unfortunately, people in this business tend to be shy of innovation."

In fact, it was not until *Star Wars* rewrote the rules of science fiction film-making that Universal began actively developing *Childhood's End*, initially as a six-hour miniseries for CBS Television, and later as a two- or three-hour telemovie for ABC. According to DeGuere, this was in the summer of 1978, just before Universal discovered that its contracts with Arthur C. Clarke — some of which dated back to 1957 — were out of date, and that Universal had lost certain rights pertaining to the story. It was another nine months before the stalemate was resolved between lawyers for Clarke and Universal, during which time DeGuere wrote a seventy-page treatment which, he felt, solved many of the problems inherent in adapting the novel for the screen. Chief among these was his decision to enlarge the role of Jan Rodericks, the black youth whom the Overlords choose as the only human permitted to oversee Man's evolution, to give the prospective audience someone to relate to throughout the film.

"That was done to *unify* the film," DeGuere explained, noting that, except for the Overlord named Karellen, the events and characters in the first half of the book, during which the Overlords do not reveal themselves to the human populace, are not related to those in the second half. "That could have been the tele-feature's only fault," he said. "It doesn't feel right to ask an audience to sit for an hour and a half and get to know some characters and a story, and then suddenly jump twenty-five to fifty years in the future and start a whole new story. You need some kind of satisfactory link to work as a framework. Having Jan Rodericks not only finish the story, but start it as well, seems to work beautifully." When the contractual difficulties were finally resolved in January 1979, DeGuere began turning his treatment into a screenplay and enlisted the services of legendary comic book artist Neal Adams to create some supporting visuals. DeGuere reasoned that a comic book artist was the ideal candidate to condense a complex scene into a single image, and Adams was his immediate first choice. "Neal has a unique ability to take a scene, read it, interpret it, understand it, and figure out a way to make it look right," he said. "It is a hell of a lot easier to have a single drawing or painting that you can take around to the technical people and say, 'This is what I want to see on the screen,' than to write a page of description and have various people interpret that and do it whatever way they like."

"What I did was what I considered to be preproduction drawings of concepts and ideas," says Adams, who now runs the New York-based Continuity Comics. Back in 1979, he travelled to Los Angeles to meet with DeGuere about *Childhood's End.* "When I do this sort of thing, I take a scene out of the script and I think of what I consider to be the ideal camera placement to show the thing — what I would call the establishing shots. But I'm an artist, so I try to put as much into it as I can — my input — and to be perfectly honest I try and twist it in my direction a little bit, as long as I agree with the person who is having me do it. So in a case like *Childhood's End*, I came up with a lot of concepts and ideas — what the alien spaceship looked like, and its bridge, to make it look different to how anyone else would perhaps see it."

Adams read the novel, and gave DeGuere a series of drawings illustrating what he saw as the key elements of the book, including: the arrival of the Overlords' enormous spacecraft over a major city, the bridge of the ship, the demonic appearance of the Overlords themselves, and the terrain of their homeworld. Drawing on the limited reference provided in the novel, Adams worked out a logical design for the interior of the Overlords' spacecraft, based on the fact that the creatures could fly. "[Humans] move in two-dimensional space because we can't fly," he explains, "but if you are in a spaceship built by creatures who *can* fly, you have to think what kind of place that would be. So you have suspended walkways, and if you've got to go to the next area down, you don't have to use a set of stairs! What you do is step off the walkway and fly down to the next level, or fly up to the level above or whatever. To them it's like taking a step." For Adams, considering the logic of the Overlords' lifestyle was a necessary part of visualising their domain. "I don't think of myself as an illustrator so much as a storyteller," he explains, "and something has to make sense to me on a logical level. I can't just draw a bunch of stuff and say, 'well, I don't know what it is.' But I can make up the logic, and come up with things that nobody else might even think of, but once you see it you [realise] that's the way it should be."

Adams's concept for the Overlord ships — described in Clarke's novel only in terms of scale — was, rather than a circular shape, that of a place setting, like a plate with two knives and a fork. "The perception that the ships were two miles long was very interesting to me, because that's so enormous," Adams explains. "I did one illustration that kind of gave the impression of something that gigantic over a city, where it would throw shadows on buildings; you would be in daylight, and suddenly you'd be in darkness." Adams felt that the ships would be so vast that clouds could be glimpsed beneath them, an idea that was reflected in at least two of his paintings. "I thought it was very original at the time," he says, "that, in effect, you would see the ship through clouds."

While a delighted DeGuere began showing the full-colour paintings — including several additional pieces rendered by another artist, Anthony Scott Thom — around Universal, Adams continued toiling on the project, even going as far as designing a workable set of the bat-like wings sported by Karellen and the other members of his species. DeGuere took

Adams to the special effects technicians based on the Universal studio lot, and the artist began explaining his concept for wings with telescopic components, based on car aerials, which would unfold when the actor wearing them raised his arms, and fold back up again, like real wings. "So I talked to the [special effects] guy, and told him that they could make wings that would unfold, and would look like they could really fly," Adams remembers. "But he said, 'We used to try to do wings, but you just can't make them work,' and I said, 'Look, I can give you a diagram that will show you exactly how to do it.' He said, 'Fine, give me all the diagrams you want, but you can't do it.' Anyway, the guy makes them, and he calls me back a couple of weeks later and he says, 'Listen, these fucking wings work! This is incredible! I am sending you Polaroids! You won't believe it!'"

Understandably encouraged by these developments, DeGuere privately established contact with Clarke himself, their brief conversations — limited by the eleven-hour time difference between Los Angeles and Clarke's adopted home of Sri Lanka — suggesting that DeGuere's story modifications had the author's blessing. "He approved of my boosting Jan Roderick's role in the novel, and also my elimination of the kidnapping of Stormgren," DeGuere noted. "Arthur revealed to me that the abduction had been an element that existed in an earlier novella that he had incorporated into *Childhood's End*, and that it didn't really pay off as far as the overall structure of the book is concerned." Unfortunately, Universal realised that the special effects required for the project were simply not viable for a television production budgeted at $10 million. Even DeGuere admitted that $40 million might be nearer the mark — a colossal investment in the era of such costly enterprises as *Star Trek: The Motion Picture* and *The Black Hole*. As Adams says, "in the end, Phil basically said, 'Well, I guess the illustrations are so good, Neal, that they helped me *not* get the thing done, because basically when [Universal] budgeted it out they discovered they couldn't make it for television. That was when it got killed.'"

However, as DeGuere commented in 1981, "Universal *has* recognised *Childhood's End*'s potential as a feature film presentation." However, he admitted, "From the studio's point of view, it doesn't have the elements that are time tested for theatrical [films]. *Childhood's End* doesn't have a clearly etched battle between good and evil, a group of people running around shooting at each other, a great deal of jeopardy, or a life and death situation as far as the characters are concerned." In addition, as Adams points out, audiences may not react positively to a story in which mankind sacrifices an entire generation — basically, every single child on the planet — in order to advance to its next stage of evolution. "As much as I appreciate the writings of Arthur C. Clarke," he says, "it is such a devastatingly unhappy view of the future, it's very hard to imagine people swallowing it. We humans don't mind evolution happening at a slightly slower pace, but a jump like this is pretty hard to take..."

Despite all of this, today's cinema audiences have arguably matured enough to accept such a film, not least because the grander themes of *Childhood's End* and its close relative *2001: A Space Odyssey* have more recently been mined in such films as James Cameron's *The Abyss* and Robert Zemeckis's *Contact*, which have intelligent, even poignant moments mixed in with the science fiction elements. "I'm inclined to think that a feature film *would* be a crossover situation, where adults would see it because of the story, and kids would want to see [it] because of the aliens and spaceships," DeGuere noted. Perhaps, he went on to suggest, it would take a personal commitment from a film-maker — Steven Spielberg, for instance — with sufficient clout to get a film like *Childhood's End* made regardless of audience considerations, in which case DeGuere's own adaptation might even serve as the basis for the film. "If somebody were to buy the rights from Universal, they'd get a copy of my script as part of the sale," he explained. "Anybody sensible enough to know what they were buying would read all the available material... hopefully they'd realise that they had a good adaptation in my screenplay."

Since DeGuere's involvement with *Childhood's End*, elements of Clarke's story — notably the arrival of enormous spacecraft over the cities of the world — have been borrowed by other science fiction productions. "I was a little surprised that some of the effects that I designed seemed to have shown up in a series called *V*," Adams notes wryly, "and since then, of course, we've had *Independence Day*." Despite this, both DeGuere and Adams feel that *Childhood's End* remains one of the greatest unfilmed science fiction novels of all time, a status it seems unlikely to retain indefinitely. "Most producers have in the back of their desks those one or two very special projects that they have always wanted to make and never forget," DeGuere admitted. "In my case, *Childhood's End* is one of them."

"It's inevitable that *Childhood's End* gets made," he added optimistically. "At one point, it's bound to happen." ∎

Where No One Has Gone Before

Philip Kaufman's *Star Trek: Planet Of The Titans* And Other *Star Trek* Voyages Never Taken

"I'm sure the fans would have been upset."

—writer-director Philip Kaufman on his plans
for the first *Star Trek* film

"**T**here's no future in science fiction." It was with these words, an unintentionally hilarious paradox, that director Philip Kaufman learned that Paramount Pictures had pulled the plug on the production of *Star Trek: Planet of the Titans*, the first proposed big screen incarnation of the popular sixties sci-fi series.

The success of *Star Trek* in syndication had led the studio to consider its options for the property and, in May 1975, the decision was made to put a *Star Trek* feature film into development. Yet it was to be another eighteen months before Paramount executives Barry Diller and Michael Eisner finally found a story they felt was strong enough to make the transition from television to the big screen. *The God Thing*, a Gene Roddenberry-penned screenplay in which, according to his assistant Jon Povill, "God was a malfunctioning spaceship", was the first to be rejected. An intriguing time travel story, on which Roddenberry and Povill collaborated, met a similar fate, followed by script outlines or ideas from such noted science fiction writers as Robert Silverberg, Ray Bradbury, Theodore Sturgeon and Harlan Ellison. As James Van Hise reported in his *Enterprise Incidents* fanzine, "[Ellison's] story did not begin with any of the *Enterprise* crew, but started on Earth where strange phenomena were inexplicably occurring. In India, a building, where a family is having dinner, just vanishes into dust. In the United States, one of the Great Lakes suddenly vanishes, wreaking havoc. In a public square, a woman suddenly screams and falls to the pavement where she transforms into some sort of reptilian creature. The truth is suppressed, but the Federation realises that someone or something is tampering with time and changing things on Earth in the far distant past.

"What is actually happening," Van Hise went on, "involves an alien race [on a planet at] the other end of the galaxy. Eons ago, Earth and this planet both developed races of humans and intelligent humanoid reptiles. On Earth, the humans destroyed the reptile men and flourished." It transpires that the reptile race have learned the fate of their brothers in Earth's remote past, and have decided to go back in time to change history, creating a kindred planet. "For whatever reason," Van Hise continued, "the Federation decides that only the *Enterprise* and her crew are qualified for this mission, so a mysterious cloaked figure goes about kidnapping the old central crew. This figure is finally revealed to be Kirk. After they are reunited, they prepare for the mission into the past to save Earth. And that would have been just the first half hour of the film!"

As Ellison later elaborated to Stephen King, "It involved going to the end of the known universe to slip back through time to the Pleistocene period when man first emerged. I postulated an alien intelligence from a far galaxy where the snakes had become the dominant life form, and a snake-creature who had come to Earth... had seen its ancestors wiped out, and had gone back into the far past of Earth to set up distortions in the time-flow so the reptiles could beat the humans. The *Enterprise* goes back to set time right, finds the snake-alien, and the human crew is confronted with the moral dilemma of whether it had the right to wipe out an entire life form just to insure its own territorial imperative in our present and future. The story, in short," Ellison concluded, "spanned all of time and all of space, with a moral and ethical problem." According to Ellison, the assembled executives, including Roddenberry, listened intently, before Barry Trabulus mentioned that he had been reading Erich von Daniken's *Chariots of the Gods*, and wondered whether the Mayan civilisation might be included. Ellison pointed out that there were no Mayans at the dawn of time, to which Trabulus rejoined that no one would know the difference. "*I'm* to know the difference," Ellison exploded. "So Trabulus got very uptight and said he liked Mayans a lot and why didn't I do it if I wanted to write this picture," Ellison told King. "So *I* said, 'I'm a writer. I don't know *what* the fuck you are!' And I got up and walked out. And that was the end of my association with the *Star Trek* movie."

During this and every other pitch meeting, Paramount's refrain remained the same: no idea was considered big enough — not even John D. F. Black's *End of the Universe*, in which the crew of the USS *Enterprise* encounters a black hole which threatens to consume all of creation. "They were preoccupied with this idea that it must have size and stature," Leonard Nimoy remarked later. "But although everyone seemed to have an idea about what a *Star Trek* movie should *not* be — a magnified television episode — no one could agree on what it *should* be."

At last, in October 1976, the British writing partnership of Chris Bryant and Allan G. Scott (*Don't Look Now*) turned in *Planet of the Titans*, a twenty-page treatment which Diller and Eisner felt had the right stuff. "My partner and I were interviewed by Gene Roddenberry," Bryant recalls, "and he said, 'How do you see Captain Kirk and all the rest of them?' And I remember saying that the nearest thing I could think of was one of Nelson's captains in the South Pacific — six months away from home and three months away by communication. And Gene said, 'That's *exactly* what I modelled him on — you absolutely have him right.' I think that's probably why we got the job."

In Bryant's and Scott's story, Kirk and his crew encounter an alien race they believe to be the mythical Titans of Earth legend and, after travelling a million years into Earth's past, introduce the concept of fire to primitive man. Adds Bryant, who admits that twenty-five years on, he cannot recall the specifics of the outline, "It also had something to do with the third eye, which we're all supposed to have, and its connection with telepathy." *Planet of the Titans* seemed to have all of the bathos, grandeur and myth of the original series, but with a story which more than suited the larger canvas. As Bryant and Scott began work on the script, Philip Kaufman (*The Great Northfield, Minnesota Raid* and, later, *Invasion of the Body Snatchers* and *The Right Stuff*) was hired to direct. "Somebody called and asked me if I'd be interested, and I said, 'Sure,'" Kaufman recalls. "I liked *Star Trek* because I felt it dealt with mature, adult themes — it wasn't a juvenile kind of science fiction.

So this was a chance to do something really unique."

For Bryant and Scott, however, turning the treatment into a screenplay which would please all parties proved more difficult than they had imagined. "Paramount really had no idea *what* they wanted," Bryant says. "I gather they must not have known what they *didn't* want either, or else they wouldn't have hired Phil Kaufman. Gene Roddenberry wanted a big, extended *Star Trek* episode, while Kaufman kept sloping in and saying, 'Well, can't you kill off all these television actors in the first reel so we can start having a proper movie?' There was no meeting of the minds at all," he adds, "which makes it physically impossible to produce a script. It was a miserable experience. The one thing I learned from that — and I've never forgotten it — was that you cannot write for a committee, ever. I never have again since, and I've done well over a hundred scripts since then."

Unable to produce a script which would satisfy the "committee" — Roddenberry, Kaufman and assorted Paramount executives — Bryant and Scott left the project by mutual agreement in April 1977. "We begged to be fired," says Bryant, "which they finally did. They threw us a wonderful party and gave us T-shirts with all the [characters] on the front, and on the back it said 'Fuck *Star Trek*.'" Their departure left Kaufman to work on the script by himself. "My version was really built around Leonard Nimoy as Spock and [Japanese actor] Toshiro Mifune as his Klingon nemesis," Kaufman explains, his subsequent casting of Nimoy in *Invasion of the Body Snatchers* proving his interest in the actor. "My idea was to make it less 'cult-ish,' and more of an adult movie, dealing with sexuality and wonders rather than oddness; a big science fiction movie, filled with all kinds of questions, particularly about the nature of Spock's [duality] — exploring his humanity and what humanness was. To have Spock and Mifune's characters tripping out in outer space. I'm sure the fans would have been upset," he adds, "but I felt that it could really open up a totally new type of science fiction."

During the eight-month development period of Kaufman's version, a formidable crew was being assembled. "Some way or other, Gene Roddenberry had reluctantly come aboard," Kaufman recalls, unaware that the *Star Trek* creator had reportedly been paid half a million dollars to act as the film's 'consultant', ostensibly to convince the fans that the feature film was the genuine article, rather than a cynical attempt to cash in on *Star Trek*'s syndicated success. "So we had Gene," Kaufman continues; "we had Ralph McQuarrie, who was George Lucas's sketch artist; [James Bond production designer] Ken Adam was doing the sets; I was able to get them to push the budget up. We were really going towards making the movie." Then, on 8 May 1977, Kaufman received the fateful phone call. "I remember [that] morning, being barely able to stand up after writing all night, coming down and saying to my wife, 'Rose, I've got it — I've got the story!' And at that precise moment, the phone rang, and it was the [executive] producer, Jeffrey Katzenberg, saying, 'We're in trouble.' He said that Paramount had decided to pull the plug on the *Star Trek* project [because] they thought maybe it could only exist on television. Of course, about three weeks after they cancelled [the movie], *Star Wars* came out... "

Incredibly, even the unprecedented success of *Star Wars* could not convince Paramount that a *Star Trek* feature film was viable. Instead, a small screen revival of the series was now seen as the cornerstone for Diller's intended launch of a fourth television network — a phase of development exhaustively detailed in Judith and Garfield Reese-Stevens' book, *Star Trek Phase II: The Untold Story Behind the Star Trek Television Series that Almost Was*. Suffice to say that if it had not been for the mooted, and later aborted, second "five-year mission" of the USS *Enterprise*, *Star Trek: The Motion Picture* might never have happened, since the story for the film originated as a script written for the series' feature-length pilot episode, 'In Thy Image'.

The pilot's plot began life as 'Robot's Return', a two-page story outline by Gene Roddenberry in which a NASA space probe returns to Earth looking for its long-dead creator, having achieved consciousness in the hundreds of years since its launch. During the development of *Star Trek Phase II*, this premise — reminiscent of the original series story 'The Changeling' — was given to science fiction writer Alan Dean Foster as the potential basis for an hour-long episode. "Roddenberry got in touch with me based on the *Star Trek Log* series I had done for Ballantine Books," Foster recalled. "He felt I was comfortable with the *Star Trek* universe, and comfortable and familiar with the characters." Foster's thirty-two-page treatment was considered strong enough to form the basis of the series pilot although, according to series co-producer

Harold Livingston, there was never any question that Foster himself would write the script. "I wanted to see something he had written, and he brought me two screenplays which I thought were terrible," Livingston said, "[so] I made a deal with Alan's agent that he would write a story and agree *not* to do the script. I then began to look for writers to turn the story into a script."

Unable to find a suitable scribe with only five weeks to go before production was due to start — under the supervision of Livingston, Povill, Roddenberry and Robert Goodwin (later executive producer of *The X-Files*), and the direction of Robert Collins (creator/producer of the short-lived *Serpico* TV series) — Livingston decided to write the script for 'In Thy Image' himself. On completion, Livingston's script and Roddenberry's unauthorised rewrite were presented to Michael Eisner at a meeting also attended by Livingston, Goodwin and Roddenberry. As Livingston recalled, "Michael had one script in one hand and one in the other, balancing them in his palms. And he said, 'Listen, this is the problem. This,' Gene's script, 'is television. This,' [my] script, 'is a movie. Frankly, it's a lot better.'" Although Goodwin remembers it slightly differently — "Eisner slammed his hands on the table and said, 'This is it! We've spent four years looking for a feature script. Now let's make the movie!'" — the end result was the same: *Star Trek: The Motion Picture* had a green light.

"The fans have supported us and consistently written us to pull our act together," Eisner remarked at a press conference on 28 March 1978, convened to announce the imminent production of the long-awaited *Star Trek* feature film, then budgeted at $15 million. The fact that the event was attended by the entire original cast was something of a small miracle, since it was well known that, for many months, Leonard Nimoy had been involved in a legal dispute with Paramount over unpaid *Star Trek* royalties and had no intention of reprising the role of Spock for the second television series. Nimoy had also been excluded from many drafts of the screenplay (ironic, since he was literally the star of Kaufman's version), and such was the weight of Spock's absence that not one but *three* new characters — Lieutenant Ilia, the bald and beautiful Deltan; the lantern-jawed Commander, Will Decker; and the Vulcan Science Officer, Lieutenant Xon — had been created to replace him. According to *Star Trek* lore, Spock was only included after four-time Academy Award-winner Robert Wise — who had replaced Robert Collins as director of the feature-length *Star Trek* once its big-screen destiny was established — was informed by his daughter and son-in-law that the film would not be *Star Trek* without Spock.

At almost the eleventh hour, rising Paramount executive Jeffrey Katzenberg (who is today part of DreamWorks SKG, where he green-lit the thinly-veiled *Star Trek* parody *Galaxy Quest*) was despatched to New York, where Nimoy was appearing in a Broadway production of *Equus*. His mission: to resolve 'the Nimoy situation' and thus ensure that the last of the original crew was aboard the new venture. But although Nimoy was happy with the sizeable cheque for backdated royalties which resulted from his meeting with Katzenberg, he was less than thrilled with the proposed feature script. Not only did he feel that his character was almost extraneous to the story of a sentient NASA space probe hijacking the *Enterprise*, he thought that this was true of the rest of the crew as well. Nevertheless, he agreed to participate in the film version on the proviso that he was granted script approval, thus ensuring that there were no empty chairs either at the press conference — where he brought the house down by claiming that the reason for his delay in signing on was the sluggish mail service between Earth and Vulcan — or on the bridge of the refitted starship, the *Enterprise*-A. This was good news for everyone except actor David Gautreaux, who was to play Spock's replacement, Lieutenant Xon; however, the other *Phase II* characters, Decker (Stephen Collins) and Ilia (Persis Khambatta), were retained.

With the release of the $15 million film optimistically scheduled for June 1979, screenwriter Dennis Clark (*Comes a Horseman*) was hired to write Spock into the latest draft of the screenplay, for which Roddenberry had assumed sole credit. The relationship between he and Clark soon broke down, however, and Roddenberry was forced to invite Livingston back into the fold; Livingston agreed to return to the project, on the condition that he would be given complete autonomy over the script. It was the beginning of a tumultuous period in the ongoing development of the film, a veritable battle of wits between the two writers. "Gene was a great idea man and a good story man, [but] he just couldn't execute," stated Livingston, who quit the film three times during production, only to be persuaded to return by Wise or

Katzenberg. "More than anything else," Katzenberg commented, "Gene was devoted to protecting the essence of *Star Trek*. Whether he went too far or not, he believed that his was *Star Trek*'s sole voice."

Small wonder that the script was nowhere near complete when principal photography began on 9 August 1978. In the following months, so many script rewrites were undertaken by Roddenberry, Livingston or Leonard Nimoy (who, according to Livingston, "enhanced the script considerably"), that amendments were not only initialled and dated, they were *timed*. Incredibly, even greater problems beset the film during production than development, the most serious of which was the loss of $5 million and almost a year's work when original special effects supervisor Robert Abel delivered virtually no usable footage, resulting in his replacement by the triple-threat effects team of Douglas Trumbull, John Dykstra and Richard Yuricich. The film's budget shot skywards, with most reports agreeing that the $30 million frontier had been left far behind. By some miracle, *Star Trek: The Motion Picture* opened in US cinemas on 7 December 1979, fifty-five months and almost as many script drafts since Gene Roddenberry was first commissioned to make a *Star Trek* feature. "On a scale of one to ten," Jeffrey Katzenberg said later, "the anxiety level on that film fluctuated somewhere between eleven and thirteen. Never in the history of motion pictures has there been a film that came closer to not making it to the theaters on its release date." Michael Eisner put it more concisely: "It was a nightmare."

Perhaps unsurprisingly, the film received an almost unprecedented mauling from the critics, and the response to the film among *Star Trek* fans is well known: initially apologists for it — basically, any *Star Trek* movie was better than none at all — most would eventually admit that they disliked it, re-christening the film 'The Slow Motion Picture' in reference to its excessive running time and sluggish pace. Nevertheless, the fans' enthusiasm, coupled with the mainstream audience's appetite for science fiction in the wake of *Star Wars* and *Close Encounters of the Third Kind*, was enough to turn the film into a $175 million success, giving Paramount the last laugh and *Star Trek* a new lease of life. A re-edited version of the film, broadcast on television and subsequently released to home video, ran eleven minutes *longer* than the original cut, yet feels pacier, since the reinstated scenes de-emphasise the film's special effects. Yet another new version, available on DVD, contains numerous special effects improvements, and purports to be the 'director's cut' Wise would have delivered in 1979 if his deadline hadn't been so pressing. *Star Trek* fans continue to debate the relative merits of the three versions.

While Paramount had spent and made a great deal of hard cash on *Star Trek: The Motion Picture*, it had also learned a few hard lessons, and realised that it had very nearly strangled the *Star Trek* film franchise at birth. Conscious not to make the same mistakes twice, the studio took responsibility for the sequel away from *Star Trek* creator Gene Roddenberry and handed it to the television division, under the aegis of producers Harve Bennett (*The Six Million Dollar Man*) and his friend and colleague, commercials director Robert Sallin. Bennett reportedly considered what was described as the ultimate Klingon story, and then a 'The City on the Edge of Forever'-style tale (in which the *Enterprise* crew travel back in time to save the life of President Kennedy, with dire consequences for future history), before becoming interested in a story loosely titled *The Omega Project*. This plotline would involve a destructive weapon, perhaps wielded by one of Kirk's former foes from the original television series. Bennett began trawling through old episodes, eventually deciding upon the character of Khan Noonian Singh, played by Ricardo Montalban in 1967's 'Space Seed'.

Bennett himself wrote a one-page outline entitled *The War of the Generations*, in which Khan leads a revolution against the United Federation of Planets, and began working out the story with TV writer Jack B. Sowards (*Bonanza*, *The High Chaparral*). Sowards' first treatment, dated December 1980, involved a battle of wills between Kirk and Khan, added a romantic relationship between Kirk and a crewmember named O'Rourke, and introduced the death of Spock — an idea proposed in order to lure a reluctant Leonard Nimoy back for a second big-screen voyage. Many of these elements made it as far as a screenplay entitled *Star Trek: The Omega Syndrome*, in which Khan plans to use his ultimate weapon to seize control of the United Federation of Planets, before wreaking personal vengeance on Kirk himself. It was art director Michael Minor who suggested that the weapon, known in the script as "the Omega system", might be a terraforming device — a method of transforming dead worlds into inhabitable, hospitable environments suitable for human colonisation — turned against an inhabited world. "Suppose you trained it on a planet filled with people and speeded up its evolution," Minor suggested. "You could destroy the planet and every lifeform on it."

With a writers' strike looming, Sowards had only three months to write the script, now retitled *The Genesis Project*. The new draft — close to the plot of the finished film, but with a twelve-page, face-to-face confrontation between Kirk and Khan — was delivered on 10 April 1981, one day before the strike began. The idea of the prototype ter-raforming device wielded as a weapon by a wrathful Khan and the almost Shakespearean machinations of Khan's revenge on Kirk, seemed to give the story both the conflict and the spectacle it needed. Nevertheless, Bennett decided to run the script by Samuel Peeples, who had, appropriately enough, written the second *Star Trek* pilot, 'Where No Man Has Gone Before', on the strength of which the series had been commissioned. "My personal objection to [Sowards'] screenplay was, contrary to other criticisms, simply that it was cast too much in the mould of 1967 *Star Trek* episodes," Peeples opined, before setting to work on an outline entitled *Worlds That Never Were*, delivered on 20 July 1981. Out went the TV villain, Khan, in favour of two aliens, Sojin and Moray, unfathomable trans-dimensional beings whose motiva-tions are so alien to us, and ours to them, that they almost destroy the Earth by accident.

"Neither the Jack Sowards or Samuel Peeples script worked," Robert Sallin later commented, noting that both felt too much like over-long television scripts. "There was a lot of intergalactic weirdness in the scripts which I felt was defeating," he added. After taking further story suggestions from another former *Star Trek* writer, Judy Burns ('The Tholian Web'), Bennett finally attempted a draft himself, unifying the most popular elements of all the scripts into a script entitled *The Wrath of Khan*. All they needed was a director who could pull it off for a mere $12 million. Enter Nicholas Meyer, whose sole feature directing credit had been the little-known sci-fi movie *Time After Time*. Meyer claimed never to have seen an episode of *Star Trek*, but he was never-theless enthusiastic about the script. "I looked at the first film and thought that there was no way that we were going to make a movie as filled with ennui as that one," he said. "I also knew we could do it for a quarter of the cost, so we would probably look like heroes!" Although, by choice, Meyer magnanimously refused a screenwriting credit on the finished film, producer Sallin insists that Meyer's reworking of the script was substantial, stating: "It is, in all candour, Nick's uncredited rewrite that is on the screen."

The film opens as the half-Vulcan half-Romulan Lieutenant Saavik (Kirstie Alley) undertakes the infamous 'Kobayashi Maru' test under the aegis of Admiral Kirk, Captain Spock and several of the original *Enterprise* crew, all of whom are 'killed' in the simulation. Elsewhere, Captain Terrell (*Quiz Show*'s Paul Winfield) and his first officer, Pavel Chekov, are searching for a lifeless planet on which the experimental Genesis device can be tested, when they are taken prisoner by Khan Noonian Singh (played, as in 'Space Seed', by Ricardo Montalban). Khan sees the Genesis device as a means to repay Kirk for abandoning him on a doomed desert world fifteen years earlier. "Revenge is a dish that is best served cold," he says icily, "and it is very cold in space." The film's climactic space battle — during which Kirk and Khan never actually meet — culminates in Spock's supreme self-sacrifice. "The needs of the many outweigh the needs of the few — or the one," the Vulcan says, during what must rank as the most emotional sci-fi movie death scene since that of HAL in *2001: A Space Odyssey*.

Despite its ultimately unspectacular box-office performance — it grossed far less money than *The Motion Picture*, although it did go into profit much quicker — *Star Trek II: The Wrath of Khan* was a critical success, propelling the series towards an inevitable third instalment, seemingly prompted by the hastily-added coda in which Spock's 'coffin' comes to rest among the burgeoning life on the Genesis planet. "It would have been very easy to say that... all the things we [had] done to modify the film's ending to be ambiguous about the death of Spock were carefully designed and that the plot for *Star Trek III* was already in my mind. Not true," insisted Bennett, adding that the more ambiguous ending was included to placate *Star Trek* fans incensed over the death of one of their favourite characters.

Nevertheless, the modified ending undoubtedly facilitated the ease with which Bennett wrote the script for *Star Trek III: The Search for Spock*, which evolved relatively painlessly during development, and the film entered production on 15 August 1983, with Leonard Nimoy at the helm. Opening in June 1984, the film was greeted with approval by critics and enthusiasm by fans, and easily matched the box-office earnings of its predecessor. Paramount wasted no time in putting a fourth film into development, with Harve Bennett acting as producer for a third time and Leonard Nimoy returning as director. This time, however, it was widely known that William Shatner was unwilling to return to the franchise unless he was given a significant pay increase, feeling that his recognition among *Star Trek* fans, coupled with the success of the previous films, warranted an appropriately large paycheque.

While Bennett and Nimoy awaited contract negotiations, an idea was put forward which would not require the services of *any* of the regular *Star Trek* cast members, since it would take place at Starfleet Academy while Kirk, Spock and the others were young cadets. "A proposal was made by me that we... could do *Star Trek* in the beginning," Bennett explained. "[It] was Ralph Winter's idea — 'Let's do them at the Academy.'" The formula, Bennett felt, had worked well enough for *Top Gun*, "but the franchise wasn't the same without the stars, and there is merit in that argument." When, after eight months, Shatner signed on for $2 million — and a promise that he would be allowed to direct *Star Trek V* — the Starfleet Academy approach was abandoned in favour of a time travel story, which would allow the crew of the newly-destroyed *Enterprise* to interact with twentieth century humans for the first time since *Star Trek*'s small-screen incarnation. Given the various time travel plotlines used in the series, the question for the story creators was not so much *how* Kirk and his renegade crew would travel back through time to present-day Earth, but *why?* "That led us to the idea that there's a problem in the twenty-third century," Bennett added, "which can only be solved by something that's now gone; extinct... We experimented with a lot of different ideas on the subject, including the idea that certain crafts and techniques might be lost by the twenty-third century."

After considering such diverse topics as violin makers and oil drillers, Nimoy began to explore the notion that there was a widespread epidemic in Earth's future, a deadly illness whose cure has been destroyed centuries earlier along with the rain forests. "But the depiction of thousands of sick and dying people seemed rather gruesome for our 'light-hearted' film," Nimoy admitted, "and the thought of our brave crew taking a 600 year round trip just to bring back a snail darter wasn't all that thrilling!" Finally, Nimoy — who had been reading a book about extinct species — landed on the idea of having a mysterious alien spacecraft arrive in orbit around Earth and attempt to make contact with a species extinct by the twenty-third century: the humpback whale.

Initial meetings with writer Daniel Petrie Jr (*Beverly Hills Cop*) came to nought — "I had a meeting once with Leonard Nimoy and Harve Bennett about doing a possible draft," says Petrie, "but I could not do the gig cause I was tied into a deal with Disney" — but by then a new consideration had arisen: Eddie Murphy, Paramount's rising star, had become taken with the idea of a role in *Star Trek IV*. "On the surface, it seemed like a terrific idea to combine two successful franchises — Eddie Murphy and *Star Trek* — in the hopes that it would draw Murphy fans who might not otherwise go to a *Trek* movie," Nimoy wrote later. "But... if it didn't work, it would hurt both Murphy and *Trek*." Therefore, Nimoy reacted cautiously, agreeing with Jeffrey Katzenberg's feeling that it was "either the best or worst idea in the world."

Nimoy met with Murphy, who asked what Katzenberg had said. "It was a direct question," Nimoy recalled, "so I responded in kind. 'He said you'd kill to be in a *Star Trek* movie!' [Eddie] flashed a grin. 'That's right!'" The pair talked for a while, but Nimoy was realistic. "I told him that Harve and I were going to be discussing story ideas, and that we'd take his request very seriously. But I also told him, 'Eddie, we like you, and you like us. You know if it's announced that you're in our movie, there'll be some sharp-shooting sceptics waiting to gun us all down if it doesn't work well. My feeling is that your part has to be terrific — or non-existent, because we don't want to hurt your career, and I know you don't want to hurt ours.' 'Then keep in touch,' Eddie said. 'Let me know how your story ideas are progressing.' I agreed, because that way, either side could get off the train if it wasn't tracking well." Ultimately, Murphy apparently allowed the studio to talk him out of combining their two biggest stars, Murphy and *Star Trek* — tantamount to putting all their eggs in one basket. "I'm a Trekkie," Murphy later admitted. "I've always loved *Star Trek* and *have* wanted to be in *Star Trek*, and that's where they got the idea of coming back in time to Earth in 1987.

The script was developed, but we eventually dropped the idea." Nevertheless, said Bennett, "So much of the development of the story was with the very distinct possibility that Eddie Murphy was in it."

Indeed, when Steve Meerson and Peter Krikes were hired to write the screenplay on the strength of *The Long Way Home*, a fish-out-of-water script about the plight of Indians in America today, they were asked to keep Murphy in mind, and went as far as writing him a major role, as a wacky college professor — a slimline forerunner of *The Nutty Professor?* — who believes in extraterrestrials and is fond of playing whale song to his students. When he meets the former *Enterprise* crew, who land in Golden Gate Park in an invisible ship 'borrowed' from the Klingons, he is convinced that his theories about aliens are true. When Murphy passed — choosing instead to make *The Golden Child*, his first big flop — his character was melded with that of a marine biologist and a newswoman to become Gillian Taylor (Catherine Hicks), the scientist who assists the crew with their capture of a humpback whale, and then accompanies Kirk back to the twenty-third century. Saavik's suggested pregnancy by a young Spock was cut, along with Krikes' and Meerson's idea of having the Klingon Bird of Prey ship put down at half time during the Super Bowl (where the crowd just assume it to be part of the entertainment).

Eventually, out went Krikes and Meerson, in favour of *Wrath of Khan* director (and uncredited screenwriter) Nicholas Meyer, who worked on a new version of the script with Bennett. Krikes and Meerson were ultimately forced to go to Writers' Guild arbitration to secure their screen credit, winning a partial victory. Meyer's version of the story had Taylor stay behind in the twentieth century, vowing to do everything in her power to ensure the survival of the humpback whales, despite the time paradox that would create. "I still think [it's] the 'righter' ending," Meyer said later. "The end in the movie detracts from the importance of people in the present taking responsibility for the ecology and preventing problems of the future by doing something about them today, rather than catering to the fantasy desires of being able to be transported ahead in time to the near-utopian future of the *Star Trek* era."

Opening in the summer of 1986, the year in which the majority of the film was supposed to take place, *The Voyage Home* became the first

Star Trek film to break the $100 million mark in the US, and received some of the best reviews of any *Star Trek* film. More importantly, it opened up the world of *Star Trek* to a mainstream audience, a development which gave Paramount good reason to believe that *Star Trek V* could be even more successful. On this occasion, William Shatner would be calling the shots. For the fifth instalment of the series, the actor's first film as director, Shatner was taken with the idea of having the crew of the brand new *Enterprise* encounter God, guided by a Vulcan holy man, Sybok, who commandeers the ship in order to facilitate a meeting with his maker. "I took the TV evangelist persona and created a holy man who thought God had spoken to him," Shatner explained. "He believed God had told him, 'I need many followers, and I need a vehicle to spread my word through the universe.' That vehicle he needed became a starship which the holy man would capture when it came to rescue some hostages he had taken." Having written an outline dubiously subtitled *An Act of Love*, Shatner approached novelist Eric Von Lustbader, only to find that the author wanted a million dollars to turn Shatner's treatment into a screenplay. Instead, Paramount offered the task to David Loughery (*Dreamscape*), who was told to lighten up Shatner's outline, and inject a sense of fun and adventure into the somewhat intense story, which went through a number of variations under Loughery's supervision.

Shatner had been hands-on during the development process, but when he briefly departed to make another film, Loughery and Bennett took the opportunity to re-build the script from the ground up, shying away from the idea of having Kirk and his crew meet a physical God, and thinking more in terms of achieving a kind of Nirvana. If Shatner felt betrayed by the new direction the story had taken in his absence, Leonard Nimoy was equally unhappy by his character's betrayal of Kirk, and the script was hastily rewritten once again to allay the concerns of the series' two biggest assets. "As originally conceived," Loughery explained, "only Kirk held out against Sybok, which gives you more of a 'one man stands alone' kind of thing, betrayed by his best friends. Leonard and De[Forest Kelley] objected and it was changed." By now, the film had spent two years in development, and Paramount was understandably nervous that the momentum generated by *Star Trek IV* was being dissipated. Production finally began late in 1988 and, after problems during principal photography led to the film's original climax — in which Kirk, Spock and McCoy were attacked by a creature made of solid rock — being dropped, *Star Trek V: The Final Frontier* was rush-released in June of the following year to disappointing box-office (less than half the gross of its predecessor) and unanimously negative reviews. Shatner shouldered most of the blame, admitting that *The Final Frontier* might well have been the franchise's final big-screen voyage: "I was sure I had marked the end of the *Star Trek* films once and for all," he wrote later.

It is true that the future of the *Star Trek* franchise had become very uncertain. So much so that a mischievous Walter Koenig managed to convince fellow cast member George Takei that the sixth *Star Trek* film would be filmed using animated clay figures. ("Are they going to use our voices?" was Takei's anguished response to the news.) Paramount would almost certainly have abandoned plans for a sixth film if studio head Frank Mancuso had not decided that the show's approaching 25th anniversary afforded them the opportunity to celebrate in style. During this time, Harve Bennett proposed that the *Starfleet Academy* concept be revived, thereby avoiding the increasing influence and multi-million-dollar pay demands of the ageing *Star Trek* actors by hiring new ones to portray the youthful adventures of James Tiberius Kirk and his fellow Academy students, including Spock and McCoy. The project was the brainchild of producer Ralph Winter, who originally pitched the idea to Bennett during the development of *Star Trek IV*. "It's a great story finding out about this young cocky character on a farm who goes to flight school," Winter explained, "and meets up with the first alien that comes from Vulcan, and how they meet the other characters. It would have been a great gift for the fans on the 25th anniversary." As Winter saw it, the future had to begin somewhere.

The fans did not agree, however. Gently yet decisively encouraged by several of the original *Star Trek* actors, who had a vested interest in continuing to play the characters which had allowed them to live long and prosper, they began writing letters to Paramount, decrying the proposal as heresy. "We were really caught off guard and surprised by the fans who reacted so negatively to the idea of this movie," then Paramount staff writer David Loughery admitted, suggesting that the negative response may have been due to rumour-mongering that the proposed film would be some kind of *Police Academy*-style *Star Trek* spoof, rather than a serious new direction for, and celebration of, the *Star Trek* franchise. Paramount was perplexed; if *Star Trek* could re-invent itself with an entirely new cast of characters on television, something *The Next Generation* had successfully achieved, why would the fans not accept a new cast of actors in their favourite roles — particularly after the low point of *Star Trek V?*

At this point, alarmed at the *Starfleet Academy* concept — which of course would not involve him playing Chekov — actor Walter Koenig decided to take matters into his own hands, boldly going to Frank Mancuso with a script outline for *Star Trek VI* subtitled *In Flanders Fields*. Koenig's story began with the Romulans joining the Federation, leading to all-out war with the Klingons; all Starfleet personnel are given statutory fitness tests and, when all of the *Enterprise* crew — bar Spock, physically and mentally superior — fail, the ship is handed over to a younger crew. When the *Enterprise* subsequently disappears, Kirk and his former crew members are reassembled and despatched to search for the missing ship, eventually finding that its youthful crew has been kidnapped, along with Spock, by a race bent on draining their life forces for its own survival. An epic rescue from these creatures — as Koenig puts it, "not stunt guys in suits, not blue-skinned furries with horns, but truly repulsive sewer-dwelling worms of slime and putrefaction... things that the monsters in *Aliens* evolved *from*" — is attempted, during which Kirk, Scotty, Sulu, Chekov and Uhura all fall on the battlefield, leaving McCoy and Spock as the only survivors from the original crew. As McCoy walks among his dead comrades, he recalls each of them in a poignant flashback (Koenig suggests several possible scenes from the television series), and ultimately rescues a weakened Spock from his captors. "In this loneliest, most desolate of moments, Spock [permits] himself the one expression of friendship that he has never before admitted to: his need of Leonard McCoy. Spock leans against the doctor for support, and the two men — adversaries in a thousand arguments over the years — walk off together."

Whether or not Mancuso ever considered Koenig's treatment, the studio ultimately abandoned its plans for *Starfleet Academy*, opting instead to give Leonard Nimoy the reins for a sixth *Star Trek* film reuniting the entire original series cast. Nimoy invited screenwriters

Mark Rosenthal and Lawrence Konner to outline the story with him, initially considering a vehicle for the two *Star Trek* captains, Kirk and Picard, to meet for the first time. Paramount's television division, which was enjoying enormous syndicated success with *The Next Generation*, was vehemently opposed to the idea. Instead, Rosenthal and Konner proposed a story — inspired by the rise of *perestroika* and the fall of the Berlin Wall — about the emergence of peace between the Federation and the Klingons. (The races had been bitter enemies in the original series and previous films, but had become uneasy allies by the time of *The Next Generation*.) What if the prospect of peace was threatened by those on both sides with a vested interest in the continuing state of war?

The story was greeted enthusiastically, first by the studio and then by Nimoy's chosen director, Nicholas Meyer, who had helmed arguably the franchise's best chapter, *The Wrath of Khan*, and contributed to the screenplay of *The Voyage Home*. For once, the story changed relatively little as Meyer developed the screenplay with novelist Dennis Martin Flinn, based on the Nimoy-Rosenthal-Konner storyline. The shooting script was completed in October 1990, a mere five months after Nimoy had first been approached about *Star Trek VI*. Yet concerns over the budget left the film in limbo for several months; at one point, the film was cancelled altogether, only to be revived again when cuts were made, both to some of the salaries (including Nimoy's and Meyer's) and to parts of the story, including a fifteen-page opening in which a mysterious Federation envoy tracks down the former *Enterprise* crew members and recruits them for one final mission. (Walter Koenig's seriously-intended suggestion that the script be improved by the death of Captain Kirk went unheeded.) Finally, on 13 February 1991, Paramount officially green-lit *Star Trek VI*, on the proviso that it beam into theatres at maximum warp — by 13 December, to be precise. Somehow, the film-makers succeeded. *The Undiscovered Country* matched the box-office grosses of *Star Treks II* and *III*, and made half as much again as *Star Trek V*. The original *Star Trek* cast had signed off in style. Or had they?

On the very day that *Star Trek VI* was screened for the first time on the Paramount lot, newly-appointed Paramount president Brandon Tartikoff asked why there couldn't be another voyage. But with *The*

Next Generation wrapping up after 178 episodes and seven successful seasons in syndication, it was obvious to everyone the direction the next big-screen *Star Trek* should take — and which captain should be in command of the *Enterprise*. "I was asked to do the movie in February of 1993," said *Next Generation* series producer Rick Berman. "The plan was, I would write two stories with two separate writers, and that I would be involved with selecting which one was the best." Three former *Next Generation* writers were chosen: Brannon Braga and Ronald D. Moore, who would take the path which would ultimately lead to *Star Trek Generations*; and Maurice Hurley, who would pursue an entirely different approach, which was never seriously followed.

"There was basically a fold in space," Hurley said of his untitled story, "and an adversary who had been in a battle was blown through it into our universe. It is trying to get home to save its species, but in order to do that — and in order to get home — it has to basically destroy us." Picard begins addressing the problem and, upon discovering that his historical counterpart, James T. Kirk, encountered a similar situation during his original five-year mission (in 'The Tholian Web'), conjures up Kirk's image on the *Enterprise* holodeck. "It basically becomes a couple of bizarre scenes between Picard and Kirk, and it gets confrontational at certain moments," Hurley recalled. "You want to bring back Kirk and not have it get confrontational? Kirk will get confrontational with anyone. In *Star Trek V*, he got confrontational with God! So it became a way to put those two classic characters together, and let them bang on each other."

Ultimately, Paramount decided to pursue the Braga-Moore idea, which involved a more literal meeting of the two captains. An early draft of the script included brief appearances by all seven of the 'classic' *Enterprise* crew, but ultimately only Scotty (James Doohan) and Chekov (Walter Koenig) joined Kirk — in roles originally intended for Spock and McCoy, until Leonard Nimoy and DeForest Kelley declined to make cameo appearances. Despite having suffered disastrous test screenings which resulted in $5 million worth of re-shoots — chiefly involving the ignoble death of Captain Kirk, who was originally simply shot in the back by Soran (Malcolm McDowell), at which fans howled in protest — director David Carson's *Star Trek Generations* was released in November 1994, grossing a not inconsiderable $75 million in the US. The film did however receive a muted critical response, which gave credence to the adage that the even-numbered *Star Trek* films were good, while the odd-numbered entries were bad. (Perhaps that was the reason why *Generations* was the first *Star Trek* film without a numeral in the title.)

Thus, having only moderately fumbled the passing of the torch from the Kirk-led *Enterprise* crew to the *Next Generation*, Paramount bounced back in 1996 with the release of *Star Trek: First Contact*, the first film in which Captain Jean-Luc Picard and his crew would carry the action without the recognition factor the stars of the original *Star Trek* series enjoyed. The result — scripted by *Generations* co-writers Brannon Braga and Ronald D. Moore, and directed by *Next Generation* actor (and occasional director) Jonathan Frakes — was a rousing action-adventure, featuring the *Next Generation* series' most formidable foes, the Borg. In a storyline echoing Harlan Ellison's pitch back in 1975 for the very first *Star Trek* movie, the Borg travel through a temporal vortex to change the course of Earth's history, with the result that the entire population of the planet — with the exception of the *Enterprise* crew, who follow them back in time — is assimilated by the Borg.

As Moore told Lou Anders, "Their whole thing is to assimilate humanity and destroy the future, so if they can't beat us in the present, they'll go back in time and solve their problem." Berman, Braga and Moore discussed several possible time periods, "[but] we decided that most of it had been mined in one way or another by various time travel stories in science fiction and in *Star Trek*." Nevertheless, he added, "We talked extensively at one point about the Italian Renaissance, because we thought that would be a neat period where a lot of scientific breakthroughs were being made. Mankind was coming out of the dark age into an age of enlightenment." However, Berman and the writers decided that the Italian Renaissance was too far removed from the audience, and that fighting the Borg dressed in tights and doublets might appear ridiculous. "Part of me kind of wishes that we had tried it," Moore admitted. "Fighting the Borg, a highly technological race, in a low-tech environment is kind of cool." Eventually, the writers opted for the relatively low-tech twenty-first century, which gave them the best of both worlds.

The earliest drafts of the script — carrying the working title *Star Trek: Resurrection* until the fourth film in the *Alien* series was announced with that subtitle — were very different, detailing Picard's efforts to repair the ship with which, *Star Trek*'s future history has it, scientist Zefram Cochrane makes the first flight at warp speed, initiating 'first contact' with an alien species. In these drafts, Braga told Lou Anders, "Cochrane is unconscious for the entire movie. He basically gets blasted by the Borg and remains in Beverly [Crusher's] sickbay and doesn't wake up until the warp flight is already done." Added Moore, "Picard basically did the launch himself, and flew the warp ship at the end of the movie. There were also some futuristic militia groups roaming the countryside. They became the villains down on the planet's surface that Picard had to fight against."

In the midst of all this action, Picard was supposed to find romance with a twenty-first century woman, Ruby. "We tried in the first draft," said Braga. "We gave it a shot, and it didn't work... because you had a Picard who was falling in love in just a couple of days while the Borg were assimilating Earth, and the Captain would never do that. Even if we could believe that he could fall in love in a couple of days, which is implausible at best, he just wouldn't take the time to do that when the Borg are about to destroy the future." The writers duly dropped the love story element — which would return in the next film — and turned Ruby into Lily (Alfre Woodard), who enabled the audience to see the twenty-fourth century from a twenty-first century person's point of view. Berman, Braga and Moore also decided to drop the militia idea, which they felt lacked dramatic tension as a subplot. As Moore explained, "We went, 'Duh! What if we just swap Riker and Picard. Throw the emphasis "upstairs," make the *Enterprise* story the primary story with Picard, put Riker down on the planet's surface and wake up Zefram Cochrane.' We could play that for more of a light adventure 'downstairs,' forget about the militias and just make the B-story about dealing with this inventor from the past who's nothing like you thought he would be. Then go 'upstairs' and have Picard facing his greatest nightmare, which is that the Borg are back... That," he added, "was really the last major conceptual jump."

Grossing $92 million in the US and a similarly substantial amount overseas, Paramount was understandably eager to capitalise on its success, immediately engaging Rick Berman to create a follow-up to what had been the biggest-grossing *Star Trek* film since *The Voyage Home*. Berman, in turn, brought former *Next Generation* writer and co-executive producer Michael Piller back into the fold, offering him the chance to co-write the story and screenplay for *Star Trek IX*. "I can tell you, returning to the franchise, that as a writer and as a viewer, I was very heavily invested in the qualities of *Star Trek: The Next Generation* and the characters of the show that had made it so special both to watch and to write in the first place," Piller told *Cinefantastique*, adding that his immediate response was to envisage a story in which Jean-Luc Picard was the hero. "I had always felt that Picard's greatest strength as a hero was that he was a man of intellect and principle, and moral and ethical guidance," he explained. Whereas Ronald D. Moore and Brannon Braga's two film scripts had depicted Picard as self-doubting (*Generations*) and vengeful (*First Contact*), Piller sought to remind fans of the qualities which made him truly heroic.

Berman was initially enthusiastic; after the dark subject matter of *First Contact*, he was aiming to challenge *The Voyage Home*'s status as the biggest *Star Trek* movie by making a "feelgood movie" which would return to the optimistic view of the future at the franchise's core. "Rick had said that he really wanted to adapt a classic story and put it into *Star Trek* terms," Piller added, noting that Joseph Conrad's novel *Heart of Darkness* — the basis for Francis Ford Coppola's *Apocalypse Now* — was the classic text selected for the purpose, albeit married to an unrelated story involving a search for the fountain of youth. To this end, Piller's first twenty-five-page outline concerned Picard's search for an old mentor — specifically, Boothby the groundskeeper, played by Ray Walston in the *Next Generation* episode 'The First Duty' — who had, like Kurtz in Conrad's and Coppola's versions, "gone native" — in this instance, on a planet whose waters grant eternal youth.

The story would have begun by showing a young and rebellious Jean-Luc Picard, raising hell at Starfleet Academy, where he also enjoys a close friendship with Boothby. The story then cuts to the present day — in *Star Trek* terms, the twenty-fourth century — where Picard is given a mission to beam down onto an uncharted world and journey upriver to the fortified home of a Colonel Kurtz-type character, who has been shooting down Romulan and Federation ships in the Neutral Zone for no apparent reason. Picard eventually reaches him, only to discover that, despite his advancing years, Boothby now looks exactly the same age as he did when the two knew each other at Starfleet Academy. Evidently, the planet holds the secret of eternal youth, and his not-so-old friend has been shooting down ships in order to protect it.

Berman liked the idea, but believed that actor Patrick Stewart — who, by this time, had been granted the right of approval over both the direction of the script and the director of the film — would not, because Picard would also be affected by the planet's youth-giving properties, growing younger as the story progressed. "By the time he gets to get the girl and swashbuckle, he's twenty-five again," Berman reasoned. "He's not going to like that." Instead, Berman suggested that the fountain of youth idea be discarded, and that Commander Data replace Boothby as the Kurtz-type character. Piller knew a good idea when he heard one. "The idea of Picard going up the river to retrieve Data, who has gone berserk, is a fascinating story to me," Piller explained. "We went down that road for several weeks," he added, "[and] came up with a story which was quite a bit darker than the one we started out to tell, [but] a story that many people at the studio liked." Despite Paramount's enthusiasm, however, the new approach was rejected by Stewart, who told Piller it was dark, grim and not entertaining enough. By way of compromise, Berman suggested that the fountain of youth concept be reintroduced into the story, with just enough of the 'Data gone berserk' plotline to avoid throwing out the baby with the bathwater. The idea was re-pitched to Stewart, who reacted enthusiastically. As Piller recalled, "When Rick said, 'We felt you wouldn't like the idea of getting younger,' [Patrick] said, 'Don't be silly. It's perfectly fine. I have no problem with that at all.'"

Piller set to work on the script, initially making one fatal error. "We tried to have our cake and eat it, too," he admitted, referring to his attempt to retain the *Heart of Darkness* story while developing the fountain of youth idea. "We tried to crush them together in a draft of the script that didn't work at all. In fact, the first half of the movie was the trip up the river to find Data, and on page seventy-eight we find Data in the fountain of youth environment. Then the second half of the movie is all about these strange things that are happening to us getting younger. It was two different movies." To solve the problem, Piller threw out the first half and expanded the second half so that it became the main storyline of the film which — after nine different names were registered with the Motion Picture Association of America (MPAA) — would eventually become *Star Trek: Insurrection*. And, while bettering neither *First Contact* nor *The Voyage Home* in terms of box-office, it was successful enough to guarantee the twenty year-old film franchise another instalment.

According to John Logan, the Academy Award-winning *Gladiator* scribe whom Paramount hired to write *Star Trek X*, the franchise's tenth voyage had an unusually painless delivery. "I went in and said, 'This is the story I want to do and these are the three things I want to happen in this movie' — and they are some bold choices — and to my great delight, everyone at Paramount said, 'Absolutely. Let's take some risks. Let's see these characters grow. And if you want to write a great antagonist and tie him into these people, go ahead and do it.' They were very supportive about it." Logan found Patrick Stewart equally encouraging. "When I came in with my rather bold ideas, Patrick was very much on board," the writer asserts, "in terms of saying, 'Let these people grow up, spread their wings and be the characters they *can* be — rather than just be bottled versions of the characters on the show.' And he was great during the development," he adds. "I would call him and say, 'Here's the story, here's what we're doing,' and he was great in terms of feedback. He'd say, 'That's not good enough' or 'That's clichéd' or 'That's great, I love that idea.'"

As *Star Trek* celebrated its thirty-fifth anniversary in 2001 with the end of one television series, *Voyager*, and the start of another, *Enterprise*, it was either the best of times or the worst of times for the franchise. Given the relatively soft box-office performance of *Insurrection*, the tenth *Trek* film was already being seen as 'make or break' for the series. At least Logan was aware of the responsibility resting on his shoulders. "I hope that we're recapturing some of the spirit of *First Contact* and *The Wrath of Khan*, in terms of [*Star Trek X*] being a big old adventure movie," he commented as the film was officially green-lit. "And while certain elements are incredibly character-driven, I hope those won't exclude the general audience. Or it will be the worst of times, believe me!" ■

Close, But No Cigar-Shaped Object

How The Evil Aliens Of Steven Spielberg's *Night Skies* Were Replaced By A Very Different Extra-Terrestrial

"I might have taken leave of my senses."

—Steven Spielberg looks back on his aborted
sci-fi/horror hybrid *Night Skies*

Nobody expects one mega-hit, let alone two," director Steven Spielberg said after the November 1977 opening of *Close Encounters of the Third Kind*. Only two years after his smash hit *Jaws*, the film earned $77 million at the domestic box-office, and solidified Spielberg's status as a film-maker with a unique ability to captivate, entertain and enthral an audience. The following year, the Academy Awards ceremony further consolidated the film's artistic merits, although, ultimately, the voters failed to convert all but two of its nine Oscar nominations into actual statuettes.

Unsurprisingly, the success of *Close Encounters* prompted Columbia Pictures, which had financed and released the film, to begin planning a sequel; the studio had purchased these rights along with Spielberg's screenplay and fully intended to exploit them. Spielberg, for his part, was less enthusiastic, yet he had no wish for Columbia to simply commission a script and assign the directing duties to another director, as Universal had done with *Jaws 2*. Therefore, to keep himself in the game, Spielberg shrewdly constructed a brief treatment for a proposed low-budget follow-up, rather than a true sequel, tentatively entitled *Watch the Skies*.

The idea for the treatment sprang from Spielberg's copious research for *Close Encounters of the Third Kind* (a film he had originally intended to call *Watch the Skies*). Noted UFOlogist J. Allen Hynek had related an incident in which a Kentucky family had claimed to have been terrorised by extraterrestrials which surrounded their farm, holding them captive and dissecting farm animals. Inspired by this supposedly true-life event, which took place in 1955, *Watch the Skies* was conceived as a contemporary thriller, in which a family is held captive in their farmhouse by a group of eleven unfriendly aliens. After failing to communicate with chickens, cows and other animals in a ham-fisted attempt to discover which of Earth's species are sentient, the aliens dissect an animal — a reference to the phenomenon of cattle mutilations often blamed on extraterrestrial experiments — before resolving to turn their unwelcome attentions on the humans.

At the time, it seemed entirely possible that *Watch the Skies* would, indeed, go ahead. Spielberg was still reeling from the aftershock of his first fully-fledged flop, the epic but misguided Second World War comedy *1941*. Adding fuel to the rumours was NASA's announcement that Spielberg had paid to reserve cargo space in what would be the inaugural Space Shuttle flight, scheduled for 1980, in order to film the Earth and the Moon from orbit for the film's opening sequence. In addition, although Spielberg had stated that he would produce the film but not direct it, since he was contractually obliged to helm his next project at Universal, he was closely involved at the earliest stages of development.

Spielberg initially approached screenwriter Lawrence Kasdan to turn his treatment into a full screenplay, but he had already been commissioned to write the second *Star Wars* film, *The Empire Strikes Back*, for Spielberg's friend George Lucas. The director turned instead to John Sayles, who had scripted Joe Dante's *Piranha*, a low-budget *Jaws* rip-off that Spielberg had admired. Sayles immediately set to work on the screenplay which, he told Gavin Smith, "eventually got called *Night Skies* because somebody had the rights to the words 'watch the skies', which is the last line Kevin McCarthy says in *Invasion of the Body Snatchers*." *Night Skies*, he explained to Smith, concerned "some farm people who were attacked by these little ETs who were mutilating their cattle." Although the story has been described as "*Straw Dogs* with aliens" — a reference to Sam Peckinpah's controversial 1971 drama about a married couple menaced by violent villagers on an isolated West Country farm — Sayles took a dramatically different reference point. "My model was *Drums Along the Mohawk*," he said, referring to the 1939 western starring Henry Fonda and Claudette Colbert, "with aliens instead of Indians attacking the farm."

Sayles even named one of the eleven extraterrestrials Scar, after the Comanche Indian who kidnaps John Wayne's niece in *The Searchers*.

As Sayles toiled on the script, Spielberg was invited by Columbia to suggest possible directors for *Night Skies*. He dutifully put forward two suggestions: Tobe Hooper, a maverick horror film-maker whose first feature, *The Texas Chain Saw Massacre*, had earned itself the dubious accolade of "The *Citizen Kane* of Meat Movies"; and Ron Cobb, a California-born fantasy artist who had worked on John Carpenter's cult movie *Dark Star*, the cantina sequence of *Star Wars* and early designs for *Alien*. Columbia evidently preferred Cobb, despite the fact that he had no experience as a director, and he was soon signed to the project, scheduled to begin shooting when Spielberg returned from the overseas locations on *Raiders of the Lost Ark*. In April 1980, a feature on Columbia's forthcoming productions in an issue of industry bible *Daily Variety* described the as-yet-unnamed *Night Skies*, and preproduction officially began that same month.

Even at this early stage, Spielberg knew that the number of scenes featuring aliens meant that he would require more sophisticated creature effects work than Carlo Rambaldi had supplied for the ninety seconds' worth of spindly, backlit extraterrestrials in the final sequence of *Close Encounters of the Third Kind*. On the advice of his friend John Landis, Spielberg hired emergent special effects pioneer Rick Baker, who was busy preparing his ground-breaking creature work for Landis's *An American Werewolf in London*. "The assignment was a dream come true... I told Spielberg what he was talking about would be incredibly difficult and expensive," Baker told *Cinefantastique* in 1982, recalling that the price he quoted Spielberg was $3 million, a figure at which the director did not seem to balk, given that there would be no other major expenses. "It was so exciting for me to do a movie that had this whole race of aliens," Baker now recalls. "There were, like, eleven different aliens in the movie. They were all from the race, [but] they're all different characters, [so] it was real character-driven stuff."

Spielberg had no script to show Baker but, from a brief outline, the effects designer was able to fashion a crude model of how he saw the lead alien. "I knew [it] had to be able to communicate its emotions through expressions," Baker told *Cinefantastique*. "Therefore, it had to have human-like features: two eyes, sort of a nose, and a mouth. But the body got very strange: it had almost a dog-like rib cage, a long spiny abdomen and frog-like legs. It was a very textural thing with wrinkles, scales and folds. It stood four feet tall when erect, but I envisioned it walking hunched like an ape." Satisfied with the design, Baker proceeded to the next stage, sculpting and painting a fibreglass model that would form the basis of the complex 'animatronics' process by which Baker intended to animate the creatures. Spielberg, who was about to fly to England to commence production on *Raiders of the Lost Ark*, gave Baker the go-ahead to produce a working prototype of the creature, at a cost of $70,000.

A few weeks later, Baker mailed off a videotape showing the complex automaton in action, receiving an enthusiastic response both from Spielberg and his co-producer, Kathleen Kennedy. "I got this call from Kathleen Kennedy saying, 'Steven is so flipped out about this! This is so incredible! This makes Yoda look like a toy! We are so excited!'" Baker recalls. "And then we just made better stuff from there." Columbia granted Baker further funds to continue research and development of the creature in Spielberg's absence, and within weeks he had established a studio with six staff and a machine shop, from which he would oversee his responsibilities for preproduction on both *Night Skies* and *An American Werewolf in London*. Finally, in mid-1980, Sayles delivered his first draft of the screenplay, which featured five different aliens (down from the original eleven), each with its own individual personality. "One of the aliens was named Scar — a real badass," Baker told *Cinefantastique*, referring to the nicknames given by the family to refer to the different creatures. Another was named Squirt, and a third — who strikes up a friendship with the family's mentally subnormal son — was nicknamed Buddy. "In the group of killer aliens who want to slice and dice this little autistic boy, there's one nice alien who makes friends with him," Sayles confirmed. "I put this autistic boy at the centre of the family."

Meanwhile, on location in Tunisia, Spielberg was having second thoughts about this story of hostile aliens. "I might have taken leave of my senses," he told *Film Comment*. "Throughout [the production of] *Raiders*, I was in between killing Nazis and blowing up flying wings and having Harrison Ford hanging from vines and all this high serialised adventure," he added. "I was sitting there in the middle of Tunisia, scratching my head and saying, 'I've got to get back to the tranquillity, or at least the spirituality, of *Close Encounters*.'" Spielberg also wanted to tell a story he claimed to have been considering since his own boyhood, when he had yearned for a playmate who could magically transform his lonely life. Spielberg ran his ideas past screenwriter Melissa Mathison, who had arrived in Tunisia to join her boyfriend (and later husband), Harrison Ford. "I asked Melissa if she would care to sit with me and let me test this out on her," Spielberg recalled. "So we sat down, and I told her the story, and she wept." According to Mathison, her interest in the story was not due to its science fiction element, but because of "the idea of an alien creature who was benevolent, tender, emotional and sweet... and the idea of the creature's striking up a relationship with a child who came from a broken home was very affecting." Mathison's enthusiasm, coupled with her informed and empathetic suggestions, was enough to encourage Spielberg to ask her to try her hand at a screenplay about a young boy's encounter with an extra-terrestrial. Mathison, who had encountered difficulties while collaborating with another powerful director, Francis Ford Coppola, on the Zoetrope productions *The Black Stallion* and *The Escape Artist*, was reluctant to accept the assignment. Pressed by Spielberg and Ford, however, she eventually agreed, beginning work on the script in October 1980.

Spielberg returned from Tunisia and Hawaii, where the opening sequence of *Raiders* was filmed, eager to close the door on the *Night Skies* project and to begin planning the film Mathison entitled *ET and Me*, but which would eventually become known to billions world-wide as *E.T. The Extra-Terrestrial*. Sayles took the rejection of his single draft philosophically, having already moved on to develop his second feature as director. Rick Baker, however, was less than thrilled to hear about the new direction Spielberg would be taking with the film he had been working on for several months. "I was working weekends, and long nights to do this stuff," Baker told *Cinefantastique*, referring to the countless production sketches, designs and sculptures he had produced during this period. "[Then] he walks in one day and says something like, 'Guess what? I'm not going to make this movie anymore.' My jaw dropped. My heart skipped a beat. I almost felt like crying. Then he said, 'But I *am* going to make another picture which is going to have an alien in it — a cuter alien, a nicer alien — and I want you to start re-designing him.'"

By this time, Baker was busy with *An American Werewolf in London* and felt that he could not fully devote himself to Spielberg's new project. "I said, 'Well, this is like we're starting all over again,'" he now recalls. "And he got pissed off that I wasn't excited about it." Spielberg was also unhappy that, although $700,000 of development funds had already been spent on the aborted *Night Skies* designs, Baker insisted that a fresh budget was required for the new project. "I told him that this is a different situation, and [that] the old movie was no more and the old contract was no good, [and] to talk to my lawyer about it," Baker told *Cinefantastique*. Kathleen Kennedy recalled similar events: "When we went to sit down with Rick and decide on a schedule, and see whether, with changes, we could do it at a lower cost, Rick wouldn't talk to us, and insisted we talk to his attorney. Steven felt that Rick wasn't as concerned [as he should be] about the money and schedule."

Baker explained to *Cinefantastique* that his use of lawyers was a precautionary tactic based on things he had been told about working with Spielberg. "I was very paranoid because I heard from so many people, 'Watch out for Steven — he'll stab you in the back.' And Steven is very paranoid of special effects guys. I was treating my situation with [him] very different than I had with any other job, because I'd heard that you had to protect yourself with this guy." According to Baker, the meeting with Spielberg ended badly. "Steven fell back and said, 'Godammit! You're so difficult!' and he went on and on. He ended by yelling, 'I'm shutting this place down!' and walked out the door. Just as he left, he said — nice and loud, so I could hear — 'Go call [Carlo] Rambaldi!' I think he thought I was going to ask for more money. He never listened [to] what I was offering to do to finish the film." According to Spielberg, however, it was Baker who invoked the name Rambaldi, at the suggestion that the title character of E.T. might resemble the Rambaldi-designed aliens who emerged from the mother ship at the end of *Close Encounters*. Either way, Spielberg *did* call Rambaldi, who accepted his offer.

Suddenly, Baker found himself literally locked out of his own studio. His notes, sketches and sculptures were confiscated — along with all of his preparatory material for *American Werewolf*. "I think Carlo Rambaldi ended up with it," he now remembers. "I *know* he did, as a matter of fact, [because] a guy that I know very well who ended up painting E.T. was there when they were doing it, and they had my stuff sitting there. And Steven would point to it, saying, 'Make this, do it like this, do this part like that.'" Small wonder, then, that Baker was further infuriated by an article about Carlo Rambaldi in *Time* magazine in May 1982, which referred to an unspecified special effects crew which "tried to make the spaceman [E.T.] and failed, spending a reported $700,000." As Baker told *Cinefantastique*, "If Spielberg and Rambaldi are claiming that the thing I did was no good, why don't they okay me to publish pictures of it? I would like to have the opportunity to prove what I did was not inadequate, but actually quite exceptional... I think I did some of the best work I've ever done on that picture, and the thanks I got was [the suggestion that] I wasn't competent."

But Baker was not the only individual to take exception to Spielberg's change of heart and *Night Skies*' change of direction. "We had a meeting or two with Steven on it," Columbia's president of world-wide productions, John Veitch, told Spielberg biographer Joseph McBride. "Steven wasn't quite positive that he wanted to do that particular story. The more he thought about it, I guess, and with Melissa getting involved, it changed." Incredible though it seems, Columbia's market research department ran demographic surveys on the new approach and concluded that spending even $10 million on what the studio privately described as "a wimpy Walt Disney movie" was not viable, particularly after the *1941* débâcle. In February 1981 — six months after fulfilling its desire for a *Close Encounters* follow-up with the release of *Close Encounters of the Third Kind: The Special Edition*, a re-edited version with several restored and newly-filmed scenes — the company put the project in turnaround. It was arguably one of the costliest mistakes in motion picture history.

Columbia president Frank Price blamed Spielberg's decision to direct the film, rather than simply produce it, noting that, "although Steven had the project in development with us, he had not decided whether he wanted to direct or just produce. When he decided to direct [the film], he told me that he had a contractual obligation to direct his next picture at Universal." Sid Sheinberg, president of Universal's parent company and a long-time friend of Spielberg, remembered it differently. "Steven had no compulsion to deliver that project to us, contractual or otherwise," he stated. "It is very simple: Steven brought us the script and said he thought we could acquire it from Columbia." Universal did so, repaying $1 million which Columbia had paid to develop the *Night Skies/E.T.* project and offering a deal by which the rival studio would retain five percent of the film's net profits. As Veitch subsequently recalled, "I think that year we made more on that picture than we did on any of *our* films." The brisk two-month shooting schedule of *E.T.* — known throughout production by the phoney title *A Boy's Life* and described deceptively by Universal as a "comedy about antics and lifestyles of boys living in southern California today" — began in October 1981, two months after Mathison delivered her final script draft. Barely a year later, it would supplant *Star Wars* as the most successful motion picture in history, a title it would retain for more than a decade.

In the meantime, however, *Night Skies* refused to die. Spielberg felt that the project had metamorphosed so radically by becoming *E.T.* that his original idea — a family besieged by malevolent aliens — was still valid. Columbia's rejection of *E.T.* — which, in retrospect, was costly enough in itself — soured Spielberg's relationship with the studio, and Frank Price in particular; when the latter moved to Universal, Spielberg reportedly insisted that their paths never cross. Instead, the director took *Night Skies* to MGM, with the stipulation that, as had always been intended, he would produce and perhaps even write the film, but not direct it. In addition, to avoid any conflict of interest with *E.T.*, he changed the malign entities which victimise the family from aliens into ghosts. *Poltergeist* was born.

At least, that's the way Spielberg tells it. According to Tobe Hooper — who was one of Spielberg's original choices to direct *Night Skies* and who would eventually be chosen to direct *Poltergeist* — it was *his* idea, not Spielberg's, to turn *Night Skies* into a horror movie about a suburban family terrorised by invisible, malicious spirits. Hooper, allegedly inspired by a book about poltergeists he found in his desk at Universal — which, it transpired, had previously been occupied by Robert Wise, director of an earlier, similar ghost story, *The Haunting* — insisted that he put the idea to Spielberg while the director was in London making *Raiders of the Lost Ark*. Veteran horror writer Richard Matheson, who had scripted Spielberg's *Duel*, also noted that, prior to *Poltergeist*'s production, Spielberg asked him for a videotape of Matheson's 1962 episode of *The Twilight Zone*, 'Little Girl Lost', in which a six year-old girl rolls under her bed and disappears into another dimension.

Spielberg, however, had his own ideas about where the story for his new take on *Night Skies* should come from, turning to best-selling horror writer Stephen King, whose début novel *Carrie* had been turned into a successful film by Spielberg's friend Brian De Palma. King was enthusiastic at his first script meeting with Spielberg, but unwisely left the negotiation of his fee to his publisher who, the author noted, "asked this incredible amount of money to do the screenplay, [especially] for somebody who had never done a screenplay that had been produced." MGM, which saw *Poltergeist* as a $9.5 million production aimed primarily at the horror market, refused to pay. "I got a letter from Spielberg saying he was really unhappy that it turned out this way," King said later, "but, in the end, I would have been hired help." Instead, Spielberg turned to a pair of aspiring screenwriters, Michael Grais and Mark Victor, with whom the producer would ultimately share script credit.

The story of the making of *Poltergeist* could arguably fill a book of its own — if only credited director Tobe Hooper would go on the record to talk about his unhappy experiences, watching Spielberg (who was present for all but three days of the film's twelve-week shooting schedule) call the shots while he sat on the sidelines. Less than a month into production, the *Los Angeles Herald-Examiner* reported that Hooper was "*not* really directing the pic anymore," prompting Hooper to respond that Spielberg's involvement "spans all aspects of this film and does not differ from those functions normally performed by the executive producer." Spielberg's agent, who made a cameo appearance in the film, saw it differently. "When I came back from the set," he told Joseph McBride, "I said, 'Well, now I know what the executive producer does... He sets up the camera, tells the actors what to do, stands back, and lets the director say, "Action!"'"

Several months later, the Directors Guild of America (DGA) successfully sued MGM, on behalf of Hooper, for running a trailer for the film in which the words 'A STEVEN SPIELBERG PRODUCTION' appeared twice as large as 'A TOBE HOOPER FILM', a violation of DGA regulations. MGM was fined $15,000, ordered to place apologetic advertisements in three trade publications and remake trailers running in major cities. As Spielberg later told the *Los Angeles Times*, responding to widespread accusations that he had taken charge of the picture himself, "My enthusiasm for wanting to make *Poltergeist* would have been difficult for any director I would have hired. It derived from *my* imagination and *my* experiences, and it came out of *my* typewriter," he added, seemingly forgetting the contributions of co-writers Grais and Victor. "I thought I'd be able to turn *Poltergeist* over to a director and walk away. I was wrong." The experience had taught him a valuable lesson. In future, he said, "If I write it myself, I'll direct it myself. I won't put someone else through what I put Tobe through, and I'll be more honest in my contributions to a film."

Despite these difficulties, *Poltergeist* became a rousing success in the summer of 1982, released virtually simultaneously with *E.T.*; non-identical twin offshoots of the original *Night Skies* idea. Although *Poltergeist* was subsequently hit by several lawsuits claiming that the film appropriated other properties — a fate which also befell *E.T.* and continues to plague some Spielberg productions to this day — the resemblance to Spielberg's original vision for *Night Skies* is obvious, despite his canny substitution of paranormal phenomena for extraterrestrial entities. In addition, as John Sayles has since observed, "The *last* scene of *Night Skies* is of the nice [alien] being marooned on Earth by his peers, and the last shot is a hawk's shadow over him, and him cowering. That's basically the first page of *E.T.*" Sayles's opening scene, in which the alien known as Scar kills farm animals by touching them with a long bony finger which gives off an eerie light, also calls to mind the glowing digit of that other, friendlier, extraterrestrial. Nevertheless, Sayles insists that there are few, if any, similarities between Mathison's script and his own, which he has generously described as "more of a jumping-off point than something that was raided for material. Melissa Mathison did an incredible job," he added. "The Writers Guild [of America] sent me her script just because they knew I was somewhere in the chain, but it had nothing to do with anything I wrote."

Arguably, additional elements of the aborted *Night Skies* project may be glimpsed in a story treatment for a proposed sequel to *E.T.* entitled *E.T. II: Nocturnal Fears*, apparently penned by Spielberg and

Mathison in July 1982. Set during the first summer after E.T.'s departure at the end of the original movie, *Nocturnal Fears* begins with
the arrival of a mothership full of unfriendly aliens — carnivorous,
albino versions of E.T. himself — who might perhaps be seen as close
relatives of the ones in *Night Skies*, not least because of the cattle
mutilations they perform upon landing. It transpires that these evil aliens
are searching for a marooned compatriot, Zrek. They kidnap, interrogate
and examine Elliott, Michael, Gertie and Elliott's *Dungeons & Dragons*
buddies. Elliott, screaming in pain, cries out for his friend E.T. before losing consciousness. His plea flies up to the stars, but will it be heard?

E.T. sends a message to Earth — ET Help Elliott Soon — and duly
appears in person, rescuing the children from the 'light cage' in which
they are held captive and re-routing the evil aliens' mothership to a
remote corner of the galaxy. The treatment concludes with Elliott and his
friends once again gathering to watch E.T. depart.

E.T. II: Nocturnal Fears did not progress beyond the nine-page treatment dated 17 July 1982; evidently Spielberg felt that a sequel "would do
nothing but rob the original of its virginity", and chose not to pursue the
proposition. He did, however, authorise William Kotzwinkle, author of
E.T.'s official novelisation, to write a follow-up novella entitled *E.T.: The
Book of the Green Planet*, based on a story by the director. Spielberg was
also closely involved in the creation of Universal Studios' $40 million *E.T.*
theme park ride, which opened in 1991. A decade later, with interest in
E.T. having been revived in at least one country by his recent role in
advertisements for British telecommunications giant BT, Universal
announced plans to re-release the original film in 2002, its twentieth
anniversary.

In the intervening years, the question over E.T.'s origins was one
that would continue to haunt Spielberg, despite the fact that Mathison
enjoyed sole script credit, while Rambaldi's read simply 'E.T. created by
Carlo Rambaldi.' Seven years after *E.T.*'s release, however, Mathison won
a Writers Guild of America arbitration, awarding her a percentage of the
film's lucrative merchandising revenues, after arbitrator Sol Rosenthal
found that the writer had "extensively detailed her main character in
her first two working drafts, before Carlo Rambaldi's model was done."
Despite Baker's belief that Rambaldi's character bore a strong resemblance to his own concepts, and Universal's insistence that Spielberg

and Sayles had described the character prior to Mathison's involvement, Rosenthal concluded that, while *Night Skies* contained "some similar references to the extraterrestrial... a review of Sayles' description (of a character with a beaklike mouth and eyes like a grasshopper's) demonstrates that E.T. was not copied from Sayles' script." Despite the ruling, Spielberg's lawyer, Bruce Ramer, later wrote to *Daily Variety* that, "as Ms Mathison would unquestionably confirm to you, Mr Spielberg conveyed his views and concepts to her respecting E.T. in the most minute detail, both before and during the writing process," implying that, since Baker was also involved at this early conceptual stage, his designs almost certainly had an influence on the final appearance of E.T.. Baker believes that if his design sketches were published, this influence would be obvious. "I hadn't looked at my *Night Skies* stuff for a long time, because it kind of hurts," he told *Cinefantastique*, "but recently I put the pictures side by side, and there *are* an amazing number of things taken from my design. Some of the mechanics are in exactly the same place, and I can point to wrinkles in exactly the same place — only [Rambaldi's] is not as well sculpted as mine."

Not that Baker is bitter, claiming that he and Spielberg eventually resolved their differences. "We talked about it," he says now, "and he told me his point of view and I told him mine, and he was pissed off that I wasn't excited about this change, but he said he could understand, and it was all water under the bridge." However, in the twenty years since his aborted efforts on *Night Skies*, Baker has produced make-up effects for a steady stream of major genre pictures, winning six Academy Awards in the process, yet has never worked under Spielberg — except indirectly through such Amblin productions as *Gremlins*, *Harry and the Hendersons* and *Men in Black*. Nevertheless, Baker regrets not only that his conceptual artwork for *Night Skies* never saw the light of day, but also that the film itself did not see the green light of production.

"It was a real disappointment," he now concludes. "They turned around and took my stuff, altered it slightly, and made [*E.T.*,] one of the most incredible movies in history." Ultimately, as he summed up to *Cinefantastique*, "I would have loved *Night Skies*, and so would people who like science fiction and horror. But I doubt if it would appeal to as many people as *E.T.*, [so] I think Steven made the right choice." ∎

The Tourist Trap

The Twenty Year Journey Taken By *The Tourist*

"I think a lot of directors read *The Tourist* and have raided it.
It's been out there in the open air in Hollywood and had its
bones picked."

—director Franc Roddam

I n 1980, the year following the release of Ridley Scott's *Alien*, writer Clair Noto completed a screenplay entitled *The Tourist* which, in the coming years, was to become one of the most famous — perhaps even *the* most famous — unproduced scripts in Hollywood. In the two decades that followed the nascent writer's first attempt at a script, which had it been produced at that time would have trumped Ridley Scott's *Blade Runner* as the first science fiction *film noir* of the colour era, Noto has seen numerous unsuccessful attempts to make the film, including a recent revival by Universal Pictures, who first optioned it in the year it was written.

The story itself is simple: in present-day Manhattan, beautiful executive Grace Ripley is one of a secret group of exiled aliens living incognito on Earth, having adopted humanoid form in order to assimilate themselves into human society. Like many of her fellow aliens, Grace is seeking to return to her homeworld and is therefore eager to track down an extraterrestrial named John Taiga, whom she believes may have discovered a way to leave Earth. The story behind the various versions of the film which failed to reach the screen has an equally tenacious heroine at its heart — Clair Noto — and arguably contains as much drama, intrigue, betrayal and conflict as *The Tourist* itself.

Originally entering the film business as an assistant editor in New York, and working briefly on Marvel Comics' *Red Sonja* title in the late seventies, Clair Noto wrote *The Tourist* under assignment to Universal Pictures, having already scripted what she describes as "a female James Bond" story for legendary producer Ray Stark. According to Noto, the inspiration for *The Tourist* came from a number of sources, most notably a single photograph in Helmut Newton's first collection, *White Women*, published in 1973. "There was a photo in it of a model named Lisa Taylor running across a lawn," Noto says, referring to a colour photograph entitled 'Lisa Running'. "She was wearing a semi-transparent chiffon dress, and her eyes were terrified, and behind her was a building that looked like a motel, with a neon light coming from it. And I looked at this picture and thought, 'What is she running from?'"

Although Noto does not call herself a science fiction fan, much less a science fiction writer — "If you put a gun to my head and asked me to write a science fiction screenplay, I'd be dead," she admits — she has said that *The Tourist* was also partly inspired by Robert Wise's 1951 classic *The Day the Earth Stood Still*, in which alien Klaatu (Michael Rennie) and his robot, Gort, visit Earth with a dire warning about Mankind's destiny. "When the film opens you see Michael Rennie in his space suit," Noto told *Cinefantastique*. "Then, from that point on, he is in a suit and tie. I loved the whole idea of a man who could walk around in a boarding house in Washington, who was from another planet and you didn't recognize his alienness. The idea of a human being who wasn't a human being had been in my mind for a long time." Noto was also partially inspired by the stylised and sexually-charged science fiction and fantasy illustrations by artists like *Alien* conceptual designer H. R. Giger in the pages of *Heavy Metal* magazine. "I wanted to create a science fiction movie for adults," she said. "I wanted to combine what I considered a serious dramatic story with the fantastic effects of science fiction — especially in terms of sex, romance and love. I wanted to portray sexual agony and ecstasy in a way I had never seen before, and science fiction seemed like the arena."

Noto was invited to develop the project by Sean Daniel, a young Universal executive (who more recently has produced the smash hit remake of *The Mummy*, as well as its sequel, *The Mummy Returns*, and spin-off, *The Scorpion King*). "He had read pages from the female James Bond project I'd been working on," Noto recalls, "and he said, 'What do you want to do?' I said I didn't have a story, but I told him about the Helmut Newton photograph of the woman running, and I said, 'She's an alien, and she's from this planet that has exiled her to Earth like a criminal, and she's trying to get back. And the flying saucers we see are not coming from other worlds — they're aliens trying to leave, because wherever it was they came from, they liked it better than life on Earth, which was very harsh.' And I told him about all these clubs in New York and Tokyo and Morocco, filled with aliens. I almost saw the aliens as existential Parisians sitting around in clubs and cafés," she adds, "but if you open their shirts, they have metal stomachs. And they're all talking about this alien named John Taiga who stays underground, and is rumoured to be able to get them out." Daniel loved the idea, and immediately commissioned a first draft.

As she wrote, Noto's ideas coalesced into a compelling story about aliens living in New York, experiencing the same combination of fascination and alienation Noto herself felt when she first moved to the city. "I wanted her to look like a New York girl/woman," Noto said of her heroine, Grace Ripley; "[to] dress well, eat in good restaurants, and have to deal with New York taxi drivers and [other] New York-type eccentrics — some of whom I wanted to be other aliens also in human form — as well as the problem of being from another world. Somehow I felt that all she wants would be to go home, so I decided that the Earth would be a dumping ground for the unwanted of other galaxies or planets; that when prison was not bad enough for some aliens, they would be sent to Earth." Once there, she decided, those aliens unable to pass for human form would be caged in a subterranean concentration camp known as 'The Corridor', disguised as an operation known as 'The Manhattan Grief Clinic', and run by an evil creature who is actually an entire species in a single organism; a very powerful being, who is looking for the same alien Grace is looking for. On the way, Grace meets other reclusive aliens living in distress in Manhattan, and by the time she finds John Taiga, the extraterrestrial who is constructing a spacecraft, she has become attached to two humans, including a one-eyed beauty named Spider O'Toole. With her desire to leave becoming confused, Grace finally decides to stay on Earth.

Daniel was impressed with Noto's first draft, but ultimately decided it was not the kind of film he wanted to make. "I think maybe he thought I'd pushed it too far in the direction of science fiction," she says. "It was different than he expected, but he gave it to some other people at Universal that were like, 'Woah, this is really interesting!'" By this time, a producer named Renée Missel (*Resurrection*) was attached to the script. As Missel recalls, "I had optioned Clair's first script, and we were working together on that, and that's how I came on to *The Tourist*, with my partner Howard Rosenman. At the time, I was under contract to Universal, so it made sense to do it there." Missel's first move was to offer the project to British director Brian Gibson, who had recently moved to Los Angeles after earning his directorial stripes on British television with Dennis Potter's *Blue Remembered Hills* for the BBC, and made his feature film début with the Hazel O'Connor vehicle *Breaking Glass.*

"I got to LA in April 1980," recalls Gibson, who has since made such films as *Poltergeist II, What's Love Got to Do With It* and *Still Crazy.* "I met Renée a few months after that, and I think that's when she first showed me *The Tourist*. It was quite striking," he adds. "I thought it would make a terrific movie. What struck me as being totally original was the idea of a rather gloomy, existentialist *film noir* with the premise of Earth being a dumping ground for monsters from various galaxies, which was very resonant with a depressed view of the human condition. It made it a movie with art-house appeal, but with a premise that had a much wider potential audience, so in a way the challenge was to make the movie that I wanted to see, which would combine the ordinary cinemagoer in me, and the art-house cinemagoer in me. There was two ways of making it: one was the way it was written, which was a low-budget movie; and the other was the way Universal wanted to do it, which was obviously a much higher-budget, higher-concept movie." Since Universal owned the property, however, Gibson could not see a way to take the former approach, since the costs involved would inevitably require a more mainstream, audience-friendly picture, something that *The Tourist* was unlikely to become.

While Gibson considered the project, Noto learned from agent

Jeff Berg that *Alien* director Ridley Scott was interested in the script, and she even met with him to discuss it: "He was working on *Blade Runner*, but people weren't moving at the speed he wanted them to move, and he was thinking about doing *The Tourist*." In fact, she adds, "I think that the Chinatown sequence in *Blade Runner* was very much influenced by *The Tourist*. I believe he even said that to me at one time." By the time Scott had passed, Universal had placed the project in 'turnaround' — meaning that another studio was free to buy them out — feeling that it was too dark. Noto believed that this meant she was free to shop it to other studios, but Missel saw it differently. "If I remember it correctly, the turnaround was in Clair's and my name," she says. "Steve Bach, who ran United Artists, was interested in making the film, because he loved dark movies," she adds. "But then Clair, on the side, sold it or gave it to American Zoetrope, without me attached."

"I got a call from Lucy Fisher at Francis Ford Coppola's American Zoetrope," Noto recalls. "I guess Renée Missel had been going around town saying she controlled it, but I said, '*I* control it, and if Francis wants it, you got it.'" Shortly after Zoetrope optioned the script, another British director, Franc Roddam (*Quadrophenia*), became attached to it, much to Brian Gibson's surprise. "I mentioned it to Franc, who is actually an old friend, when we were playing tennis, around the spring of 1981," Gibson recalls, "and the next thing I knew, Franc was attached to it! Franc and I have sort of been friendly rivals, if you like, over a twenty-five year period," he adds. "I'm fond of him, and I think he's talented, but he's got his own way of doing things and I was somewhat annoyed that Franc had hustled in there so quick."

Roddam duly began to develop the project with Noto, who describes the director as "incredibly supportive. I have no idea what he would eventually have done, but he got the whole idea. Franc and I spent a lot of time going through the script, page by page, trying to work out what it was we were trying to do." The problem, they knew, was that the film was not traditionally structured. "It was like a Nicolas Roeg or Donald Cammell film," Noto explains. "It didn't follow the Robert McKee story structure. And there were these long musings of dialogue, but when you cut those out, you didn't have anything, because it wasn't the events that made it work, it was the people and their angst and their malaise, and the fruitless search. In a sense, the journey becomes more interesting than the ending, because in the end she doesn't want to leave."

Both Noto and Roddam say that their work on a new draft was successful, and that Zoetrope considered *The Tourist* a 'go picture.' Unfortunately, Coppola's company was too busy haemorrhaging money on *One from the Heart*, the ill-fated musical which would eventually bankrupt the studio, to realise Coppola's vision of an artistic haven where film-makers like Michael Powell, Jean-Luc Godard and David Lynch could make films outside of the Hollywood system. "I was surrounded by ten people in this little unit," Roddam told *Cinefantastique*, "and we were all going to make fantastic films for Francis. Not only did none of the films get made, there was absolutely no money for our preparation of these films — no money for our secretaries and no money for us. And Francis, meanwhile, is spending millions and millions of dollars refurbishing his studio and making *One from the Heart*. What was supposed to be the greatest ideal studio to go to and work with an artist-producer, Francis, and was supposed to be heaven, turned out to be pure hell. It was worse than any journey he did up in the fucking Philippines."

At one point, Roddam tried to force the issue, "to get the film made, to get my secretary paid and to keep my family alive. I remember once going into the executive's office saying, 'Where's my money?' They said, 'We can't. The deal's held up with the lawyers.' I said, 'You employ the lawyers. You get them on the phone and tell them to send me a cheque right now.' For a while, they were going to have me arrested for kidnapping an executive for four-and-a-half minutes." Meanwhile, Roddam continued to toil with Noto on *The Tourist*. "We're both passionate people," he observed. "We were talking to art directors and discussing how the film should be made, but there were no funds coming. In the end, Francis' studio [was] going under."

Roddam's involvement in the project had got as far as the casting stage, with a range of possibilities, beginning with Noto's bizarre first choice, German actress Hanna Schygulla (*Dead Again*), and continuing through Kathleen Turner, Madonna, Michelle Pfeiffer, Hazel O'Connor and Noto's own favourite, Theresa Russell. "It was passed on by a lot of the actresses that I was interested in," Noto admits, "and some of them the studios didn't think were big enough to carry an expensive movie. I was looking for a kind of blonde, cool, strange individual, who was not fashionable but chic in her own individual way, who had this mysterious under-life, who fascinates and repels you at the same time. And finding an actress at that time that embodied all of that was tough."

Finally, after spending eight months "pissing around, talking to actresses," Roddam realised that *The Tourist* would never be made at Zoetrope, and began shopping the idea to other studios. "We tried to set up a deal with Dino De Laurentiis and other people to try and get *The Tourist* made elsewhere, because it's a fantastic script," he explained, "[but] the deal got held up because Francis wanted a fee. He wouldn't just let it go free and clear. He wanted money even though he hadn't put any money into it." With only two months left on the option, it was clear to both that Zoetrope would not be able to afford the renewal payment of $150,000. "Then, suddenly, Renée Missel came into it again at Universal saying, 'Hey, there's a legal problem here anyway,'" Roddam added. "So it floundered."

Missel apparently claimed part ownership of the property she had optioned from Noto, leading to a potentially litigious stand-off with which Roddam was unwilling to become involved. "I had the joint turnaround, so I had to sue them," Missel states flatly. In a final attempt to salvage the situation, Roddam suggested to Noto that Renée Missel return as producer for Universal Pictures, to whom the option was due to revert. "I said, 'You really don't know what you're in for — this is a really crazy woman,'" Noto recalls. "I just did not want her involved and he didn't pursue it, and the project went away." Today, Noto regrets this decision. "I feel that it was a very transitional point for Franc, and if I could go back and do it again, I would let him do it, because he showed good faith in me, and I don't think he would have double-crossed me. I feel like I did him a real injustice."

If so, Roddam certainly seems to bear Noto no grudges. "If you look at the journey of the script," he told *Cinefantastique* in 1994, "it seems to me that it's a fight on the part of the writer to try and retain the integrity of the piece as she saw it... I think, in a sense, that Clair thought she created the work and therefore her thoughts should be respected, and I agree with that. At the same time, sometimes as a director you say, 'I respect it and I'm going to see it clearly for you,' but sometimes the verbal vision has to be altered to make it work on film. The real story of this piece is Clair's attempt to protect her vision," he added. "I can't speak for Renée, because I don't know what she did, but it's quite common that a producer will take a piece [of a property] and just say, 'I own it and I'm going to do what I like with it.' And that wasn't the original deal."

When Zoetrope's option lapsed after a year, Roddam went on to direct *The Lords of Discipline* for Paramount and *The Tourist* returned to Universal, where Sean Daniel once again began actively developing it. "Sean said, 'We want to start it again, but we don't want to work with Clair," Missel recalls. "[He] said, 'She's too dark; too difficult.' And I have to be honest with you and tell you that, having been with Clair on the project for two years and another project before that, the fact that she went to Franc Roddam and American Zoetrope [made me] not so keen to work with her either. I really felt betrayed." Instead, Missel contacted Brian Gibson again, who became attached to the project, but soon found that working with Noto on the script would be impossible. "Very early on, I had to part company with Clair Noto," Gibson recalls. "It was pretty evident after about one meeting. Clair is a very talented and very unique writer, but I made one suggestion — 'Let us investigate the following' — and she hit the roof. [It's] the kind of rage that Clair is famous for," he adds. "I made some suggestion, and I got an absolute, hardline kind of 'No' which indicated that it would be pretty impossible to work with her."

Says Noto, "I had a meeting with Brian Gibson at this house he was renting in the Hollywood Hills, and he was really aggressive; like, 'I don't need you — anybody can rewrite this.' I think he got this from Renée Missel. She was personally trying to do me damage, and Gibson made no attempt to listen to what I had to say. So I did my revisions, handed it in, and she said, 'You're finished. You're written out.'" As Missel explains, "I felt that she couldn't keep rewriting. She was stuck. She had created something that had its own *gestalt*, and even she could not fix it where people thought it needed fixing. And whether we were right or not in thinking it needed fixing, it just was not fixable. So then began the process of trying to make the movie without Clair Noto."

Missel knew, however, that pursuing the project without Noto would be difficult, given the intensely personal nature of the script. "Usually in Hollywood, many projects have many writers," she explains. "However, there are certain projects that are so bizarre and so original that to work without the original writer, to undo the weave of the story, is impossible. Clair, in her brilliance, had woven a script that could not be taken apart." Noto understood. "There are certain projects that have a form and a structure to them that any good writer can really come in and deal with," the writer explained to *Cinefantastique*. "This didn't have that. When they took it away from me," she added, "they were very nasty, like, 'Fuck you — we're going to put it together.' I couldn't get Renée Missel on the phone. It was terrible, just terrible. She kept belittling the project, saying, 'Nobody's even going to want to make this movie. Or if they would, it would be a cult movie that would play at midnight like *Rocky Horror*.' [She was] totally insulting about it."

At one point, Missel sent it to science fiction writer Harlan Ellison for his advice. "He called me and said, 'How can you make *Resurrection* [the uplifting supernatural fable Missel had produced in 1980] and then make *The Tourist?*'" she recalls. "'Do you really want to have such a gloomy vision put out into the world? It's sick and dark and disgusting, and it doesn't believe in humanity.' And that's what the studios kept saying: that it had to be pro-humanity, ultimately. They wanted a mainstream movie with a lighter tone." Says Gibson, "Life would have been a lot less complicated if it had been a lower budget movie, because it wouldn't have necessitated the kind of ambitions a Universal main line studio film would involve. When I came into it, it was already costing hundreds of thousands of dollars in turnaround," he adds. "I think it could have been developed into a great movie that could have kept the best of what Clair wrote, and also made it more accessible. But we just never got there."

In an effort to lighten the tone, Missel and Gibson brought in a writer named Patricia Knop to try her hand at another draft. Knop had not previously rewritten another screenwriter's work, but accepted the assignment because *The Tourist* seemed to be close to getting a production green light. "Brian Gibson was so gung-ho about it, and so was Universal, especially Ned Tanen," Knop recalls, referring to the then-head of production. "Our quest was to preserve the quirky wonderfulness of the script, but at the same time, lighten it a little bit. What Ned Tanen wanted, what he felt would make it work, was to lighten it just enough so that it would be more palatable to a wider audience." Knop's rewrite involved some story changes, she says, "but I tried to keep the major wonderful things, like the big warehouses with the people who are disintegrating — that vision which, at the time, was profoundly unique, I think. I loved it when we went into it, and I was trying to be very careful about the elements that seemed to be really wonderful about the script." Both Gibson and Missel felt that Knop had largely succeeded in her goals. "The draft that I worked on with Pat is probably the best combination of Clair's original vision with a more human drama," says Gibson. "She was the only one who came close to adding a bit of sunshine to the palette," agrees Missel, "but so that it still made sense. And that's when we were almost green-lit."

As the script edged closer to a version which Universal seemed likely to approve, Gibson invited *Alien*'s Oscar-winning conceptual artist, H. R. Giger, to create a series of conceptual illustrations for the film. "Giger was very excited," Gibson recalls. "We went over to Zurich to meet with him at least once, maybe even twice. We were there for several days, and went through the various scenes, and he then started to develop various creatures that were based on our discussions, and there were one or two designs that were brilliant. That's when the project was at its most exciting." As Giger recalled in his book *H. R. Giger's Film Design*, "I was commissioned... to airbrush the extraterrestrials from the rewritten script, the most important parts of which were translated into German for me." The sequences — which, Giger says, were taken from a draft of the script dated 16 February 1982, credited to Noto, Missel and Gibson, but almost certainly the Knop rewrite of Noto's script — included one in which one of The Corridor's inmates, described as "a humanoid being with a grotesque harelip", attacks Grace Ripley with a tentacle.

Giger even oversaw the creation of a one-fifth scale model of the creature by Cornelius de Fries and had his agent, Ueli Steinle, take it to Hollywood, to present it to Universal.

Noto believes that it was she who suggested Giger as one of several possible designers for the proposed film. "I had mentioned Giger, I believe, to either Renée or to Brian Gibson," she told *Cinefantastique*. "My feeling was that the best way to proceed for the alien designs would be to have many different designers do their own versions of the aliens," she added. "What I wanted to try to do was a version of the *Star Wars* cantina that was more reality-based, where you had one designer's view of an alien sharply contrasted with another designer's view, so that they were sharply different, giving you the impression that these aliens could be from vastly different places. If you put Giger's alien next to somebody else's, they would not look like they were made by the same person. I tried to figure out a way to really jolt people, to do something new with the way those aliens looked. Juxtaposing images of very different sensibilities so it would have taken more than one person, I think, to complete this thing as I originally saw it."

Nevertheless, Noto was excluded from the development process during the period in which Giger was involved; indeed, the first time she saw his nightmarish concepts for *The Tourist* was in May 1988, when several of them were published in an issue of *Cinefantastique* devoted to Giger's work. Noto was disappointed with the results, she told the same publication in 1994, "but I was not the one directing what Giger was doing. It was Brian Gibson, really, who was working with him. If I had spoken to Giger, there are other things that he had done and other ideas that I would have encouraged him to pursue." Noto could not even tell which parts of the script Giger's designs pertained to, and realised that he was working from a draft that she had never seen.

At this point, Missel believes that Universal liked the direction the project was taking. "We were ready to go," she says, "and I thought, 'Well, we've finally done it.' They kept saying, 'There's certain things that don't quite work, but we're getting closer.'" Gibson agrees that the project had a lot of support from junior Universal executives like Thom Mount and Sean Daniel, "and they gave the impression that they had the power to greenlight the movie. But part of my education in Hollywood at that time was understanding who actually gets to greenlight a film. Everyone will tell you when you're a young writer or director that they have the power to bring your movie to life, but very few actually do." According to Patricia Knop, she and Gibson worked on numerous drafts, "before we finally had this very pressing deadline to get it into Ned Tanen, who was waiting with baited breath." Then, she says, Gibson found himself sitting next to Franc Roddam on a plane. "So suddenly, here sat these two guys, and Franc began talking about how the only thing that made *The Tourist* extraordinary was its darkness, and he began going into a litany of wondrous praise for the darkness of this film. This was after six months of very carefully trying to lighten it, while retaining its quirky originality. So we were literally handing in the script the next day, and suddenly Brian came back in a state of panic and said, 'We have to make this darker!' And here we had Ned Tanen waiting to put it into pre-production with everything based upon its lightness." Gibson, however, is swift to dismiss Knop's story. "What a lot of bollocks," he exclaims. "I would never be influenced by another film-maker, least of all Franc Roddam! The whole thing about being a film-maker is [that], even if someone comes up with the greatest idea on Earth, the ego of a film-maker is such that you'd never want to be influenced by another film-maker."

Certainly, Gibson's version of events during this period of *The Tourist*'s journey seems more credible. "The problem was the sensibility of Ned Tanen," he explains. "When we handed him Pat Knop's draft — which we worked on for at least six months, perhaps longer — he announced that he never wanted to make *The Tourist* in the first place. I'm not sure he even read the draft. I'd not been in LA that long," he adds, "so it was a kind of rude awakening about the carelessness with which a studio can pick up the project, agree to get it re-developed, re-develop it, and then not appreciate it." This was despite the fact that Universal had put a considerable amount of money into *The Tourist*, even paying for H. R. Giger's conceptual designs. "The Giger designs were just the icing on the cake," says Gibson, "and Ned Tanen, who was the person who greenlit movies at the time, didn't like the cake. A few months after that, because of

Ned Tanen's lack of interest, the project was put in turnaround." Missel believes that Tanen was enthusiastic about *The Tourist*, but that by the time Knop's draft was delivered, he had been replaced by Bob Raimi, who "took one look at the project and said, 'We don't want to make it,' and put it in turnaround again." As Knop puts it, "It was going full tilt ahead, and suddenly it screeched to a halt, and then went into reverse."

By this time, Universal had released Steven Spielberg's *E.T. The Extra-Terrestrial* to universal acclaim and enormous box-office. "I remember seeing *E.T.* at a preview and thinking, 'Oh, yes — this is what the studio would have wanted' — an alien movie with an upbeat and more childlike sensibility," says Gibson, who feels that the studios took some time to realise that the decade that began with *Easy Rider*, and ended with *Raging Bull*, was over. "The seventies saw some very successful *films noirs*, but there we were at the beginning of the eighties, and I don't think anyone really appreciated that there'd been a bit of a change," he explains. "It took time to catch up with where the audience was. At that time, there was a greater confidence that dark subjects could be successful than later turned out to be the case," he adds. "We were at the end of that era, and it was the beginning of a more adolescent, automatic, franchise-[friendly] film-making. I found *The Tourist* interesting because it was a kind of *film noir*, and had the movie been made, it might have been very successful. But the environment, the belief system, was turning into something that was more child-oriented film-making." At this point, as far as Gibson was concerned, *The Tourist* disintegrated. "We tried to go into turnaround" — ie, interest another studio in the project — "with the Pat Knop script, but we couldn't set it up. And then Renée wanted to re-develop it, but by then I wasn't really involved." Although still technically attached to *The Tourist*, Gibson had already begun work on his next feature, *Poltergeist II*, for which he again commissioned Giger to work on production designs.

In an effort to reignite interest in the film, Missel had brought in journalist and nascent screenwriter Tom Topor to write yet another new draft. The result, she says, was disastrous. "He botched it totally. It was horrible. His draft was unusable, and he cost us a lot of money." Topor, who has since worked on many screenplays, including Ridley Scott's aborted virus thriller *The Hot Zone*, was relatively new to the film business, but felt that his work on *The Tourist* was adequate. "I delivered what was a perfectly acceptable but not very interesting script," he says. "It 'worked', quote-unquote. But the thing about *The Tourist* was that it really depended on Clair Noto's vision, and I had said to Renée and Brian when they approached me that this was a very special point of view, and what they needed to do was stay with Clair Noto till they got what they wanted." Although Topor had never met Noto, he was aware of her reputation, and knew that Missel and Gibson were unlikely to take his advice. "I'd heard that she was really monstrously crazy to work with," he says, "and apparently being in a room with her was the worst kind of masochism. And her script was a mess, but it had a very distinctive voice — her voice. [I felt it] really had a lot to do with Clair Noto's sexual fantasies and neuroses, placed in a science fiction context. So the more accessible I made it, the more I drained it of its original impulse. Brian and Renée were not happy with what I turned in," he adds, "and I said, 'I understand that you're not happy. *I'm* not happy. All it is, is a competent, skilful piece of work, but it doesn't have what Clair brought into it.' And my guess is that was the problem they ran into each time."

Naturally, Noto shared Topor's view that she alone had the best chance of remedying the problems that continued to plague the script, but Missel refused to rehire her. "[Renée] didn't want to go back to my script, because she didn't want me to have credit," Noto told *Cinefantastique*. "She was trying very, very hard to make sure that if it ever got made, my name would never be seen on the screen. At one point, they changed the city from New York to San Francisco, which did not work at all. They changed a lot of the characters' names, and had all these politically correct aliens running around San Francisco. [It was] very boring." Missel claims to have had other ideas, however. "I had always thought that the way of going with *The Tourist* was to make it in Europe, perhaps in Amsterdam, and to have [someone like] Paul Verhoeven direct it. I always thought, 'Why are we doing it as a big studio movie?'"

Gibson agrees with Missel's view. "It was a unique combination of the punk and the existential, and that particular combination is a very difficult sensibility to turn into a mainstream picture," he says. "I think the film probably took a wrong turn months before I was involved, and the wrong turn was to think of it as a mainstream movie which would have cost millions of dollars. In retrospect, Clair would have been much better advised to develop the film herself, independently; try to retain control, and make a lower budget movie, a couple of notches above Roger Corman, which retained her unique sensibility. Because once it had been bought by Universal, with the kind of overhead that involves, it has to have a larger audience than the art-house audience that the original [version of] *The Tourist* would have been for. The movie as written by Clair was convoluted and bizarre and self-contradictory and strangely structured, and not in any way an elegant screenplay. So to turn it into a piece of movie-making that would be embraced by millions of people was a very difficult task. I think we had one moment of opportunity," he adds, "which was the Pat Knop draft with the Giger drawings. And when that didn't happen because of the complexion of the head of the studio, Renée lost confidence, and she over-developed it, brought in every bloody writer she knew, and it got a huge amount of money against it in turnaround, and basically just fell apart."

Instead of rehiring Noto, Missel asked her husband, journalist and novelist Roger Simon, to attempt a rewrite of his own. "I said, 'Would you do me the favour of rewriting this for free, because we're going into turnaround, and I can't sell the Patricia Knop draft.'" Simon agreed, and wrote another new draft of the script, which was picked up by yet another studio, Paramount, where Michael Eisner, Dawn Steel and producer Joel Silver were all enthusiastic. According to Missel, Paramount paid Roger Simon to write another draft, but ultimately decided not to pursue the project, not least because the development costs accrued against the picture had amounted to $1 million. Although Missel asked Universal to waive the costs, so that the picture could be made elsewhere, the studio refused. As a result, having spent six years developing *The Tourist*, during which time she had earned only $25,000, Missel gave up on the project, moving on to produce *My Man Adam* and, later, Jodie Foster's *Nell*. "Renée ran with it for a long time," Tom Topor says of *The Tourist*, "because it was a thing that intrigued a lot of people, and she could always find an executive who was sort of interested. No one was ever interested to the point of green lighting the picture, but people would occasionally spend money on another draft. Eventually another picture came out, *Starman*, which dealt with many of the same things, and I have a feeling that, once *Starman* was out there, it probably put a stake through the heart of *The Tourist*."

Although Noto moved on to other screenwriting projects, including a widely-regarded true-crime script based on a case of kidnapping and murder known as 'the girl in the box case', she refused to give up on *The Tourist* as it passed from studio to studio without ever reaching the screen. "Every time somebody got a hold of the script, they just held onto it," she told *Cinefantastique*, adding, "Warner Bros had it for seven or eight years, optioning it after they knew they weren't going to make it, [because] they didn't want to hand it back to Universal and have them make it into a successful picture, which would have made Warner Bros look bad. It's like a stupid chess game. Universal spent a shitload of money because of the Giger designs, and paid for several rewrites with different writers." To Noto, the widely read screenplay seemed to have taken on a life of its own. "What constantly amazed me, and continues to amaze me, is that it struck people in a certain way," she says now. "There are very few twenty year-old scripts that people still talk about, but I kept meeting people in the business who had read it and wanted to talk about it for an hour. It's a really dark screenplay," she adds, "and one of the reasons it didn't get made is that a lot of the higher level studio executives felt it was sick and twisted because of the sexuality, which is now pretty tame. It was so unique that nobody was trusting their own feelings about liking it. They'd say, 'It's not going to play in the Midwest — it's just going to be New York and Los Angeles, and nobody else would get it.'"

Nevertheless, in early 1997, Universal put the project back into active development under two producers with more than a passing interest in the science fiction genre: Lawrence Gordon, whose many films include two *Predator*s, two *Die Hard*s, *Waterworld*, *Event Horizon* and *Lara Croft: Tomb Raider*; and Michael Levy, producer of *Predator 2* and *Demolition Man*. "I had worked with Michael at Silver Pictures, and I knew he had been a fan of *The Tourist* for years," says

Noto. "Michael is a producer who loves movies, and I had tons of meetings with him — hours and hours — figuring out a way to update it. A good producer is a good editor," she adds. "They're not trying to write the script — they're trying to edit it in a way that doesn't harm what you're saying, but brings out what you want to say in the clearest way possible. He had a real love for the story in a way that Renée Missel never had, and I had no problem rewriting it seventeen years later, because I knew what I had to do."

Noto handed in a new draft in July 1997, the very same weekend that saw the opening of Barry Sonnenfeld's *Men in Black*, which, like *The Tourist*, depicted a New York infested by aliens disguised as humans. According to Noto, "Universal said, 'We can't do it now, because *Men in Black* has stolen [the idea].'" Says Brian Gibson, who came closest to making *The Tourist*, "The whole premise of aliens trapped on Earth, and that flying saucers are [aliens] trying to get off, not trying to get on, is what made *The Tourist* original, combined with an almost Bergmanesque alienation movie sensibility. *Men in Black* is a totally different movie — a populist, popcorn-eating kind of movie, hugely enjoyable in a comedic way — but if you made *The Tourist* now, the audience would say, 'Well, it's like *Men in Black*.' I mean, *The Tourist* even climaxes at the end with [the aliens] trying to get to a flying saucer and get off the planet! I think it's highly likely that the developers of *Men in Black* were influenced by *The Tourist*." This belief is one which Gibson and his "friendly rival" Franc Roddam share. "I think a lot of directors read *The Tourist* and have raided it," Roddam told *Cinefantastique*. "It's been out there in the open air in Hollywood and had its bones picked. You'll see elements of it in other people's movies." Despite this, Universal reconsidered its position in the late nineties, and the project remains in development under Sean Daniel's supervision, with Noto still very much involved.

"Now it's a question of finding the right director," Noto says. "There were several people they had meetings with after [the latest draft of the script] was sent out," she reveals. "One of them was Jake Scott, Ridley Scott's son, who got interested in it right after *Plunkett & MacLeane*. Jake Scott had a very interesting take on it, and I don't even know why he fell out with it. But ultimately, I think if anybody was going to interpret it in a way that would have the same impact as the script had, it might be me." Despite their differences over the years, Renée Missel thinks that this might be the perfect solution. "I have heard, throughout the years, that Sean Daniel has tried to start it again," she says. "But I know, having tried with four writers, that the only way to do it is to let Clair direct it, and let it be what it is, and live with that. She wrote a brilliant, brilliant movie. I think there are holes in it," she adds. "I never thought she solved the third act problems. But I think you could live with them if you weave the mystery properly. And I really think that only Clair could weave it and unweave it."

The idea of Noto herself directing the script she has struggled for more than twenty years to bring to the screen may not be as unlikely as it sounds, given that the screenwriter's stock rose sharply in 2001 thanks to her authorship of another well-received script: *Julia Pastrana*, based on the true story of a man who falls in love with a disfigured woman living in London in the 1860s. Taylor Hackford (*An Officer and a Gentleman*, *Proof of Life*) came on board to direct the film, and Oscar-winning actress Hilary Swank (*Boys Don't Cry*) signed to play the title role. While Noto believes that this may revive interest in her other unproduced scripts, others feel that *The Tourist*'s time has long passed. "The tragedy was that *The Tourist* could have been a film way ahead of its time," Franc Roddam told *Cinefantastique* in 1994. "If *The Tourist* had broken through... it would have been a great movie, I think. It was a project I felt very close to and, when it fell through, it was a project that I very reluctantly put out of my life."

Renée Missel admits to having been equally reluctant to let go, and agrees with Roddam's view that Clair, as a writer, and *The Tourist*, as a concept, were both ahead of their time. "I loved *The Tourist*," she says. "There were thoughts and ideas and scenes in that movie that were fabulous, and yet *it did not work*. For me, it would only have worked done for a low budget *just as is*, so you make it a dark little nihilistic film out of Germany or Holland. That's how it should have been done from the beginning. But we were in Hollywood, and we went where we knew we had pull, and in a way we went to the wrong place. I think we over-develop projects in

Hollywood, and there are some pieces that stand on their own, and you should just shoot them." In other words, Missel feels she learned an important lesson from the six years she spent working on *The Tourist*. "What I learned from the experience was that you have to take the gamble and shoot it," she says. "And that's why it should have been done for a low budget, because then the gamble is not so terrible."

Tom Topor agrees. "David Brown, a legendary producer who used to run Fox with Richard Zanuck, said that the problem with almost all screenplays is that there's a first draft by the tenth writer instead of a tenth draft by the first writer, and I think that's true in this case. If you made the picture for three or four million dollars, with an [independent studio]," he says, "and you basically accepted the fact that it wasn't the most clear and accessible script in the world, there might be enough people out there for you to get your money back. It should never have been a studio picture, but this was the early eighties, and there *were* no indies."

Patricia Knop also believes that the studio should have taken a gamble and filmed the script that they had. "Under other circumstances, it would seem as if they should just have gone with that," she says. "Every time a very original script is mucked around, a lot of times it suffers. So I don't know if it got better or not. All I know is that there was an effort being made to pacify the studio feeling that it should be a film for mass audience consumption. I like to think [my draft] was better, but how do you know? I felt wonderful things about it at the time, and that's why I jumped on board. It could have been a real first in terms of doing some sort of wonderful strange vision." Tom Topor is not so sure. "This is hindsight, and hindsight is always cheap," he says, "but I have a feeling it was doomed from the beginning, because it was very much a female perspective, which is really unusual in a science fiction movie, [because] science fiction is the last macho form, like westerns. And it was quirky without being charming. It was not something that could seduce the audience."

Despite Noto's claims of renewed interest in the project, Brian Gibson is not optimistic. "I would predict that, unfortunately, *The Tourist* won't get made," he says, "the reason being that there have been too many movies — more than anything, *Men in Black* — where people have deliberately, or inadvertently, or coincidentally, used some of *The Tourist*'s premises. I think it was the resonance of the metaphor — that a whole lot of people live their lives on this planet secretly feeling like aliens — that would have made it a unique movie. But now, because the premise has been begged, borrowed or stolen, the metaphor no longer has that ring of something surprising. So I think it's going to [end up as] a chapter in your book, but it's not going to be a chapter in film history."

Noto, however, is not yet ready to give up on her dream of making the film. "*The Tourist* has always had incredible supporters and incredible detractors," she told *Cinefantastique*. "Right from the very beginning it aroused very strong feelings one way or another... There is something about that script. It has a life of its own. [It was] something that Giger could have been involved with, that other people were involved with on such an emotional level, millions of dollars spent, [with] option money paid year after year." With the project still in development, and yet another version of the script written, *The Tourist*'s journey isn't over yet. Noto remains upbeat: "The update is more successful in some ways," she concludes. "There's a new twist that I've done in the latest draft which I don't want to expose. The new version contains an idea that has still not been done..." ■

Profits Of *Dune*

Unrealised Visions Of Frank Herbert's Seminal Science Fiction Fable

"A lot of people have tried to film *Dune*. They all failed."

—*Dune* author Frank Herbert

In 1963, the acclaimed science fiction magazine *Analog* began publishing 'Dune World', a three-part story by author Frank Herbert, whose only science fiction novel, a 21st century submarine adventure entitled *The Dragon in the Sea*, had been published seven years earlier. The following year, the periodical published 'Prophet of Dune', Herbert's three-part continuation of the story. A complex sociological, ecological, political and theological saga spanning several worlds and set thousands of years in the future, the two stories were collected as *Dune* in 1965, winning the Hugo and Nebula awards, and signalling the arrival of a major new science fiction visionary. The book has remained in print ever since, spawning five sequels, *Dune Messiah* (1969), *Children of Dune* (1976), *God Emperor of Dune* (1981), *Heretics of Dune* (1984) and *Chapterhouse: Dune* (1985); a trilogy of official prequels, the *Prelude to Dune* series by Kevin J. Anderson and Frank Herbert's son Brian; and two screen adaptations, a 1984 feature film by David Lynch and a 2000 miniseries produced by the Sci-Fi Channel and adapted by John Harrison. While literary fads have come and gone, Herbert's legacy endures, placing him as the Tolkien of his genre and architect of the greatest science fiction saga ever written.

The story begins in the year 10,191. The universe's most precious substance is the spice, melange, which extends life, expands consciousness, is vital to space travel — and is found on only one planet: the desert world Arrakis (Dune), home to gigantic worms and a mysterious race, the Fremen. Yet the Emperor, Shaddam IV, seeing a potential rival to the throne, hands spice mining over from House Harkonnen, led by a diseased Baron and his idiot nephews, to House Atreides, ruled by Duke Leto and his concubine, Lady Jessica, a member of the telepathic sisterhood known as the Bene Gesserit. His gesture is a trap, designed to bring down House Atreides. Prophecy foretells the coming of the Kwisatz Haderach, a messianic figure which the Bene Gesserit have been manipulating bloodlines to produce, without success. But Leto and Lady Jessica's son Paul may hold the key: his premonitory dreams and precocious skills suggest that he is more than human.

While the Harkonnen plot to bring down their enemies with the help of a traitor, Atreides arrives on Arrakis, visiting the spice miners just as a giant worm attacks. Back at the palace, the duplicitous Dr Yueh disables the protective shields and betrays his Duke, blackmailing him into killing the Baron (who killed Yueh's wife) in return for sparing Jessica and Paul. The Harkonnen overrun the defenceless palace, killing Yueh and sending Paul and Jessica to their deaths in the desert. Using Paul's growing powers, they escape to safety among the Fremen, where they discover huge underground water reservoirs. The Duke dies in his unsuccessful attempt on the Baron's life, but Jessica becomes the Fremen's new spiritual leader and gives birth to a daughter, Alia, with formidable power. Meanwhile, Paul's own powers increase and he leads the Fremen to victory over the Baron's troops, eventually bringing down the evil Emperor, restoring peace to the universe and fulfilling the messianic prophecy: he is the Kwisatz Haderach, destined to change the face of Arrakis... with rain.

Arriving on bookshelves during the rise of sixties hippy culture, *Dune* was an almost instant success, for reasons which even its author was hard pressed to explain. "I didn't set out to write a classic or a bestseller," he told Ed Naha, author of *The Making of Dune*. "In fact, once it was published, I wasn't really aware of what was going on with the book, to be quite candid. I have this newspaperman's attitude about yesterday's news, you know? 'I've done that one, now let me do something else.'" Like write five sequels, each seemingly larger and more epic in scale than the last. Added Herbert, "The publishers didn't really think it would be big. They didn't know what they had. When the book hit, it hit, largely, via word of mouth. The publishers couldn't keep up with the demand."

Based on the sales figures alone, Hollywood's interest in the hugely successful saga was inevitable, despite the sprawling story's apparent unsuitability to the cinema form. However, it was not until Stanley Kubrick's *2001: A Space Odyssey* gave science fiction cinema a swift kick up the evolutionary ladder that the special effects required to bring *Dune* to the screen seemed possible. The book was first optioned in 1972 by *Planet of the Apes* producer Arthur P. Jacobs, as Herbert recalled: "He took a nine-year option out on the book. Nothing really came of that deal. Jacobs died [in 1973] and the project was tied up in his estate for quite a while." In 1975, however, a French consortium backed by Michael Seydoux, a wealthy Parisian eager to break into the film business, purchased the rights from Jacobs's estate. With six years still to run on the original option, the project landed in the lap of Chilean-born director Alejandro Jodorowsky, the revered and occasionally reviled film-maker behind the cult movie *El Topo*, who set to work on another attempted adaptation of the rather unwieldy narrative.

"*Dune* is much more than a science fiction novel," said Jodorowsky. "It deals with themes like the creation of a messiah, the ascension through different levels necessary to dominate over circumstances which are harmful to humankind. There are also the themes of a search for eternity, for superior mental powers, drug addiction, and, basically, of loneliness. It's the story of a man who develops his mind enough to reach a summit, but once up on this summit, he had lost all human contact. Then, to find human contact again, he has to try and bring all the human race up to where he is now." All of the messiahs, from Buddha to Christ to Mohammed, have had to face the same question, he observed. As for the evil Harkonnen, he added, "I saw it as a vision of contemporary Man. A vision of a world where nothing is sacred, where Man is born in a dustbin, where the whole world is garbage."

Jodorowsky's first move was to begin conceptualising the various visual elements of the book, with the help of three very different artists: French comic book artist Jean Giraud, aka Moebius, who would work on designs for creatures and characters; Dan O'Bannon, a gifted artist, special effects technician and would-be screenwriter who had co-starred in John Carpenter's *Dark Star* and would soon enjoy success as the author of *Alien*; and British illustrator Chris Foss, best known for his painted science fiction book covers, which had recently been collected in his first book, *21st Century Foss*. "Jodorowsky was absolutely thrilled with the book," Foss told *Cinefantastique*, "and out of the blue, I got a phone call asking if I'd like to work in Paris. I was specifically brought in to work on the hardware. And I might add that there is not a lot of hardware in *Dune*, but by the time Jodorowsky and I had finished with it, there was certainly quite a bit of exotic machinery."

For four months, from August to December 1975, the triumvirate worked with Jodorowsky on countless designs for spaceships and spice miners, characters and creatures, palaces and props. "It was a phenomenally creative period," Chris Foss wrote in *Skeleton Crew* magazine, "and, goaded by the guru-like Alejandro, I produced some of my most original work. We were literally a gang of three working under the master to create a multi-million dollar movie... in a palatial, no-expenses-spared office block with materials instantly provided on demand, and — *most important of all* — a director who knew what he wanted." One of the things Jodorowsky wanted for his three-hour 70mm epic, then budgeted at $9.5 million dollars, was Spanish-born surrealist Salvador Dalí to play Emperor Shaddam IV. The artist surprisingly agreed, subject to a previously-unheard of salary of $100,000 an hour.

It was during this pre-production period that Swiss artist H. R. Giger heard about the project through Bob Venosa, "an American painter of fantastic realism", who lived in Cadaques and frequented Dali's house. "Bob Venosa telephoned me and explained that the director Alejandro Jodorowsky was interested in my work," Giger wrote in his book, *H. R. Giger's Film Design*. The artist duly gathered his portfolio and left Switzerland for Cadaques, where he met with Dali but was disappointed to find that Jodorowsky had already left for Paris. However, in December 1975, while Foss, O'Bannon and Giraud had returned to their respective homes for the Christmas break, Giger was visiting Paris and stopped by Jodorowsky's studio to leave his contact details. "As a result," Giger stated, "Jodorowsky telephoned me, and then later showed me the groundwork for *Dune* in his studio.

"Four [sic] science fiction artists were in the process of designing spaceships, satellites and entire planets," Giger recalled, noting that several copies of images from his own portfolio were being used as inspiration. "Jodorowsky told me that he would be happy if I would co-design the film. I could build an entire planet and would be given complete free reign. Three-dimensional models would be built according to my designs, into which the actors would be incorporated. I would also have the opportunity to make costumes, masks, etc. according to my own ideas." Giger's planet was to be Geidi Prime, the home of the Harkonnen, ruled by black magic and steeped in violence and perversion. "In a word," Giger observed, "it was my speciality. Only sex could not be shown," he added. "Therefore I was to design it as if the film was made for children. Jodorowsky was sick of his films always being censored."

Giger was told that a team of thirty specialists would execute his ideas in three dimensions, and although Jodorowsky insisted that Giger's fee would have to match Foss's — 4,000 Swiss francs a month — the artist was assured that the publicity resulting from the project would be priceless. "We parted with the understanding to talk by phone again about the fee," Giger recalled, "and he gave me the script, so that I could immediately start with my work." Back home in Switzerland, the artist was surprised to be told by Jodorowsky's agent to make a painting of the planned castle and take it to Paris, to see if it was suitable for the picture. "That's how 'les petits Suisses' get treated," he complained. Nevertheless, Giger set to work immediately, sketching and airbrushing numerous images of the Harkonnen castle, built in the image of the grotesquely fat and almost Buddha-like Baron Vladimir Harkonnen himself. Meanwhile, Seydoux's consortium withdrew financing for the film. As Foss told *Cinefantastique*, "The producer and, I think, Jodorowsky, went to Los Angeles shortly before the Christmas of 1975, with the hope of getting American interest in the film and setting up a co-production deal. I believe that there was a disagreement in Los Angeles about how the film should be made. Bearing in mind how large the budget had by then become, the French company was unable — or possibly unwilling — to finance it totally on its own."

Thus, Jodorowsky's over-ambitious plans to adapt Herbert's gargantuan novel were shelved, much to the regret of the artists involved. "Basically it was a glorious experience, and then it was over," O'Bannon told *Phobos* magazine. "I was sent back to the States around Christmas of '75 to try to find some special VistaVision equipment, and while I was back there staying with friends, I got a telegram informing me that *Dune* was postponed indefinitely. And everything fell apart." Foss knew how his friend felt. "Dan was equally under Alejandro's spell," he lamented, "so his disillusion was as great as mine when one million pounds, four months, and a *lot* of work later, the project did not resume after the Christmas break." As Herbert himself told Ed Naha, "Alejandro Jodorowsky spent a couple of million dollars in pre-production on his version, [but] nothing ever happened. I'm not quite sure why it fizzled," he added, before providing a perfectly adequate explanation: "Without exaggeration, his script would have made an eleven- or twelve-hour movie. It was the size of a phone book. It was pretty anti-Catholic, too. I used to kid Alejandro about that. I told him that his biggest disappointment in writing the script was probably not finding a way to horsewhip the Pope in it." Instead, Jodorowsky moved on to his third feature, *Tusk*, and apparently never looked back. "Being an ardent adept of Karmic Yoga, I am interested in the work I do, but not in the result of this work, whether good or bad," he said philosophically. "So, I deeply enjoyed working on *Dune*, and for me, anyway, the film *was* made."

With the project in limbo once again, it took the success of *Star Wars* — arguably influenced by Herbert's novel, with its desert planet, quasi-religious group and young hero with mystical powers — to prompt a resurgence of interest in science fiction, and *Dune* once again came under close scrutiny from several producers, among them Dino De Laurentiis. "I had a special feeling about *Dune*," the veteran film-maker told Ed Naha. "I knew about the book since before I moved my headquarters to America from Italy; since the late 1960s. Once I established myself here in America, many producers approached me about working with them on this project. But I was scared. Frankly, *Dune* was the kind of movie that I wanted to have a strong hand in. If I was going to make it, I had to be able to call the shots. Here were these offers with another producer already attached. That would limit my input. So, I stayed away." Nevertheless, when the remaining four years of the option went up for sale, De Laurentiis saw the opportunity to work on the project with his daughter, Raffaella, and purchased the film rights to the book and its sequels for $2 million.

Having already brought an equally unwieldy theological and sociological book — the Bible — to the screen, De Laurentiis seemed unafraid of the scope of the project. "I don't know why other people hadn't succeeded with *Dune* before," he stated. "There's no logical reason why they failed. Maybe they were scared about the script. Maybe they were scared about the money. Maybe they were scared about so many major roles. I'm too long in the business now to get frightened by things that should frighten me," he added. "You take a chance every time you make a movie. I knew I would be taking a big chance with *Dune*. It would be very risky.

It would be very expensive. But I never worry about money. If you have the right idea, the money will come. You just have to be patient."

Herbert himself was contracted to write the script but, when his 176-page draft proved unworkable, De Laurentiis took a different approach, hiring Ridley Scott, fresh from his *Alien* success, to direct the film. Scott, in turn, selected novelist and screenwriter Rudolph Wurlitzer (*Pat Garrett and Billy the Kid*) to write a new screenplay. "The *Dune* adaptation was one of the most difficult jobs I ever did," Wurlitzer later admitted. "I did three drafts of that script before I was even *beginning* to become satisfied with its structure. Even the initial result was more of a working outline than a script," he added, "but eight months later I felt Ridley and I had a very strong working screenplay of *Dune* that, at the very least, kept true to the spirit of the novel. I will say, however, that we rarefied it, and injected a different sensibility into the script than that of the book."

Indeed, Wurlitzer's infamous first draft toned down the messianic impulses of Paul Atreides, weakened the Fremen and the Baron Harkonnen, and — most controversially of all — added an incestuous relationship between Paul and his mother, which has the result that Alia, the unearthly child-woman who is born with the mental capacity of an adult, becomes not only Paul's sister but also his daughter. "I took what I always felt to be a latent but very strong Oedipal attraction between Paul and the Lady Jessica, his mother, one step further," Wurlitzer explained. "I injected a lovemaking sequence between these two. I meant that act as a supreme defiance of certain boundaries, which might make Paul even *more* heroic, in the sense that he *willingly*, but lovingly, broke a taboo." This development displeased both Herbert and De Laurentiis, and the subplot was duly removed in subsequent drafts.

While Wurlitzer continued to revise and refine the screenplay, Scott set up a pre-production office at Pinewood Studios, inviting his *Alien* collaborator H. R. Giger back on board as production designer. By this stage, Giger had become interested in the idea of producing a range of furniture in his unique skeletal style, and saw the revival of *Dune* as an opportunity to see his visions realised. "My involvement with the renewed *Dune* project provided the opportunity to construct my designs as the Harkonnen furniture pieces and to also have them featured in the film," he explained. "It was agreed that my contract would allow the copyright of my designs to remain with me."

Giger duly designed a Harkonnen chair, and also produced two new *Dune* paintings: one placing the chair against an elaborate airbrushed background; and one depicting one of the worms of Arrakis. Having still not signed an official contract with De Laurentiis, Giger received a telephone call from Ridley Scott informing him that the producer had handed over the production of the film to his daughter, Raffaella, and that Scott had decided to quit. "After seven months I dropped out of *Dune*," the director later explained to Paul M. Sammon. "By then, Rudy Wurlitzer had come up with a first-draft script which I felt was a decent distillation of Frank Herbert's [book]. But I also realised *Dune* was going to take a lot more work — at least two and a half years' worth. And I didn't have the heart to attack that because my [older] brother, Frank, unexpectedly died of cancer while I was prepping the De Laurentiis picture. Frankly, that freaked me out. So I went to Dino and told him the *Dune* script was his."

Herbert was philosophical about the collapse of this latest effort. "I found it all grist for the mill," he told Ed Naha. "After a while, though, I honestly didn't think that a movie would ever be made. The nine years were almost up." As Scott's replacement, Raffaella suggested David Lynch, who had followed the cult success of his first feature, *Eraserhead*, with a mainstream movie, *The Elephant Man*, nominated for eight Academy Awards. Lynch, having turned down *Return of the Jedi* and failed to find a home at Francis Ford Coppola's Zoetrope for his own science fiction project, *Ronnie Rocket* (see chapter 7), accepted their offer to direct, immediately rejecting all of the existing pre-production concepts, including H. R. Giger's. Says Lynch, "I didn't like [his approach], I didn't like the design in the book and I didn't like any designs that I'd seen. It was a problem." Instead, Lynch hired *2001: A Space Odyssey* alumni Tony Masters and Ron Miller as conceptual artists and Bob Underwood (*Excalibur*) as costume designer, and began writing his own adaptation of the novel with *The Elephant Man* co-writers Eric Bergren and Christopher De Vore. At 200 pages, their first draft was even longer than Herbert's, and it was another year before Lynch's *sixth* draft was finally given the go-ahead. As Raffaella De Laurentiis told *American Film*, "It took David to break the code for how to make this book into a film."

Chris Foss, however, was not so easily convinced: "The *Dune* that finally made it to the screen was pitiful in comparison to Alejandro's vision." ∎

Twin Freaks

Sci-Fi From Another Place: David Lynch's *Ronnie Rocket* And *One Saliva Bubble*

"It might be a picture that I would love, but I don't know if too many other people are going to dig it. It's very abstract."

—David Lynch on *Ronnie Rocket*

I t has always been difficult for David Lynch to make films. His first feature, *Eraserhead*, took four years, plagued by a variety of problems, mostly money-related. Over twenty years later, the making of *Mulholland Drive* took almost as long, if for entirely different reasons. The problem tends to be that, despite being acclaimed as one of America's most stylish and *avant-garde* directors, Lynch has never enjoyed real commercial success anywhere but the small screen.

Lynch's problems with the financing of certain projects began as early as 1977, when he intended to follow the release of *Eraserhead* with "an absurd mystery of the strange forces of existence" entitled *Ronnie Rocket*. The eponymous hero of the story was a diminutive and malformed creature with blank features and a bald head, who had been surgically altered against his will, and now sported a shock of red hair. 'Shock' was the right word, for, as the surgeons discovered, Ronnie was able to conduct electricity and needed to be plugged into the mains every fifteen minutes. "Ronnie was like a man-made kid," explains Dexter Fletcher, the *Elephant Man* actor who was Lynch's original choice for the title role, "and these young [musicians] found him somehow, and they could plug him into the mains and he would make these amazing sounds, and they started to use him as a musical instrument in their band."

The script is set in a dystopian urban wasteland, occupying either a post-apocalyptic future or parallel universe, where a mysterious and frightening individual named Hank Bartell plagues the populace with a kind of electrical disturbance. He also dispatches truckloads of 'Donut Men' — creepy individuals dressed in long black coats who spontaneously combust when informed that their shoelaces are untied — to assault anyone in range with cattle prods, which cause all manner of bizarre side effects: people have seizures, attempt to eat their own hands, stand on their heads and even die. Into this strange landscape comes the even stranger figure of Ronald De Arte, who lies in a hospital bed, disfigured beyond recognition by some unthinkable event and rendered unable to do more than emit strange sounds. A detective visits him, leaves with some odd symbols scribbled on a piece of paper and sets out on a journey into the mysterious city, full of weird and psychotic characters.

Meanwhile, Ronald is kidnapped from hospital by two outlaw plastic surgeons, Dr Dan Pink and Dr Bob Platinum. With special techniques and machines they jolt him to life, Frankenstein style, christening him 'Ronnie Rocket' after a 10,000-volt mishap which shoots him into the air like a rocket and transforms him into a kind of living superconductor. Frightened yet fascinated by Ronnie's transmogrification and feeling responsible for his welfare, the doctors promptly dispatch the diminutive figure to high school, where his studies are somewhat hampered by his need to plug himself into a socket every fifteen minutes.

Running low on juice one school day, Ronnie finds himself in the basement where a rock band are rehearsing and plugs himself into their equipment, following which an extraordinary sound issues from his mouth. The band are amazed, and their manager blackmails Bob, Dan and their girlfriend Deborah into letting Ronnie perform with the band which — thanks to its newest member — becomes an overnight success. But the effort weakens Ronnie, and Bob and Dan decide to rescue him.

Meanwhile, the detective's investigations lead him into the inner city, and towards the power station. He makes two important discoveries: that pain is the key to staying conscious during the fatal blasts of bad electricity; and that his unique ability to stand on one leg may provide the key to defeating Hank Bartell and his evil currents. He runs into Bob, Dan and Deborah, and together they decipher Ronnie's scribbled symbols and resolve to confront Hank and his deadly Donut Men. The group finds Hank at the heart of the power station and, during a bizarre display on a stage, manage to reverse the flow of electricity, allowing the detective to defeat Hank. The city is bathed in golden light. Everyone is saved. Ronnie sings a beautiful love song and turns into a golden egg which envelopes the city. A dancing blue lady with four arms smiles as she touches the golden egg and speaks the name Ronnie Rocket.

Lynch originally hoped to make *Ronnie Rocket* at American Zoetrope, the studio founded by Francis Ford Coppola with a view to encouraging such individualistic directors as Jean-Luc Godard, Michael Powell and Lynch himself to pursue pet projects they would be unable to finance elsewhere. Many such directors moved to the Zoetrope lot; most spent a frustrating year or two failing to secure finance for their films while Coppola's company lost vast amounts of money on expensive flops like *One from the Heart*. *Ronnie Rocket* was just one victim of Zoetrope's eventual collapse into bankruptcy, and by 1980 Lynch had been forced to accept the assignment of directing *The Elephant Man* — a career-making move, as it turned out — rather than his beloved *Ronnie Rocket*.

The director returned to the script after the Oscar-winning success of *The Elephant Man*, which had earned Lynch a good deal of respect. "I hope my project *Ronnie Rocket* is in the future," he told Joy Kuhn in 1980. "I want to make films that take you into a different world, a place you could never get to unless you saw the movie. *Ronnie Rocket* will go into some rather strange areas." Although he had made his first two films in black and white, he added, "I would like to make the next film in colour. I love the way Jacques Tati uses colour, and some of the old three-strip Technicolor movies are so beautiful. I think it will take some time experimenting to find a good look for the next picture."

Meeting with Dexter Fletcher while the then-teenaged actor was appearing in a Royal Shakespeare Company production of *King Lear*, Lynch realised that he had grown too tall for the title role, forcing the director to consider other actors. As Lynch explained, "When we shot *The Elephant Man*, Dexter was small, but I really needed someone much smaller than Dexter. He was growing up fast." Instead, Lynch placed an advertisement in *Variety*, effectively an open casting call for the role of Ronnie Rocket. Three-foot-tall Michael J. Anderson, a former electronics expert with NASA contractor Martin-Marietta, and now working as an extra in music promos for The Alan Parsons Project ('Stereotomy') and Yoko Ono ('Hell in Paradise'), was one of those who saw the ad. Anderson sent Lynch a copy of a video about his work on the space shuttle programme and was promptly invited to lunch.

"I met Michael Anderson in New York," the director recalls. "He showed up in a gold suit and he was pulling a wagon, and it was really a great meeting. We got on great." Potential financiers did not take too well to Lynch's unequivocally bizarre tale, however, not least because he refused to tell anyone what it was about. "It's not a commercial picture," he admitted to David Breskin. "It's an American smokestack industrial thing — it has to do with coal and oil and electricity. It might be a picture that I would love, but I don't know if too many other people are going to dig it. It's very abstract." As Dexter Fletcher observes, "I should imagine that the big money heads at whatever studio it was couldn't get their brains round it at all. It's fine for the artist to read and enjoy, but for accountants it was probably a very different proposition. But that's David Lynch all over in a lot of ways."

After three years of unsuccessful negotiations, Lynch was hired by veteran producer Dino De Laurentiis as director of *Dune* (see chapter 6), which he followed with *Blue Velvet* for the same producer, before turning to the small screen and the hugely successful but short-lived *Twin Peaks*. In the summer of 1990, Lynch denied that *Ronnie Rocket* was dead — "No, no, no, no, never, not in a million years" — but added that he wasn't sure it would ever be made. "It's definitely not dead," he insisted to David Breskin. "I've talked about it so much and scripts of it are around. I'm waiting for the next step to happen to do it, if there is a next step. I'm waiting for a time where I don't really care what happens, except that the film is finished," he added. "I do care, now, enough so that a film like *Ronnie Rocket* is frightening, because it's not a commercial picture."

Nevertheless, in April 1991, *Ronnie Rocket* looked like it may finally make it into production, courtesy of Lynch's new three-picture deal with French financier CIBY-2000. Actor Michael J. Anderson — by now known to millions as the Man From Another Place in *Twin Peaks* — told the *New York Daily News* that he was "deliriously happy" to be cast as the title character, "[who] has a limited awareness of normal reality but a large awareness of transcendental reality." However, after making the first of his three films for CIBY, *Twin Peaks — Fire Walk With Me*, Lynch cooled on the project. "After so many years, now I have the opportunity to make it if I want to," he told the *Los Angeles Times* in May 1992. "But when I read it, it doesn't do the things it should to me. I've lost the electricity in it; it's like a light bulb with no electricity."

Today, Lynch admits that it has been "a long time" since he last looked at *Ronnie Rocket*, and feels that the moment to make it has truly passed. "If I had gotten the money to do it right when I wrote it, I think it would've been a different story," he says, "but I didn't. I couldn't get it going. I'd have meetings and I wouldn't tell anybody what it was about, so it stands to reason that they didn't wanna know! And now the script got out," he adds, referring to the availability of several drafts on the internet, "and that really hurts me." Not that people who have read the script would know what the film would be like, he says; after all, "the script is only a blueprint. But at the same time, I like to keep things private. Those kinds of things, for sure." Besides, even if *Ronnie Rocket* did get made, he would probably have to search again for an actor to play the title role. "Mike [Anderson] is probably too old to play Ronnie Rocket," he says mournfully. "I'd have to find somebody else if I did it."

Lynch encountered an altogether different set of impediments to the making of another absurd science fiction tale, *One Saliva Bubble*, the film with which he originally intended to follow *Blue Velvet*. The project began as an original screenplay co-written by Lynch and former *Hill Street Blues* writer-producer Mark Frost, who would later collaborate with Lynch on *Twin Peaks*. After *Blue Velvet* the pair had worked together on *Venus Descending*, a stillborn adaptation of Anthony Summers's Marilyn Monroe biography *Goddess* and, when that project failed to find favour with any studio, they considered another collaboration. "Nothing ever happened with *Goddess*," Lynch says, "but I asked Mark one time if he would be interested in comedy, and he said, 'Sure.'" The resulting project was *One Saliva Bubble*, which Lynch has described as "an out-and-out wacko dumb comedy [with] clichés one end to the other. Mark and I were laughing like crazy when we wrote it." As Frost told *Empire* of the collaboration, "David is somewhat inaccessible to other people and very solitary, but there was some chemistry between us and we had a lot of fun... We'd just sit in a room together — I'd sit at a computer because he doesn't really type — and just kind of hammer it out as we went along. It was like a badminton match, just knocking the dialogue back and forth. The thing I remember the most is laughing ourselves ill."

The widely circulated first draft of *One Saliva Bubble*, dated 20 May 1987, concerns the chain reaction of chaos and absurdity sparked by a single saliva bubble. As the story opens, a goofy security guard blows a raspberry, producing a perfect saliva bubble at the precise moment that scientists remove a panel from a top secret military satellite. The bubble lands deep inside the machine, causing a tiny short circuit... Meanwhile, in Newtonville, Kansas — the lightning capital of the world — car salesman Wally Newton has failed to sell any cars again, and goes home to his violent son, nagging wife and very unfriendly dog. In the corporate world, 'Company A' hires a genius professor to get ahead of the competition, 'Company B', which has, in turn, hired a hitman named Horton Thursby to take out the Professor. The Professor, a harmless simpleton named Newt Newton, a troupe of Chinese acrobats and a group of Texan businessmen all arrive at the airport just as the satellite's countdown climaxes, sending an energy beam directly to Earth, striking them and causing them to swap identities. Wally and Horton switch places, Newt swaps with the Professor, the acrobats with the Texans, and so on. Zany happenings ensue as Company A finds the Professor behaving like a simpleton, the Texan businessmen try to form a human pyramid and Wally makes a killing in his car firm. A military containment team is sent out to deal with the accident, and decides to use another blast from the satellite to put things right. After a few hilarious hiccups, it works. The saliva bubble deep inside the machine pops. Newtonville finally returns to normal — or as normal as they ever were in the lightning capital of the world...

"I thought of this idea on an airplane," Lynch explained to David Breskin. "Steve Martin and I had met and [he] loved it... I think the problem for me is that there's not enough meat to it. I feel like a lot of people could do it." Nevertheless, Lynch came close to shooting the film for Dino De Laurentiis "right after *Blue Velvet*", with a cast headed by Steve Martin and Martin Short. "I almost was going to make *One Salvia Bubble* then," he admits. "We had all our scouts, had it cast; [it] was right there ready to go. Dino kept delaying it, delaying it, delaying it. It became obvious it wasn't going to happen [because] there wasn't any money. Shortly thereafter the company went bankrupt." It took three years for Lynch to reclaim the rights to the project, only to find that De Laurentiis would still be due a share of the first profits if the film were produced, due to the development money he had already sunk into it.

Today, Lynch is not sure he would make *One Saliva Bubble* even if the finances weren't a problem. "It hasn't dated," he says, "and I could probably get [the money]. But I just don't have any interest in doing it." ∎

Alienated

In Space, No One Can Hear You Scream. In Hollywood, They Can Hear You — They Just Don't Take Any Notice

> "I hoped that one could reinvent and reinvigorate it. Because of the difference between Ridley Scott and James Cameron, it seemed at that stage that it was the only one of these sequels where they would allow anybody with any vigour to make it. And as it worked out, I was wrong."
>
> —one-time *Alien*[3] director Vincent Ward

Aliens, writer-director James Cameron's 1986 follow-up to Ridley Scott's seminal 1979 science fiction horror film *Alien*, had been open at US cinemas only a matter of days before the studio behind both films, Twentieth Century Fox, decided it wanted another film in the series — and fast. It had taken seven years for the studio to capitalise on the success of Scott's film — "They felt there was no market for a second one," writer-producer Walter Hill told *Starlog*, "but we finally convinced them to let us develop an *Alien II*" — despite the fact that Cameron's screenplay had been written in 1983. With a potentially vast adult-oriented franchise in the making, Fox was not about to wait another seven years for a third *Alien* film.

Alien had begun life ignominiously, as a script for a Lovecraftian horror tale entitled *They Bite*, written by screenwriter and *Dark Star* co-star Dan O'Bannon. "The producers I showed it to felt it was too weird and that it would be too expensive to do because of the special effects involved," he said of the aborted screenplay, which he intended to re-work as a novel. "But they all did admit that it frightened them. When I got ready to write *Alien*, I pulled a couple of concepts from *They Bite* and put them in deep space." After the collapse of Alejandro Jodorowsky's proposed film adaptation of *Dune*, on which O'Bannon had worked for several months (see chapter 6), the writer needed another screenplay fast and, with the help of his friend Ron Shusett, wrote *Alien* — then titled *Star Beast* — in the space of three months.

The script was sold to Fox-based development company Brandywine Productions, a partnership between Walter Hill (*48HRS.*), David Giler (*Fun with Dick and Jane*) and Gordon Carroll (*Pat Garrett and Billy the Kid*), in 1977. "[Walter Hill] showed me the style of scriptwriting he had developed; a simplified, easy-to-read format that looked like blank verse," O'Bannon explained. "It had become a sure-fire format for him, and he promptly sat down and [re-]wrote *Alien* into that format in order to sell it to Fox." Fox had given *Alien* a green light in October 1977, and pre-production officially began the following January, with American artist Ron Cobb (*Dark Star*), British science fiction illustrator Chris Foss (Jodorowsky's *Dune*), Swiss avant-garde artist H. R. Giger and French comic book artist Jean Giraud (aka Moebius) working on conceptual designs for the film, which went into production under director Ridley Scott (*The Duellists*) on 15 July 1978. "I stepped into *Alien*, in a way, almost by accident," Scott told Paul M. Sammon. "But when the script was sent to me, I had been burying myself in the area of *Heavy Metal* comics and graphic novels and other similar things, and *Alien* seemed well suited for those types of design possibilities."

Released in 1979, *Alien* became the last great science fiction film of the seventies, and one of the first to be targeted at an adult audience; despite the film's prohibitive 'X' rating, the film grossed an impressive $60 million from a $10 million budget, won an Academy Award for H. R. Giger's conceptual designs and spawned a franchise whose popularity continues to thrive today, with fan clubs, magazines, conventions, theme parks, computer and console games — and countless imitators. In almost every respect, it was a watershed film: reimagining the future as a place in which blue collar workers bitched and moaned about their overtime pay, and became expendable cannon fodder for their corporate bosses; and launching the 'A-list' movie careers of former commercials director Scott and unknown actress Sigourney Weaver.

Despite the success of *Alien*, Scott was not re-hired for the proposed sequel. "We talked to Ridley briefly," Sigourney Weaver claimed, "but he could never get it together." The assumption has always been that Scott turned down the opportunity to continue the franchise that made him famous, but a source close to the director insists this is not the case. "People have suggested he might do another *Alien* [movie]," says conceptual artist Sylvain Despretz, who worked with Scott on the aborted adaptation of *I Am Legend* (see chapter 10) and *Black Hawk Down*, "but Ridley says he's never been approached, and that nobody at Fox has ever shown any interest in him doing another one." Instead, Fox offered the sequel to James Cameron, who had written and was preparing to film the science fiction thriller *The Terminator*, released in 1984. "Fox basically said, 'Here's $18 million. Give us a call in a year once it's done,'" Cameron recalled to *Skeleton Crew*. "I couldn't complain about that."

Cameron, who was also working on a script for another sequel, *Rambo: First Blood Part II*, claims only to have watched *Alien* once before embarking on his script for *Aliens*. "Then, later on, I looked at sequences on video to get a feel for the creatures — what we did and didn't see — so as not to violate anything. *Alien*'s strength was that it was so simple," he added. "*Aliens* did complicate it all and I worried about that to a degree. In doing a sequel you tend to have not only everything you want to say, but everything that needs to be reiterated from the first film, so it can get overloaded. My instinct was to go for more story, [and] character, to make the plot denser. The original was almost deliciously simple. It was an exercise in style, which Ridley excels at — look at *Black Rain* — but that isn't my *forté*."

If *Alien* had been a monster movie set in outer space, James Cameron's film was Vietnam reimagined as a ground war between cocksure US Marines and a seemingly unstoppable wave of vicious attackers. For Cameron, steeped in Vietnam war research thanks to his script chores on the *First Blood* sequel, it was a perfect assignment. "The only thing they gave me was 'Ripley and soldiers' — that was all they had in mind," Cameron revealed. "They thought the concept of grunts in space was wonderful." In the resulting film, Sigourney Weaver reprised her role as Ellen Ripley — "Although it seemed obvious to have Ripley as the focus of the sequel, not everyone at Fox thought the same way," Cameron claimed — but was joined by an entirely new supporting cast, including newcomer Carrie Henn and several actors from *The Terminator*. Lance Henriksen, Michael Biehn, Bill Paxton and Jenette

Goldstein. Released in 1986, *Aliens* earned $81 million at the US box-office, and enjoyed considerable critical acclaim (including a Best Actress nomination for Sigourney Weaver), cementing Cameron's status as a commercial *auteur*, and giving Fox a new science fiction franchise to nurture (following George Lucas's decision not to film his proposed second *Star Wars* trilogy — at least, not for a decade or two). As far as everyone at Fox was concerned, *Alien III* was just around the corner. But as it turned out, the third part of the *Alien* trilogy would have an even more painful birth than the creature that emerged from John Hurt's torso in *Alien*.

Shortly after the release of *Aliens*, producer David Giler read 'cyberpunk' author William Gibson's début novel, *Neuromancer*, on a beach in Thailand. Returning to the US, he signed the Canadian novelist to write *Alien*'s second sequel, convincing fellow producers Walter Hill and Gordon Carroll that Gibson's cyberpunk aesthetic was precisely what was needed to make *Alien III* as different from *Aliens* as Cameron's film had been from Scott's. Gibson was equally impressed with Hill and Giler, recalling to *Cinefantastique* that "they were arguing at the time about what the alien metaphor meant," with Hill viewing the alien as a metaphor for cancer and Giler suggesting the creature as a metaphor for the HIV virus. "I expected this kind of discussion of subtext from academics," said Gibson, "not from producers." The author even admitted the influence *Alien* had had on his own work. "I found a lot of things in the original that were interesting even when it first came out," he said. "I thought there were germs of stories implicit in the art direction. I always wanted to know more about [the *Nostromo* crew members]. Why were they wearing dirty sneakers in this funky spaceship? I think it influenced my prose SF writing because it was the first funked-up, dirty, kitchen-sink spaceship, and it made a big impression on me. When I started writing SF, I went for that."

Gibson was given the scripts of the first two films and a twelve-page story outline by Hill and Giler, whose rather sterile concept involved a Cold War-style confrontation between the Weyland-Yutani Corporation, mentioned in the previous films, and a rival organisation with socialist or even communist leanings. At the time, Gibson was glad to have a concept to work with, but was already beginning to feel the limitations of the proposed scale of the production. "Budget parameters argued against introducing the aliens into something that was the equivalent of the *Blade Runner* set, which I admit would have been my natural impulse," he said. "Failing that, I worked through a series of semi-abandoned space station ideas, my favourite of which was a space station that seemed to be a shopping mall under construction, [like science fiction writer] Somtow Sucharitku's *Mallworld*, but unfinished. The most fun I had with it, though, was working out this kind of futuro-socialist third world culture that seems to be in opposition to the [Weyland-Yutani] company, but in fact was just as corrupt. It's like the crew of the *Enterprise* running into a spaceship full of Stalinists."

Gibson began his screenplay in 1987, but immediately found the process more difficult than he had imagined. "If you look at my style as a novelist," he explained, "I'm heavy on cultural detail. That's really something that, as I've subsequently learned to a certain extent on other screenplays, is the province of the art director. In a screenplay you only want a little telling detail. I was writing down what people were wearing and how their watches functioned." Pressurised by an impending Writers' Guild strike which forced him to work on his first screenplay at a much faster pace than he would have preferred, Gibson wrote at breakneck speed, finally handing in his draft in early 1988. The result, he said, was akin to "arty science fiction novelist attempts to come to grips with cinema form. The *TV Guide* synopsis would read, 'Space commies hijack alien eggs — big trouble in Mallworld.'"

Gibson's story began where *Aliens* ended, with the ship carrying Ripley, Newt (Carrie Henn) and Hicks (Michael Biehn) in hypersleep, drifting in space. It is intercepted and searched by commandos from the Weyland-Yutani's rival, the Union of Progressive Peoples (UPP), who are promptly attacked by an alien facehugger hiding in the entrails of the wrecked android, Bishop (Lance Henriksen). The soldiers blast the creature into space, remove Bishop for further study and return the ship to its original course: Anchorpoint, the Company-run space station/shopping mall described by Gibson. With Ripley comatose following an on-board fire, Hicks becomes the focus of the story, uncovering a plot by Weyland-Yutani to breed an army of aliens — precisely what the UPP is busy doing. After a pitched battle with the alien infestation on Anchorpoint, the script closes with representatives of Weyland-

Yutani and the UPP uniting against a common enemy, and vowing to trace the aliens back to their homeworld and destroy them at source. "This is a Darwinian universe, Hicks," Bishop tells his friend in the closing scene. "Will the alien be the ultimate survivor, or will Man?"

Giler and Hill were evidently no more impressed with Gibson's first draft than the author himself. "We got the opposite of what we expected," Giler admitted to *Cinefantastique*. "We figured we'd get a script that was all over the place, but which would have many good ideas we could mine." What they got, instead, was a competently written screenplay which was not as inventive as they had hoped. "That was probably our fault, though," the producer added, "because it was our story. We had hoped he'd open up the story, and don't know why it didn't happen." By this time, with the Writers' Guild strike in full swing, the producers had hired Finnish film-maker Renny Harlin (*A Nightmare on Elm Street 4: The Dream Master*) to direct the new instalment of the *Alien* series. Harlin met with Hill, Giler and Gibson to discuss a possible rewrite, but Gibson, already involved with script adaptations of two of his own stories, *Burning Chrome* and *Johnny Mnemonic*, declined to give further input. In his place, Harlin suggested that screenwriter Eric Red (*The Hitcher*, *Near Dark*) be brought aboard to revise the script to his satisfaction. Hill and Giler agreed.

In the meantime, negotiations with actress Sigourney Weaver were not proceeding well; she refused to sign on to the project until the script met with her approval, a prospect which seemed a long way off. "At the start of each of them, all I ever said is, 'Please give me something interesting to do,'" she told the *Alien³ Movie Special*. "I didn't want to do what I did before." Weaver also insisted that, if she returned as Ripley for a third time, she did not want the film to be as hardware-oriented as Cameron's contribution. "I didn't want to be in a movie with guns," explained Weaver, a spokesperson for anti-handgun lobby group Handgun Control, who felt she had been hoodwinked into joining such a hardware-heavy production as *Aliens*. "When I read the script, I was working very hard, and I skipped over a lot of the stage directions, which went on and on about the guns. And I didn't realise they were the star of the film until I started to see this amazing hardware they brought out every day. I was a member of Handgun Control, and I was amazed to find myself in this very warlike picture." Weaver denied that she was being unreasonable in trying to influence the story's direction. "It's not important for me to dictate those things," she added, "but to me it was more original to investigate what real courage is. If you can't get along with each other, how can you go about fighting this monster?"

Although the producers were suddenly forced to consider the prospect of an *Alien* movie without an important element of the connective tissue between the first two films, Weaver herself claims that this was an idea they had already considered. "When *Aliens* came out," she told the *Alien³ Movie Special*, "the producers said to me, 'Wouldn't it be interesting to do a third one without Ripley, about their returning to the original planet and screwing up? Then, back to back, to shoot the fourth movie, in which Ripley comes back and saves the day or something?'" Although the idea of back to back sequels, which had previously proved successful with *Back to the Future Part II* and *Part III*, was rejected, screenwriter Eric Red was asked to exclude Ripley from his draft. "The basic problem when I was involved, for five weeks, was they didn't know what they wanted," he told *Cinefantastique*. "They went through a real waste of talent because of that. Another major problem was that they didn't want Sigourney back, so I had to go through a whole series of new characters. As for the producers," he added, "they simply weren't involved. I think it's the responsibility of the producer or creative entity to have a creative concept or to make sure it's moving forward efficiently. But these guys were aloof. I only met once with each of them."

Ripley's replacement in Red's script was a special services commando with a grudge against the aliens since his platoon was wiped out after boarding the ship in which Ripley, Newt and Hicks escaped LV-426 at the climax of *Aliens*. The alien is unwittingly brought aboard a space station populated mostly by farmers, gestates inside the body of a cow, and emerges as a brand new version of the creature, wreaking havoc on the terrified and ill-equipped inhabitants. "When I met with Hill," Red recalled, "I said, 'In *Alien* you had one creature, in the second, [you had] a hundred,' and that in this film you needed a new type of creature." Thus, he said, "I gave them the 'cattle alien'."

Hill and Giler were not impressed by Red's script, however. "It was a disaster," commented Giler, "absolutely dreadful. And that was the end of both them," he added, referring to Red and Harlin, who departed the project soon after Red turned in his script. "I specifically worked with two writers who sold me on their very ambitious plans to develop a story about the future of mankind and what type of intelligence was really behind the aliens' evolution," the director told *Cinefantastique*. "But what they turned in was nothing more than a re-hash of the two previous movies." Harlin hated the Eric Red draft to such an extent that he asked to be released from his contract to direct *Alien III*. "At that point I'd lost all passion for the project and thought it would be embarrassing to follow Scott and James Cameron's great epics with a tired carbon copy of both."

By now, having lost their director and looking increasingly unlikely to sign Sigourney Weaver — then in the midst of suing Fox over alleged unpaid profits from *Aliens* — the producers were back to square one, and hired a third screenwriter, David Twohy (*Critters 2*), to go back to the politically-minded Gibson draft, relocating the story first to a Russian space station and then to a prison planet. The fact that Ripley did not appear in either story made it ironic that Weaver liked it. "They put together quite a wonderful script without my character," the actress told the *Alien³ Movie Special*, "but [Fox chairman] Joe Roth said, 'We can't do an *Alien* picture without Ripley.'" Roth, for his part, explained his reasoning. "She is the centrepiece of the series. She's really the only female warrior we have in our movie mythology. In successful sequels you have a fine line between old and new ingredients... We feel it would be cataclysmic to proceed without her." Thus, said Weaver, "We started work on putting my character into another screenplay."

Meanwhile, the search for a director had narrowed, with stylish New Zealand film-maker Vincent Ward, director of the medieval time travel drama *The Navigator*, being the front runner. Although Ward liked the idea of directing *Alien III*, he was uninspired by any of the previous script drafts, and asked to work on a concept of his own, incorporating minor elements of earlier drafts. As he put it, "Sigourney would land in a community of monks in outer space and not be accepted by them." By this time, Weaver had settled her lawsuit over *Aliens* profits and had signed to *Alien III* for the sum of $5.5 million — then the highest salary ever paid to an actress — with a contract that gave her approval over the script *and* the director. Weaver duly approved Ward, whom she said "came in with a very original idea and a very arresting piece, as far as I was concerned. Ripley was unconscious for half the picture, [and] it had a great, unusual male lead." Since time was of the essence, Ward was paired with legendarily fast screenwriter John Fasano (*Another 48 HRS*), who set to work even as Twohy continued to refine his draft. "We were supposedly writing *Alien IV*," Fasano noted, "but if ours came in first, it would be *Alien III*." Twohy, who has since written and directed the *Alien*-influenced science fiction thriller *Pitch Black*, was furious about being edged out of the project. "At that point," he said, "I just slapped my script together and went off to make my own film. And that was the last I ever heard from them. The old adage is true," he added. "Hollywood pays its writers well, but treats them like shit to make up for it."

The Ward-Fasano collaboration resulted in a radically different reworking of the prison planet idea, set on a wooden planetoid just five miles in circumference. It's inhabited by a group of political prisoners, which has evolved into a religious colony whose technological level is that of medieval Europe, living a simple and self-sufficient monastic existence, until the crash-landing of Ripley's escape pod brings the alien into their midst. Ripley's insistence that an alien menace has arrived leads her to be denounced as a dangerous heretic by the Abbot, who is eager to conceal another kind of impending doom facing the shaven-headed monks: that the planetoid's supply of heating fuel is almost depleted, a fact of which only the Abbot is aware. Ripley, renamed the "Comet Woman" because she fell from the sky, is thrown into the dungeons, where she meets an android in the mould of Ash from *Alien* and Bishop from *Aliens*. Rescued by a sympathiser who believes that the scourge she describes is prophesised in arcane texts, Ripley and the android attempt to escape the doomed planetoid, while pursued by the alien creature which, having gestated in the body of a sheep, is a four-legged variety, with several of its host's characteristics. Rich with religious imagery, iconography and metaphor, and replete with a vast number of special effects, the Ward-Fasano script was delivered in early 1990, by which time the director had flown to Britain to begin overseeing the construction of sets for the prison planet, Arceon.

Realising that one of the key factors in the success of the original

Alien was the contributions of Oscar-winning conceptual artist H. R. Giger, Ward flew to Switzerland to meet with him. "Vincent came to Zurich," Giger told the *Alien³ Movie Special*, "and had these ideas for a wooden planet inhabited by medieval monks who manufactured glass, which I thought were very good, very different. One particular scene I liked took place at the end of Ward's script, when the alien would be seen to come out of Ripley's mouth. I even fashioned a device for extracting the creature," he said. "But I later heard that Vincent didn't like me, possibly because I found it hard to understand all his ideas. I was never officially involved at the same time as him."

At that point, however, the producers had begun to lose confidence in Ward's radical approach, despite the director's assertion that "initially, everyone was very excited by the idea." According to Giler, it was not the ideas but the logic behind them that presented the problem. "We couldn't figure out why [the planetoid] should be made of wood," he told *Cinefantastique*. "We could never get a simple answer from them. Why would they fly all that wood out there — the film is set in another galaxy, no less — and why was it crummy wood, at that?" While the film would have looked amazing, Giler acknowledged, it would have made no sense. "There were just a lot of 'why?' problems. What were these monks about? What was their creed? They were sort of Luddites, but it never gets explained properly." Ward and Fasano reportedly fell out over the direction of their next rewrite, which was followed by a draft from screenwriter Greg Press, notably the first to kill off Ripley at the climax — a proposition which, understandably, appealed to Weaver more than it did to the studio. Next, Fasano was recalled to provide a solo reworking of the script, toning down the ambitious scale of Ward's vision, and bringing it closer to the ambitions dictated by the budget.

Meanwhile, relations between Ward and the producers became increasingly strained, ultimately leading to the director leaving the project. "I essentially had a difference of opinion with one of the producers on the script," says Ward. "Initially, he embraced it, and then seemed to change his mind over the basic tenets I had, which made it very hard for me to continue, because that's what I'd come to the film with. I'd said that if I did the film, this is what it would be, and I couldn't see any way to realise that." In other words, Ward had been hired for his vision, and then let go for the same reason. According to Ward, however, there were other fundamental problems. "I think there were several things," he says. "I'm not sure which was the most important, because things were complex." One major difficulty was that a release date — the Easter weekend of 1990 — had been announced before a script was completed which, Ward says, made the studio nervous. "We were trying to write the script even as we were fast approaching production, and sets were being built," he explains. "So when you want to be a little adventurous, which this was, *and* didn't have the script nailed down, *and* didn't have a $100 million-grossing American director or a well-known screenwriter…

"The studio system here makes people tend to follow what's been done, and feel secure with safe decision-making, because it's such a large investment of money," Ward adds. "I'd always hoped that it could be like a prequel; something that had the main elements they needed — ie, the alien; Sigourney Weaver; a whole lot of people under threat; and some sort of resolution to that — but I hoped that one could reinvent and reinvigorate it. Because of the difference between Ridley Scott and James Cameron, it seemed at that stage that it was the only one of these sequels where they would allow anybody with any vigour to make it. And as it worked out, I was wrong." Ward was paid off, investing the money in his next film, *Map of the Human Heart*. "I wrote a story for *Alien³*, and drew storyboards, which they filmed," he told *Cinefantastique*. "I got paid for it, meaning I could carry on with my prime concern, *Map of the Human Heart*, without financial worry. I have *Alien³* solely to thank for that."

With sets already under construction at Pinewood Studios, the producers wasted no time in finding a replacement for Ward: twenty-eight year-old *wünderkind* David Fincher, an award winning commercials and pop promo director eager to make his feature début. Weaver, who had the right to veto the director, remembers hitting it off with Fincher at their first meeting, during which she asked him how he saw the character of Ripley: "He said, 'Well, how do you feel about *bald?*' At that second, I fell in love with him." Once hired, one of Fincher's first moves was to bring H. R. Giger back into the fold, flying to Switzerland on 28 July 1990, accompanied by producers Fred Zinnemann and Gordon Carroll, for a meeting with the artist. Giger began work conceptualising four elements of the revised alien design: an aquatic 'facehugger'; the infant form of the four-legged alien, nicknamed the 'bambi-burster' by the crew; a fully-grown alien quadruped; and the alien skin. "It was a shame they didn't keep my original idea, which showed the creature sliding out of a large ox in a hangar, as it burned its way through the animal using its acidic blood," said Giger, adding, "I also created a 'super facehugger' based on an old design. One of the first scripts had it swimming, so I visualised how it would move: the fingers would retract, so that it would crawl just under the water's surface." Giger faxed daily designs to Fincher and received detailed comments in response, but ultimately failed to earn an appropriate credit on the finished film and was forced to sue Fox to secure his payment.

Meanwhile, work continued on the script, for which Fincher was paired with Larry Ferguson (*Highlander*, *Beverly Hills Cop II*), by now the seventh screenwriter to work on the project, in an effort to modify Fasano's most recent draft to the satisfaction of all concerned. Weaver, however, reportedly thought that Ferguson's version of Ripley made her sound like 'a very pissed-off gym instructor', and rejected his draft. "Ferguson's quite a good writer," Giler commented, "but he was working under enormous pressure, working very quickly, and it wasn't what we wanted." Eventually, Giler and Hill decided to take over the writing chores themselves, which, as Giler admitted, backed the director into a corner. "It's a difficult position to be both the producer and the writer," he told *Cinefantastique*. "It's easy for the director to argue with the writer, but not the writer-producers. You can't get rid of the writers when they are the producers. You bring the studio into it too, and that creates trouble."

The Hill/Giler draft of *Alien III*, dated 18 December 1990, combined the monastery and prison planet ideas, so that the inmates of the Weyland-Yutani prison facility on planet Fiorina 'Fury' 161 have found religion as a metaphorical form of escape from lifelong incarceration. Although this screenplay — which ends like Ward's script and the finished version of the film, with Ripley clutching the alien queen as she throws herself into a furnace — reads close to the theatrically-released version, Fox apparently did not favour their approach. Yet another screenwriter, Rex Pickett (*From Hollywood to Deadwood*), was brought in to reshape the second half of their script, while Giler threw up his hands and quit. "They snuck this guy in on us," Giler said of the studio's surprise move. "No one knew who he was, no one had ever read anything of his, no one knew why he should be hired... It was just a farce."

With a mere four weeks to go before principal photography was due to commence, Pickett worked through Christmas 1990 to January 1991 on what he later described as "a complete rewrite of the second half of the Walter Hill/David Giler screenplay due to certain major character and narrative changes mandated by Walter Hill. Once that was accomplished I was to attend to the first half and write an amalgamated version, which was to include scenes from their draft and new scenes that I wrote." In short, he stated, "this was a 'crunch time' rewrite," with the resultant screenplay containing "scenes that I was instructed to include whether I wanted to or not." Having taken delivery of Pickett's draft, Fox was reminded of another clause in Sigourney Weaver's contract: that she was only obliged to appear if Hill and Giler were retained. Giler was invited back on 11 January 1991, working on yet another draft of the script — now entitled *Alien³* — and a further *ten* revisions dating from 16 January to 10 April 1991, by which time the film was well into production, although it had already missed its original projected release date by some margin.

Around this time, Fox rather unwisely put an *Alien³* teaser trailer into theatres, its single visual image and voiceover narration suggesting, erroneously, that the storyline would take place on Earth. Even at this stage the announced release date of Christmas 1991 seemed optimistic, and so it was to prove, as the first screening for the studio brass led to extensive re-shoots, including a revised version of the 'bait and chase' sequence at the film's midpoint. (The revised sequence, twenty-one pages in length and appended to the shooting script, is apparently credited to 'Alex Thompson', and dated '12.00pm/Tuesday/5.3.91'). The logistics involved in bringing the cast and crew back for re-shoots was further complicated by the fact that, by this time, Weaver's hair had grown back and she was unwilling to shave her head again — perhaps unsurprising, since she was already contracted to play Queen Isabella in Ridley Scott's Christopher Columbus bio-pic *1492: Conquest of Paradise*. A further problem arose when it emerged that, by sheer coincidence, the ending of James Cameron's *Terminator 2: Judgement Day*, released in the summer of 1991, was unmistakably similar to that of *Alien³*. "We were about two weeks into shooting when someone learned about the similarity," Fincher said, "but we were just too far into it to change it."

An extensive period of editing and post-production followed, and the film was previewed again in September 1991. This time, it was to a specially invited test audience, who were reportedly puzzled how a four-legged alien came to be running around the prison camp. "We previewed it to audiences," Fincher explained later, "and people would ask, 'Where did the alien come from?'" This problem arose from Fincher's excision of the 'bambi-burster' sequence, which the director felt had suffered due to budgetary restrictions. "[It] just never played," he explained. "To really do it right would have cost a couple of hundred thousand dollars, and we only had sixty thousand. It looked stupid." Thus, with barely two months to go before the scheduled release date, the studio agreed to finance another two-day re-shoot, with *Aliens* alumni Alec Gillis and Tom Woodruff Jr being called upon to film the creature's emergence from its four-legged host — not an ox, as in the script, but a dog, which Fincher felt would give the new alien greater agility and intelligence, and more aggressive characteristics. "The change to a dog broke everybody's heart, because it had been done before in *The Thing*," Fincher admitted, "but it helped when we got into the big chase sequence at the end."

Alien³ finally made it into US cinemas on 22 May 1992. After a promising opening weekend, driven largely by audience curiosity after the many postponements and pre-release horror stories surrounding the film, the film struggled to an overall US box-office take of just over $50 million, little more than half the gross of *Aliens* six years earlier. The critical response was withering, while fans who expected to leave the cinema saying 'Wow,' as they had coming out of *Alien* and *Aliens*, mostly scratched their heads and asked, 'Why?'

Despite his departure from the project, Ward's contribution was rewarded with a story credit — the result of an acrimonious Writers' Guild arbitration over who had written what — although the director admits that the elements he liked most about his proposed version did not make it into the finished film. "The things that I thought would have made it really fantastic aren't there at all," he says. "The little things are in there, and the plot devices, but those were the things that to me were the least interesting." Upon seeing the finished film, original *Alien III* screenwriter William Gibson found only one of his ideas had been used: a barcode tattooed on the back of a character's head. Overall, says Ward, "I thought David Fincher made the best of a difficult situation, given the politics of it, because it was a virtually impossible job — I don't think it was a 'win' situation. He came in very late, it wasn't his script, and the main ideas which had driven that script were stripped out so that it didn't make any sense any more."

Fincher, who survived the *Alien³* debacle to make *Se7en*, *The Game* and *Fight Club*, was philosophical about his first feature. "Everybody did a phenomenal job, considering the restraints we had," he said. "In the end, *Alien³* is $60 million worth of the best ideas we could come up with on any given day. It was a logistical nightmare, a production nightmare and it was a micro-management nightmare. The whole movie was a matter of hitting the ground sprinting and making the best decisions we could," he added. "We started shooting with only forty pages [of script], and the script changed so much and so fast that we were receiving stuff off the fax and shooting it the next day. It was just insane."

Yet the *Alien* series was not the only film franchise with which Twentieth Century Fox had apparently committed 'franchicide.' In 1990, the studio had killed off another potentially successful film series with *Predator 2*, Stephen Hopkins' follow-up to the hit Arnold Schwarzenegger movie which told the story of a highly intelligent, virtually invisible and seemingly invincible alien who comes to Earth to hunt humans for sport. While *Predator* took place deep in the jungle, the sequel brought the action to near-future downtown Los Angeles, where — in the absence of Schwarzenegger, who passed on the film in favour of *Terminator 2* — *Lethal Weapon* star Danny Glover, *Aliens* alumnus Bill Paxton and Maria Conchita Alonso take on another visiting warrior. Despite nail-biting action set-pieces and a strong script, *Predator 2* grossed just $30 million at the US box-office, barely half that of the original. By 1992, with the failure of *Alien³*, and despite rumours of a third *Predator*, the chances of another film in either series seemed slim. That the franchises were kept alive in fans' minds, not to mention on the desks of Fox executives, is at least partly due to a licensed comic book, combining creatures from both series, which had become the fastest-selling independent comic of all time.

Predator 2 cheekily hinted at the prospect of an aliens/predator match-up, by having an alien skull displayed in a trophy case of the predators' spacecraft. But the concept was fully realised on the page in 1990, when Dark Horse Comics began publishing *Aliens vs Predator*, a four-issue limited series written by Randy Stradley and pencilled by Phill Norwood. The premise was simple: in a constant search for new species of big game to hunt, a pack of predators have taken to seeding distant worlds with batches of alien eggs, returning to hunt them when the creatures have hatched and matured. On the desert world Ryushi, however, their sport is complicated by a colony of humans, caught in the middle of a bloody battle between two of the deadliest species in the galaxy. As the battle rages, an uneasy alliance develops between a Japanese female named Noguchi and the predator leader, Broken Tusk, as they both face the alien onslaught.

The comic was an instant success, thrilling fans of both film franchises on both sides of the Atlantic, and attracting the attention of one British fan in particular: would-be screenwriter Peter Briggs. Using the Stradley/Norwood comic as a foundation, Briggs took it upon himself to write a gripping 107-page 'spec' script: *The Hunt: Aliens vs. Predator*. Under normal circumstances, getting anyone at Twentieth Century Fox to give the script more than a cursory glance would have been difficult; on this occasion, however, the stars were in alignment: Briggs's script found its way onto the desk of *Predator* producer Lawrence Gordon, who contacted the young writer with an official commission for a second draft. By late 1991, with *Alien³* undergoing post-production and re-shoots, Briggs had handed in another draft, now under sanction from Fox.

However, while obviously enthusiastic at the prospect of an *Aliens vs Predator* movie, fans of the comic book took issue with Briggs' free adaptation, which failed to acknowledge Stradley's contribution, either financially or in terms of story credit. The fact that Fox owned both intellectual properties arguably makes this a moot point, but Briggs was widely vilified in the science fiction press, and went to great lengths, first to point out the differences between his screenplay and Stradley's comic script, and then to acknowledge the influence of the latter on the former. "The comic was the jumping-off point," Briggs later told the website *Coming Attractions*. "I've never denied the thing was liberally based on it... My decisions were to take what was *good* about the comic, and pump up the octane level... just to make [it] better, for the good of the 'cinematic experience.'" Nevertheless, where Stradley's story wasn't broke, Briggs saw no reason to fix it, and only amended details he felt were out of synch with the films. For instance, he said, "in the comic, the predators essentially slaughter a helpless family as a revenge killing. I didn't like that. I've always thought of the predators as being samurai, with their own noble code." Indeed, in *Predator 2*, the hunter refuses to kill a helpless female because it can sense that she is pregnant. "I'm sorry Mr Stradley hasn't read my printed acknowledgements of the terrific work he did for the comic. I certainly owe him an enormous debt, that I may probably never be able to repay," a contrite Briggs told *Coming Attractions*, adding that, if the film were ever produced, he would expect to see a screen credit, "Something to the effect of 'Based on material created by Dark Horse Comics.'"

Briggs admits that he did not expect what was essentially a 'fan' script to provoke the reaction it did, either from real fans or a real producer. "It was a fast write, and it was *never* intended to get the attention it had," he said. Besides, he added, with each new draft, the story drifted further from the original comic book scenario, introducing such concepts as a holographic swordsman programme, new supporting characters, and — perhaps most intriguing of all — an alien/predator hybrid. "In my second draft of *Aliens vs Predator*, the opening scene was different — it took place on a deep space exploration vessel," Briggs recalled. "They're drifting along, and get 'pings'. They find a damaged predator 'egg pod', and bring it on board. Something nasty happens. Cut to the ship floating with no power. Something clangs onto the hull. Shapes come onboard — everything's in zero-g, with emergency lighting. Predators in armoured space gear 'de-cloak'! Find blown-open human corpses floating around — and then the aliens attack. One [predator] makes a very stupid move with a blaster, and blows an alien apart. Cue zero-g acid exploding equally in every direction, chewing through all the hulls and decks! [It] would have been wild..."

It would, indeed, had the various interested parties agreed. "The reason the project stalled was producer in-fighting," Briggs explained. "I was kept abreast of the situation by my agent, and there was a lot of backwards-and-forwarding over something like a twelve-to-eighteen month period." Producer David Giler, in particular, was resistant to the idea, preferring to see Ripley's return, despite the fact that she had met her demise at the end of *Alien*[3]. After all, as Giler told *Cinefantastique*, "It's science fiction — there are nine million ways to bring Ripley back." Besides, as *Alien: Resurrection* writer Joss Whedon (*Speed*, *Buffy the Vampire Slayer*) told *Cinescape*, "Some of us felt [the *Aliens vs. Predator* concept] might have sullied the *Alien* films. It becomes like *Destroy All Monsters* — you know, Godzilla, Rodan, Mothra and all the rest. Or *Freddy vs Jason*. Actually, I think the reason it fell through is that it was so unbelievably complicated legally. There are something like nineteen producers involved, and I don't think they could do it."

Sigourney Weaver subsequently indicated her own dislike of the *Aliens vs Predator* premise in an interview with *The Boston Herald*. "I'd heard they wanted to make it *Aliens vs Predator*, and I wanted to get as far away from that as I could," she said. "I thought, 'Why are they doing this?' We did three quite amazing films, and now they're just going to put it through some grist mill to make money. That's one of the reasons I wanted to die in the third film... I didn't want my part to go on forever." Eventually, she said, "They came to their senses, and decided not to make *Aliens vs Predator*. And basically what I said was that we needed to restore the alien's superiority and elegance, to bring back the idea of what and who it is. I wanted to restore a lot of the mystery to the series and also, frankly, to play the Antarctic side of Ripley..."

It is reasonable to assume that the *Aliens vs Predator* concept died when Sigourney Weaver signed to make a fourth *Alien* movie, scripted by Whedon and directed by French film-maker Jean-Pierre Jeunet (*Delicatessen*). By Whedon's own admission, however, his first draft did not include the franchise's heroine. "I got the gig by writing a treatment that did not involve her," he told *Cinescape*. "Then they said, 'We want her.' I guess the idea of doing an *Alien* movie without the anchor, which she is, makes them a little nervous. So I wrote a new treatment." Whedon also says that he discounted the possibility of setting the film on Earth early on in the writing process. "First of all, it would require an enormous budget and gigantic scope," he explained. Besides, he added, "Ultimately, it would have just been a backdrop that wouldn't affect the main part of the story or what the characters would be."

While Whedon acknowledged that fans of the franchise have long expressed an interest in having a story set on Earth, he claims that nobody could say what it was about the idea that interested them. "Nobody, including me, could answer that," he said. "We know the Earth won't be like anything we recognise, so it's not like you'd be afraid the aliens are under your bed. Ultimately, I didn't know what we could extract from that idea, except a mankind versus the aliens epic, this all-out war kind of thing." Thus, although the ending sees Ripley and Call (Winona Ryder) heading for Earth — a shortened version of the original ending, in which they crash land off the coast of a Terran city, and pursue the Newborn alien through sewage pipes — Whedon's script took the story back into space for a relatively safe entry in the series, artistically speaking, returning to the franchise's roots as a kind of monster-on-the-loose-meets-monsters-versus-military — a deliberate merger of the first two films.

Today, a decade after Briggs's 'spec' script caught the attention of producer Lawrence Gordon — not to mention millions of alien and predator fans worldwide — the prospect of an *Aliens vs Predator* film seems increasingly unlikely, not least because Fox has failed to develop the *Predator* franchise, despite *Daily Variety's* assertion in October 1996 that writer-director Robert Rodriguez (*From Dusk Till Dawn*) had handed in a draft for a third *Predator* film. Dated 2 August 1996, and entitled *Predators*, the script was reportedly set on the creatures' homeworld, and was rumoured to feature Dutch, the character played by Arnold Schwarzenegger in the original *Predator*. Little more has been heard of the screenplay since then, however.

It is likely that the *Predator* franchise will remain dormant if Fox intends to include Sigourney Weaver in *Alien 5*, which has been mooted since before *Alien Resurrection* opened to disappointing reviews and box-office. "I have never read [the *Alien 5* script], and I have never asked to read it," Weaver told *TV Guide Online* in early 2001. "I think the plan is to make it *Alien* [sic] *vs Predator*, and I would just as soon not be in that — although I am sure I could whip them both." Nevertheless, she told *Cinescape*, "I sort of left [Ripley] in an interesting place, and I want to see what happens next. There's a cool Jekyll and Hyde thing going on inside her, and I'm not sure who will win. I don't think another sequel is a bad thing," she added. "Nowadays I think there's a whole generation of moviegoers who think of these movies as episodes in a long adventure. And I don't think this adventure is completely finished." ■

Lights, Cameron, No "Action!"

Even The Self-Styled "King Of The World" Couldn't Get Spider-Man, Terminator 3 Or Avatar Off The Ground

"There is no doubt that Jim is the best man on
Earth to do the *Spider-Man* movie."

—*Spider-Man* creator Stan Lee

I n 1978, twenty-four year-old James Cameron made a twelve-minute, 35mm, special-effects laden promo reel for a science fiction film he hoped to make entitled *Xenon Genesis*. It was the beginning of a science fiction legacy that would stretch through his first screen credit, as art director on the Roger Corman production *Battle Beyond the Stars*; to his inauspicious directorial début, *Piranha Part Two: The Spawning*; two-and-a-half *Terminator* films (including *T2-3D: Battle Across Time*); *Aliens*; *The Abyss*; an uncredited rewrite for ex-wife Gale Anne Hurd's production *Alien Nation*; an original screenplay, *Strange Days*, directed by another of his ex-wives, Kathryn Bigelow; right up to the hit TV series he co-created, *Dark Angel*.

Having made *Terminator 2: Judgment Day* — at $120 million, one of the most expensive movies ever made, but at $517 million in receipts world-wide, also one of the most successful — writer-director James Cameron considered a number of projects as a follow-up. One possibility was *The Crowded Room*, based on the true-life story of Billy Milligan, a man with multiple personalities who is put on trial for murder. Cameron had signed a deal with Sandra Arcara, who owned the rights to the story, shortly after completing work on *The Abyss*, and began writing the screenplay with writer-actor Todd Graff in early 1990. Having made four science fiction films in a row, Cameron was understandably taken with the idea of making an $11 million courtroom drama focussing on the central performance of a single actor (albeit effectively playing several roles).

Yet the lure of science fiction was one that Cameron found difficult to resist, and while he continued with pre-production on *The Crowded Room*, he began developing ideas for a near-future thriller, set during the New Year's Eve celebrations of 1999. Tentatively titled *Strange Days*, the resulting treatment ultimately became the 1995 film co-written by Cameron and Jay Cocks, and directed by Kathryn Bigelow (*Blue Steel*, *Point Break*). He was also offered, through his close friend and collaborator Arnold Schwarzenegger, the chance to remake *La Totale!*, a French comedy about a married man who hides the fact that he is a James Bond-style spy from his wife. "I wanted to do a comedy as well as a big action and visual picture," Cameron told the *Los Angeles Times*. "Comedy was something totally new for me and so I knew it would be a challenge. And besides, the whole James Bond-spy genre had not really aged well. I felt it was time to pump some new blood into it." But even as he sketched the outline for this film, released in 1994 under the title *True Lies*, Cameron's ideas for an epic love story based around the sinking of the *Titanic* began to coalesce, although it was to be another five years before he would bring this story to the screen, winning eleven Oscars and earning a billion and a half dollars world-wide. And in the midst of it all, there was Spider-Man.

Like millions of Americans, Cameron had been a fan of superhero stories since his youth, preferring Marvel Comics titles like *The Amazing Spider-Man* and *The Uncanny X-Men* to DC Comics' *Superman* and *Batman* tales. By the age of twelve, he had decided that he would grow up to be a comic book artist, and began copying his favourite characters. "I basically learned how to draw comics by copying the characters out of Marvel Comics," he told the *Hollywood Reporter*. "I would spend long hours drawing Spider-Man and The Incredible Hulk." For Cameron, Spider-Man must have been of particular interest, having at its centre a teenage boy named Peter Parker, socially awkward but precociously bright, much like the young Cameron himself. Thus, when the success of Tim Burton's *Batman* opened the floodgates for a new wave of films based on comic books, Cameron became the logical choice to bring his web-slinging idol to the big screen. An initial meeting between the director and Spider-Man creator Stan Lee took place in 1991, following which Lee stated simply: "There is no doubt that Jim is the best man on Earth to do the *Spider-Man* movie. He wants to do it, and I want him to do it."

Carolco, the company behind *Terminator 2*, also wanted him to do it, and acquired the rights to a Spider-Man feature film from 21st Century Film Corporation. 21st Century's founder, Menahem Golan, had inherited them as part of the dissolution of his previous company, Cannon, which had licensed the rights from Marvel in 1985. "I was crazy for *Spider-Man*," Golan told *Premiere*. "Comic books were down, and nobody was interested. But I thought they would come back." To retain the rights, 21st Century were contractually obliged to put *Spider-Man* into production by April 1989, and Golan wasted no time in announcing the film, with Stephen Herek (*Bill & Ted's Excellent Adventure*) at the helm: "The world's best-selling comic book hero battles his multi-limbed arch-enemy, Doctor Octopus, in a fun and action-packed adventure comedy."

Desperate for money to finance the film before the deadline, 21st Century sold the home video rights to Sony-owned Columbia TriStar, and international television rights to Paramount's parent company, Viacom; Golan even struck a new deal with Marvel Comics, extending the deadline to January 1992. But still the movie failed to materialise, and when 21st Century collapsed in 1991, cash-rich Carolco swooped in to pick up the remaining rights, paying Marvel $3 million to extend its option through May 1996, and inviting Cameron aboard as writer, director and producer. Although Cameron continued to pursue several other projects, he was interested enough in *Spider-Man* to write a 57-page 'scriptment' — a combination of script and treatment, not unlike the one he had written for *The Terminator* a decade earlier. Cameron's first draft was completed on 3 August 1993, the same day *True Lies* began shooting. Stan Lee immediately proclaimed the story treatment to be "brilliant" — unsurprising, given that Cameron had been almost obsequiously faithful to Spider-Man's comic book origins. "What Jim managed to do was do *Spider-Man* exactly the way *Spider-Man* should be," he enthused to *Premiere*. "The same personality, the same *gestalt*. And yet it all seems fresh and different, something we have never seen before."

Opening with an image of the web-slinging crimefighter suspended upside down from the uppermost radio mast of New York City's tallest building, the World Trade Center, Cameron uses first-person narration to describe how Peter Parker, an orphaned but otherwise unremarkable seventeen year-old living with his aunt and uncle in Flushing, New York, is bitten by a spider whose genetic code has been altered by its ingestion of a mutagenically-activated fruitfly. That night, Peter has a dream in which he imagines himself as a spider — and wakes to find himself eighty feet up a high tension tower dressed only in his underwear!

Peter soon begins to display other arachnidan qualities, apparently brought on by the spider bite: he can climb vertical surfaces, land safely on his feet from virtually any height, perform incredible acrobatic feats and tune his senses to superhuman levels. He can also secrete a pearlescent white fluid from his wrists, which turns out to be his equivalent of a spider's silky thread (these organic webspinners, a change from the original comic's mechanical ones, were fully intended by Cameron to be seen as a metaphor for puberty and the urges that go with it). Peter, like Gregory Samsa in Kafka's *Metamorphosis*, has awoken to find himself turned into a bug. Peter hides his secret from his family and his classmates — even the object of his unrequited affection, pretty classmate Mary Jane Watson. Instead, he dresses himself in a mask and makeshift spider costume, and — under the name 'Spider Man' (with no hyphen) — begins performing gymnastic feats for money, first in the street, and later on television variety shows — but always, somehow, retaining his anonymity. But when his elderly uncle is murdered by street thugs, Peter decides to use his powers for more than just financial gain and small-scale fame. He begins a solitary hunt for Ben's killer, and eventually becomes a kind of nocturnal vigilante, a masked 'superhero' who invokes the wrath of legitimate law enforcement *and* the enmity of the criminal underworld. Soon, these feelings are shared by the public at large, whose fear of the costumed vigilante stalking the city at night (wearing the classic red-and-blue Spider-Man costume) is fuelled by a local newspaper. Already unpopular at school, Peter now finds himself a despised public figure.

Soon, Spider Man's superhuman feats come to the attention of evil tycoon Carlton Strand, who developed the ability to control electricity after surviving a lightning strike. Using his powers to turn himself from small-time crook to billionaire supervillain, he now controls his empire along with his beautiful but deadly consort, Cordelia, and shapeshifting sidekick, Sandman (not to be confused with the early DC Comics character revived by Neil Gaiman). Strand tries to lure Spider Man into his criminal empire, but Peter rejects the offer, and continues his fight against crime, despite the fact that the line between good and evil is often as blurry as his vision was before he gained his 'spider-sense.' A furious Strand frames Spider Man for murder, turning the crime fighter into a hunted criminal. Meanwhile, romance is blossoming with Mary Jane, but not for Peter — it is Spider Man who seduces her, and she has no more idea that Peter Parker is the man — or rather, *boy*— behind the mask than anyone else in the city. Eventually, in classic comic book style, Strand uses Mary Jane to lure Spider Man into his web, and when Spidey comes to her rescue, an almighty battle atop the World Trade Center ensues. Strand is killed, Mary Jane discovers Peter's secret identity, they fall in love, Peter graduates... and the one-time hated vigilante becomes — you guessed it — your friendly neighbourhood Spider Man.

The closest Cameron came to directing the film was in 1995, and in interviews given for *True Lies* he regularly referred to *Spider-Man* as his next project. "I'm doing the origin story and then going way beyond that and delving into the whole story of teenage angst," he told *Platinum* magazine. "What if you were seventeen years old and you could do whatever the fuck you wanted, anytime you wanted? There's going to be all the webs and stuff, but it's also going to be deeply philosophical." Cameron had met with his future *Titanic* star Leonardo DiCaprio to discuss the central role, believing that Spider-Man himself was a big enough star to carry the movie. Besides, he said, "I think the big star factor is obviated by the fact that the guy's supposed to be just seventeen or eighteen. He's a senior in high school, and I'm playing it the way it was originally written."

Cameron also gave a hint as to the visual style of the proposed film. "One of the things that really interests me, possibly in *Spider-Man*, possibly in some other later project, is going into some very bizarre and surreal imagery that can only be done using computer-generated images," he added. "I want to try something really wild. Before, there were limits to what you could do in special effects, but now there are no impossibilities. If you can imagine it, you can definitely put it up there on the screen." Cameron may have been referring to a sequence in which Peter has an arachnid nightmare after being bitten by the spider, described in his scriptment as a dark, David Lynch-style montage of fevered images, including prey wriggling in webs, shining eyes and shadowy rooftops.

As fate would have it, by the time Cameron was free to make the *Spider-Man* movie, the feature film rights were caught in a web of their own, arising from the bankruptcy of Carolco in 1996, the result of such costly failures as *Cutthroat Island* and *Showgirls*. A year earlier, Twentieth

Century Fox — which had struck a deal with Cameron after *True Lies* hit big at the box-office — offered to buy the rights for $50 million, but Carolco, which had spent in the distinctly *un*friendly neighbourhood of $11 million developing the project, stubbornly refused to sell. Now, the collapsing company was forced to hand over production and distribution rights — excluding television and video, still held by Viacom and Columbia respectively — to MGM, which acquired both Carolco's and 21st Century's rights in the bankruptcy sell-off.

Before MGM could make a move, however, Marvel Comics filed a lawsuit claiming that the rights to make a Spider-Man film had reverted to Marvel in May 1996, since Carolco had failed to put the film into production before the deadline. Marvel was understandably desperate to reacquire the rights to its tent-pole character, since by 1996 it was facing bankruptcy proceedings of its own, precipitated by a slump in comic book sales and a disastrous attempt at direct-sales distribution. MGM promptly responded to Marvel's litigation with a three-pronged countersuit, claiming that if it did not own the rights under the Carolco agreement, it did so under its agreements with 21st Century and Cannon, both of which it had acquired from Carolco. To further complicate matters, Sony stepped in to assert its claim to the video rights, while Viacom threw its hat into the ring with a particularly creative lawsuit, claiming that, rather than merely owning the TV rights it purchased from 21st Century in 1989, it actually held the rights to produce and distribute a cinematic feature. "It's a tangled web," 21st Century's attorney, Sam Perlmutter, told *Premiere*. "More of a web than Spider-Man ever could have made in one of his stories. Almost all the studios have a seat at the table, claiming they have a piece of [the rights]."

As the litigation continued throughout the making of Cameron's next film, the gigantic hit *Titanic*, Twentieth Century Fox head of production Tom Rothman kept a close watch on proceedings, hoping that whoever came out of the legal mess with the rights to make a *Spider-Man* movie would be interested in a *Titanic*-style co-production deal with the studio most favoured by Cameron. "It's a great, enduring character — it's mythic," Rothman told *Premiere*. "I like it, and kids today are into *Spider-Man*, too. It's a property we're quite interested in, and we really hope we can make it." Nevertheless, he said of the legal battle, "Without a doubt, it's the most complicated and tortured rights process I've ever seen." Added

Sony lawyer Robert Schwartz, "the shame of it is you have a valuable property that is just sitting there. No one knows where it's going to go."

The Spider-Man saga was briefly put on hold during Toy Biz's takeover of the Marvel Group in the summer of 1998, by which time the prospect of Cameron directing a *Spider-Man* movie looked distinctly doubtful. "Jim's a big fan and has the utmost respect for Stan Lee," admitted Rae Sanchini, president of Cameron's production company, Lightstorm Entertainment. "But who knows if it will ever get made? So many people want to make it, and that has been one of the greatest impediments to getting it made." As Stan Lee told *Dreamwatch*, "For years now, lawyers have been working on this, trying to untangle this terrible legal knot and get the rights back [for Marvel]. The minute the rights come back, I hope Jim will do the movie, and I hope by then he's not busy with another movie, or he hasn't lost interest. As far as I know," Lee added, "he says he wants to do it, and as far as I know, he has no movie to do at the moment, and I have heard that we're close to getting a resolution with the legal thing." Lee felt that Cameron's participation was crucial. "He's not just a writer who's going to get the assignment and going to have to learn who Spider-Man is," he explained. "Jim has told me he's wanted to do a Spider-Man movie since he was about fourteen years old. So you have the desire and the ability in one guy, and the knowledge and the skill. I don't say other people couldn't do it... but I think it would be awful if it isn't Jim Cameron, if only because we've both been waiting so long for this."

The legal web surrounding Spider-Man finally became untangled in February 1999, as the US courts dismissed MGM's claim to the rights, leaving Marvel free to make a new deal — and thus, a new movie — with Sony Pictures Entertainment. "This is a great day for the studio," Sony chief John Calley declared. "I am delighted that we will be able to bring this long sought-after comic book hero to the world of Sony film and television entertainment." Describing the Spider-Man property as the "jewel in the crown of Sony's franchise vision," Calley confirmed that Cameron was still the studio's first choice, but admitted, "We haven't even looked at [his] treatment yet." By this time, however, and in the wake of *Titanic*'s critical and commercial success, Cameron felt that the ship had sailed. "Here's where I am philosophically," he told *Premiere* in November 1998. "I'm forty-four, I make a movie every two or three years — it should be something that I create. I've always done that, with the exception of *Aliens. The*

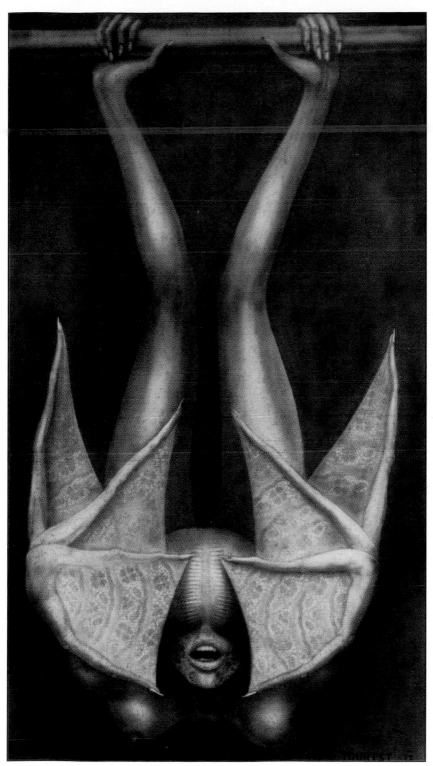

The Tourist IX, Hanging Alien, 1982, H. R. Giger.

Dune II, Harkonnen Castle, 1975, H. R. Giger.

Dune Worm XII, 1979, H. R. Giger.

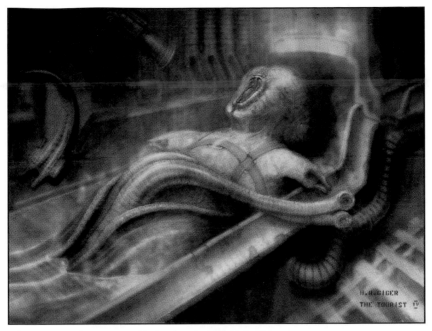

The Tourist IV, The Creature with the Tentacle, 1982, H. R. Giger.

Drawing for *Dead Star, The Demon* (detail), 1991, H. R. Giger.

Childhood's End: An alien Overlord, by Neal Adams.

Childhood's End: Adams's concept art for the arrival of the Overlords.

The Stars My Destination: Adams's vision of future Manhattan.

The Island of Dr. Moreau: A selection of preproduction paintings by Graham Humphreys, showing Richard Stanley's original vision for the film.

What could have been: an excerpt from the *Aliens vs. Predator* graphic novel.

Terminator was my creation, so were *Titanic* and *The Abyss*. With the amount of time and energy that I put into a film, it shouldn't be somebody else's superhero. I don't want to labour in somebody else's house."

Understandably disappointed by Cameron's departure, Sony wasted no time in discussing the project first with Roland Emmerich and Dean Devlin, the writer-producer-director partnership behind *Independence Day* and *Godzilla*, and then with David Fincher, director of *Alien³*, *Se7en*, and *The Game*. "I went in and talked to them about it," he told *Cinescape*. "I've always loved Spider-Man. [But] I wanted to do a much more operatic version of it, and everybody went, 'Gulp! We want the creation story.'" Exploring the character's origins was not something that Fincher wanted to do. "I was never interested in somebody getting bitten by a radioactive spider," he explained. "If we had a scene where a guy goes, 'Ouch! What is that?' I mean, I couldn't keep a straight face." Finally, genre favourite Sam Raimi (*The Evil Dead*, *Darkman*, *A Simple Plan*) signed on to direct an entirely new version of the story (though one which retained Cameron's idea for organic webspinners), scheduled for a May 2002 release.

With Spider-Man out of the picture, Cameron began considering the options for his next film: a sequel to *True Lies*; a third *Terminator* feature; a new version of Russian sci-fi epic *Solaris*, to which Cameron's Lightstorm Entertainment owned the remake rights; and a remake of *Planet of the Apes*, with Arnold Schwarzenegger in the Charlton Heston role. ("I would have gone in a very different direction," is all he would say about his version of the project, ultimately directed in 2001 by Tim Burton.) In early 1998, Cameron admitted that *T3* and *True Lies 2* were both possibilities, but added: "I have a better idea for a second *True Lies* than I do for a third *Terminator* right now." Nevertheless, he had outlined one possible future for the *Terminator* series back in 1995, telling *Platinum*: "There's a very rich, though bleak, futurography out there, that you could delve back into at any point. Arnold played the Terminator. And then he played the other Terminator. So he could easily come back as yet another. There's a factory somewhere in the future cranking these suckers out, so we could always go back to it if we wanted to."

Except that they couldn't, because the rights to produce another *Terminator* film were mired, like those of Spider-Man, in the downfall of Carolco, which owned a fifty per cent share of any sequel, prequel or television production. At the company's 1997 bankruptcy auction, Carolco cofounders Mario Kassar and Andy Vajna bought their former company's share in the *Terminator* property for $8 million, and subsequently paid a further $8 million to original *Terminator* producer Gale Anne Hurd, who owned the other fifty per cent. Now, Vajna and Kassar's new company, C-2 Productions, was free to make a third *Terminator* film. The only problem was that Cameron had publically stated that he would not be working on a *Terminator* sequel, with Lightstorm president Rae Sanchini confirming to *Premiere* that "[Cameron] is not now, has never been, and has no plans to be involved with [rights holder] Andy Vajna on *Terminator 3.*" In addition, Arnold Schwarzenegger had sworn he would not make a *Terminator* film without Cameron, and actress Linda Hamilton had recently become the latest of Cameron's ex-wives. C-2 vowed to carry on regardless, failing to snag Hamilton, but managing to lure the seemingly all-important Schwarzenegger when Cameron gave his blessing.

In any case, although the idea of *True Lies 2* still appealed to him, Cameron had other ideas, beyond sequels and remakes. One was *Bright Angel Falling*, an asteroid disaster film which the director wisely shelved after two similar pictures, *Deep Impact* and *Armageddon*, divided up the box-office between them in 1998. Another possibility was an adaptation of the novel *Ramses the Damned*, a cerebral and erotically charged retelling of *The Mummy* from Anne Rice, author of *Interview with the Vampire*. A more likely alternative, however, was *Avatar*.

Completed in 1997, *Avatar* was an original science fiction scriptment by Cameron, set on a polluted, overcrowded Earth, some time in the late 21st Century. The story begins with Josh Sully, a wheelchair-bound victim from some nameless war, who is picked to take part in a military and scientific project on planet Alpha Centauri B-4, a lush green world of untapped resources, also known as Pandora. The chosen subjects become 'controllers', who, under the guidance and orders of the brass, get to 'control' living aliens on Pandora, via psionic link. The officials have specifically grown the alien bodies so that they are mindless without the psi link; essentially, they are shells, or 'avatars'. The plan is that the controllers, in the guise of native aliens, infiltrate the inhabitants of the planet and discover as much useful information as possible about the planet's supply of Unobtanium, a room-temperature superconductor that is Earth's last, best hope for a renewable energy source. This material is held mainly in the giant floating mountains of Pandora, the biggest of which is nicknamed 'Big Rock Candy Mountain'. Sully joins the programme, and there are initial humorous scenes as he becomes used to 'controlling' a completely new alien body. But as he mingles more with the local inhabitants, Josh becomes increasingly involved with the plight of the natives, who feel — correctly — that the Earth people are intent on raping and destroying their planet. To complicate matters, at least for the humans, Pandora is home to an astonishing array of bizarre and deadly wildlife, and Cameron's script does not shy away from showing these beasts in full and deadly effect as they fight and tear around the planet.

The plot, however, was not the most intriguing aspect of *Avatar*. What most excited Cameron was the possibility of shooting the film live-action, but with six characters — the genetically-manufactured avatars themselves — being created entirely using the computer-generated imagery (CGI) Cameron had pioneered in films like *The Abyss* and *Terminator 2*. "We're developing a broad-spectrum toolset for integrating animation, motion capture, and live action in a photo-realistic way," Cameron told Paula Parisi in 1996, suggesting that the film would boast "organically believable lip-synching characters" indistinguishable from real actors. "These are supposed to be real people, real characters," he added as CGI tests began at Digital Domain, the special effects company co-owned by Cameron. "If we can pull it off, *Avatar* will be the coolest film ever made. If not, we'll have egg on our face."

The initial test phase at Digital Domain seemed to proceed well enough, and by February 1997, the company reportedly produced a reel of CGI footage in which a photo-realistic figure stood up from a chair, turned a somersault, and walked around the room. However, the time it allegedly took the company to render the sequence did not bode well for *Avatar's* special effects budget, which was pegged at twice that of *Titanic*, and may have led to an overall budget of up to $350 million. By June, reports spread that Cameron had lost interest in the project and in December Cameron confirmed as much in an online forum sponsored by Microsoft: "*Avatar*, I am not doing," he said simply. But did he mean that he wasn't going to do it *yet* — in other words, until technology had caught up with his ambitious plans? Or that he wasn't going to do it *ever*, having simply lost interest in it? With the IMAX project *Destination Mars* and *True Lies 2* on his schedule, it is difficult to say. After all, as Cameron said in 1999, "I want to keep on doing what I'm doing. I just want to keep making films." ■

Legend Of The Fall

Will Ridley Scott's *I Am Legend* Rise From The Dead?

"Vampires were passé, Summers' idylls or Stoker's melodramatics or a brief inclusion in the Britannica or grist for the pulp writer's mill or raw material for the B-film factories."

—from *I Am Legend* by Richard Matheson

I n 1954, American-born writer Richard Matheson published *I Am Legend*, arguably the first great vampire novel of the twentieth century. As Matheson commented — within the text in true postmodern fashion — vampires had passed, in a matter of centuries, from folklore and superstition into literature and on into the realms of pulp fiction and B-movies, their finest hour being in Bram Stoker's 1897 novel *Dracula* and F. W. Murnau's 1922 film *Nosferatu*. For three decades, the notion of the vampire as the subject of a serious, literate work had lain dormant, only to arise again, true to form, in *I Am Legend*.

Set in 1976, in the aftermath of some unspecified post-war plague possibly linked to biological warfare, Matheson's story took a novel approach to the vampire myth, imagining a blue collar worker named Robert Neville as the last human being in a world where every other living being — and many previously dead ones — had been turned into nocturnal nightmares. Pale-skinned, white-fanged and with an insatiable bloodlust, the creatures have many — though not all — of the traditional trappings of vampirehood, including aversions to garlic, running water, sunlight and crucifixes (one of which Neville has tattooed on his chest), and a single means by which they can meet a permanent end: a wooden stake through the heart.

Having watched his wife and daughter die of the same blood disease which has afflicted billions worldwide, Neville has spent the past five months as a virtual prisoner in his own home. He spends the nights listening to the pitiful cries and curses of his former friends and neighbours baying for his blood, and the days collecting supplies, repairing the damage inflicted by his hunters the previous night and carefully cultivating the garlic crop which, along with his collection of wooden stakes and crucifixes, are all that stands between him and the fate which, for no reason he can fathom, this "weird Robinson Crusoe, imprisoned on an island of night surrounded by oceans of death", has thus far been spared. The novel's ominous title held a pleasing double-meaning: the vampires which, nightly, hurled rocks and curses at Neville's fortified Los Angeles home, were a legend come to life. Neville, meanwhile, had become a legend in his own lifetime, as the last human in a world of vampires. But hopelessly outnumbered and increasingly in danger of losing his mind, if not his life, how long before the last man on Earth was nothing more than a legend?

I Am Legend was greeted with almost universal acclaim upon its first publication and remains one of the most influential novels of its kind. "I think the author who influenced me the most as a writer was Richard Matheson," Stephen King has commented. "Books like *I Am Legend* were an inspiration to me." Others in King's field agreed. "A long time ago I read *I Am Legend*," stated British writer Brian Lumley, "and I started writing horror about the same time. Been at it ever since. Matheson inspires — it's as simple as that." For Dean Koontz, *I Am Legend* was simply "the most clever and riveting vampire novel since *Dracula*."

But it was not just those who shared Matheson's talent for terror who admired *I Am Legend*; the cinema was quick to make a claim to his legendary vampire tale. In 1957, Matheson himself wrote an adaptation of his novel for Hammer Films, the British company then riding high with the success of their first full colour horror feature, *The Curse of Frankenstein*. But Hammer sold the script on to producer Robert L. Lippert, and it was re-written by William P. Leicester (Matheson took his name off the project, preferring the pseudonym 'Logan Swanson' on the final screenplay credit). The eventual result was *The Last Man on Earth*, a relatively faithful adaptation starring Vincent Price as Dr Robert Morgan, filmed in Italy by Ubaldo Ragona in 1961, and released by American International Pictures in 1964. A mere seven years later, the story was filmed again as *The Ωmega Man*, in which Charlton Heston battles the nocturnal visitations not of vampires exactly, but of a sinister brotherhood of diseased albinos, dressed in robes as black as their faces are white and organised into a nightmarish collective known as 'The Family'. In this equally effective version, adapted by John William and Joyce H. Corrington (*Battle for the Planet of the Apes*) and directed with considerable style by television veteran Boris Sagal (*The Twilight Zone*), Neville develops an antidote from his own healthy blood to the disease afflicting the remaining population, but finds that the Family members are more interested in converting him to their 'cause' than in finding a cure for their affliction. The film, replete with religious imagery up to and including the final shot, ends on a cautiously optimistic note, as Neville sacrifices himself so that the few other healthy individuals he discovers during the course of the story have a chance of continued survival. Matheson was not impressed with the adaptation, however, suggesting that "it was so far removed from my book, I don't know why they bothered. It was no more *I Am Legend* than *Little Miss Marker*."

Although both film adaptations had played fast and loose with the source text they shared, making frequent and often significant departures from the storyline, Matheson's novel nevertheless had a clear influence on many other films, not least George A. Romero's *Living Dead* zombie trilogy, which turned Matheson's vampires into an equally, if not more, formidable form of the undead, shuffling through streets and shopping malls in a brainless, soulless and utterly hideous parody of their former lives. Romero's numerous imitators, and the rapidity with which their films lost favour with audiences, chiefly by slipping into self-parody, arguably led to a lack of interest in *I Am Legend* as fuel for a further cinematic adaptation.

However, by the early 1990s a tentative resurgence in science fiction and horror as mass-market genres led to a revival of interest in Matheson's forty year-old urban gothic horror novel, the options on which were regularly renewed even though no new film was forthcoming. Then, around 1996, a producer at Warner Bros, the studio behind *The Ωmega Man*, optioned Mark Protosevich's 'spec' script, *The Cell*, and offered the writer a job on one of three projects the producer Lorenzo di Bonaventura was developing. "The first one that he mentioned was *I Am Legend*," says Protosevich, "and as soon as he said it, it wasn't even worth talking about the other two. Here was one of my favourite science fiction books by one of my favourite writers, and *The Omega Man* had been one of my favourite movies when I was a kid, and here I was being offered the chance to do it. It was just incredibly good luck." That night, Protosevich worked on a treatment and was promptly offered the job.

Protosevich's first draft was set in San Francisco in the year 2002, some four years after an catastrophic viral outbreak had turned the entire population — save, of course, for Robert Neville — into nocturnal creatures known as Hemocytes, one of which Protosevich describes in detail: "A demonic visage. Ghostly white flesh so devoid of pigment we can see the blue and purple veins beneath the surface. His eyes are an unearthly cold blue/grey and white. He is completely hairless — nothing on his pate, no brows, no facial hair. His lips a deep ruby red. This thing was once human, but now, now... " As Protosevich explains, "Although these creatures consume blood, are allergic to light, and bear other similarities to vampires, they are not. They are something new, something we have never seen before, something strikingly different. There is nothing about their existence or behaviour that is based in the occult or supernatural. They are real."

Sprinkled liberally with flashbacks detailing the coming of the plague (an experimental viragene which escapes from a scientific facility), the story begins as Neville goes about his daily routine: making a videotape recording for posterity; broadcasting a message over the local radio station, in the vain hope that a fellow survivor is listening; feeding his dog; watching videotapes of old TV news programmes to deceive himself into thinking life goes on as normal; and finally, heading out to begin the grim and literally soul-destroying exercise of hunting Hemocytes which, he knows, will begin attacking his fortress home at sundown. One day, however, Neville falls foul of one of his own mantraps, and is still at large in the city when darkness falls. He survives the journey back home — barely — but his beloved dog, his only companion, is bitten by an infected mutt and he is forced to cut the wretched creature loose. Neville, as devastated as the empty world he calls home, is close to breaking point when he meets a fellow survivor: an uninfected young morphine addict named Anna, with whom a difficult first encounter soon becomes an uneasy companionship. But Anna betrays him to the Hemocytes, who are holding her little brother hostage, along with other human survivors being harvested for their blood. Neville is captured and crucified, but manages to escape, driving a subway train into the Hemocytes lair, rescuing Anna, her brother and as many other uninfected survivors as he can manage, and puts to sea. They are few, but where there is life, there is hope.

This draft, which Protosevich says was probably the purest version of the script, was greeted enthusiastically by Warner Bros, who immediately put it on the development 'fast track' under prolific producer Neal H. Moritz (*Volcano*, *I Know What You Did Last Summer*, *Urban Legend*, *Cruel Intentions*). The first actor to be linked to the project was Tom Cruise, a self-confessed science fiction fan whose sole excursion into the realms of fantasy at that stage was Ridley Scott's *Legend*. Cruise's interest was never officially confirmed — it is safe to say that, in the nineties, he was offered every script with a white male lead — but at various stages a number of other A-list actors, including Mel Gibson, Michael Douglas and Arnold Schwarzenegger, were reported to be considering the role.

Then, on 6 June 1997, Schwarzenegger's apparent interest was confirmed when *Variety* reported that the Austrian-born star — who had co-starred with *The Ωmega Man* himself, Charlton Heston, in James Cameron's *True Lies* and whose heritage seemed to merge neatly with Matheson's vision of Neville as being of Anglo-Germanic stock — was in talks to play Robert Neville. So much for the meek inheriting the Earth. "At the time," says Protosevich, "Arnold was shooting *Batman & Robin*, where he was playing Mr Freeze, and I think Warner Bros had huge expectations for that movie, and for Arnie, and they were eager to get him into something else." Although Schwarzenegger was the last actor Protosevich expected to take the role — he had written the script with *The Last of the Mohicans*-era Daniel Day-Lewis in mind — he believed that it could work. "The character was conceived as an everyman who, because of these extreme circumstances, turns himself into a very physically capable person," the writer observes, "so physically speaking, Arnie was perfect, and I knew he could handle the action. And if he had a real emotional performance in him, this would be the chance for

Schwarzenegger to show it. More importantly, perhaps, he would ensure that the movie got made."

The same *Variety* report revealed that British director Ridley Scott looked likely to sign on as the film's director, despite the fact that his last two films, *1492: Conquest of Paradise* and *White Squall*, had been box-office failures, a fate which would soon be shared by *G.I. Jane*. The director had also recently suffered the very public collapse of an adaptation of Richard Preston's best-selling novel *The Hot Zone* which, like *I Am Legend*, dealt with the consequences of a devastating viral outbreak. For Scott, the film would mark his third science fiction production, after *Alien*, a blend of sci-fi and horror as potent as *I Am Legend*, and *Blade Runner*, an equally dystopian worldview. "There was a huge output of sci-fi books in the thirties, forties and fifties, but there were only a few that were any good," Scott later told *SFX*, evidently feeling that Matheson's book was one of the few. "I think the real power of sci-fi is when you look ahead and it feels uneasy because it feels like you are portraying what could be. It could be accurate." This ultra-realistic approach would clearly be as fundamental to Scott's version of *I Am Legend* as it had been to *Blade Runner*.

Despite the widespread approval for Protosevich's script, however, Scott apparently found it dramatically wanting, and his first order of business — after paying off producer Neal H. Moritz and assigning *Predator* and *Judge Dredd* producer Beau Marks in his place — was to bring in his own writer, John Logan, who would later share an Academy Award with David Franzoni for Scott's *Gladiator*. Nevertheless, out of courtesy, Warner Bros asked Scott to meet with Protosevich, the writer whose script had initially attracted him to the project. "It just felt like I had no chance," Protosevich says of the meeting. "It was like John Logan was hiding in a closet somewhere, because that's all Ridley wanted to do. He just wasn't interested in even giving me a chance." This probably had less to do with Scott's opinion of Protosevich as a writer than with the fact that he had written the script under contract to the studio. "From day one, a lot of directors perceive the studio as the enemy, and I was the studio's writer," he says. "And the next thing I knew, I was fired."

With Protosevich out of the picture, Scott immediately hired Logan to work on a new draft of the script. "When Ridley gets involved with a project, he has to totally re-envision it to make it the movie that he wants to make," Logan explains. "I don't think I've ever reworked anything as radically as *I Am Legend*," he adds. "It was an heroic undertaking." Logan and Scott sat down for an intensive period of story meetings, during which they explored the anthropological, sociological and even theological ramifications of having the human species reduced to a single man. "We kept saying, forget movie conventions — what if this really happened? If the human population was wiped out by a biogenic plague, what would happen? We approached it from a scientific perspective. We talked to scientists and survivalists, to find out what the civil defence response would be, and what the [public] response would be, and then Ridley and I started working together in terms of trying to create that. And what we came up with was a very bold approach to the material."

Essentially, Logan says, they brought down human civilisation in the first fifteen minutes of the film. "In the first draft, we did this almost entirely without words, through images of civil defence, and bodies burning, all set to Wagner's 'Siegfried's Funeral March' from *Götterdämmerung*, so that it became almost an opera of the end of the world. It was so great. So we did this amazing sequence, almost all visual, of the plague spreading and people getting sick, people dying, the end of the world. Then, after that, we opened on a day in Neville's life." It was at this point that Logan's draft made a radical departure from Protosevich's version. "We said, if he's the last man on Earth, let's *really* make him the last man on Earth," he explains, "so he has no one to talk to — he's just there by himself, struggling to survive. The most radical thing we did was take away other humans, and the dog, and anyone for him to interact with. So, literally, for the first hour of this movie, *no one* spoke — it was entirely visual storytelling." Scott had already rejected the idea of having Neville narrate the film, as the protagonist in *The Last Man on Earth* and *The Ωmega Man* had done, feeling that if the audience was to truly empathise with Neville's isolation, they should not have a voice to guide them. As Logan explains, "We rejected voiceover without even thinking about it, because Neville has no one to talk to, and there's no one to talk to him, so to mitigate that by having him talk to the audience in some abstract way seemed to take away the purity of the notion."

Eventually, it was decided that an hour of total silence was taking things too far, and a different approach was tried. "The idea we were working with was that a man scrounging for survival in a desolate landscape would exist on memory, and feed on the memory of when he was happier, and when others were alive," Logan explains. "So we created the conceit that when his wife was dying, she made audio tape recordings for him. And we would play bits of those during the first hour of the movie, so she would narrate his life as he was listening to these tapes, about what it was like to be sick, what the world was going to be like after everyone was gone, how much she cared for him. So for the first hour of [that] draft, the only voice you heard were these strange elliptical nostalgic romantic voiceovers from his dead wife. It was amazingly bold," he adds. "Maybe a little *too* bold."

While Logan toiled on the script, Scott set up an art department consisting of production designer Arthur Max (*Se7en*, Scott's *G.I. Jane*), conceptual illustrator Tani Kunitake (*Armageddon*, *The Matrix*) and storyboard artist Sylvain Despretz (*Alien Resurrection*, *The Fifth Element*). Initially, their task was to channel Scott's vision of *I Am Legend* onto paper in visual terms that would eventually become the blueprint for the film. "People are always accusing me of being too visual," Scott told *SFX*, "but I always start with the concept. It's all about the concept; the single idea. You have to have that great idea." Scott had already spent three weeks scouting for locations in the Los Angeles area, and considering the back lots of the sprawling Warner Bros studios in Burbank — including the triangular intersection popularly known as 'Ridleyville' since Scott filmed *Blade Runner* there a decade and a half earlier — where areas of Los Angeles could be duplicated, as decayed and deserted. By this time, the studio had rejected Protosevich's idea of setting the film in San Francisco for reasons of practicality: while several other cities could convincingly double for Los Angeles — Scott favoured Houston in Texas, and spent several days scouting possible locations there with location manager Jim McCabe — the distinctive appearance and unique environment of San Francisco made it impossible to match using alternate locations and studio backlots.

"Imagine Ridley shooting downtown LA in silence for almost an hour," says Logan, who helped orchestrate the script's shift from San

Francisco to Los Angeles. "Just watching this man survive, and the gathering storm of the Hemocytes — what *are* those things? On one hand we had great scenes in old landmarks like the Ambassador Hotel lobby or the wax museum," he says. "Then there was the place where he lived, which was like an ultramodern architectural movie-star home which was very secure, but he'd done a lot of things to make it even more secure." Tani Kunitake, who worked on conceptual renderings of the building, explains further: "The idea was that it was a very modern fire station, with all these abstract angles, and fragmented shafts of light coming through." The building's defences included a moat filled with gasoline, 'arrowslits' through which sighted weapons could be trained, and a perimeter defence of floodlights and land-mines. "It was going to be a total build from top to bottom, with electrics and everything, on a hillside overlooking Los Angeles," Kunitake says of the proposed location. Neville had also filled his house with paintings and sculptures purloined from the abandoned J. Paul Getty Museum. After all, Scott reasoned, Neville would need to feed his soul as well as his body.

Scott's view of Los Angeles circa 2005 was of a city which had advanced in subtle ways, but had suffered arrested development when the disease took hold. "Everything had stopped," Sylvain Despretz explains. "Time had stood still, so you just had carcasses of cars, a lot of dust everywhere, animal footprints. There was a subway system, which was influenced by a lot of techy Parisian designs, and you saw a few solar-powered phone booths, so there were changes, but they were subtle. It sort of gave you a feeling about what might have happened around 2005, which was then about eight years off." Despretz recalls sitting down with Scott to discuss a scene-by-scene breakdown of the film. "He's a director who is so seasoned visually that when he does his own storyboards, they blow a lot of people away because he can already control all the information that would be essential to a director like him, which is unusual, and probably makes it easier to work with him. He's got an incredible visual intelligence," he adds. Scott was also smart enough to move the pre-production team off the Warner Bros lot to offices in Santa Monica, an hour's drive away, so that studio executives would be less inclined to 'pop in' to see how things were progressing. During this period, Despretz and Kunitake storyboarded a significant percentage of the ever-changing script, sketching out various versions of Neville's fortress home and numerous sequences showing a devastated Los Angeles, as well as scenes set during the riots which broke out after the disease first swept the city.

"There is actually a blood disease that affects the skin's resistance to ultraviolet rays," Despretz points out, "and the implication [in the film] was that some event had triggered a bizarre retrovirus that had spread extremely fast, turning into an epidemic over the course of a few months, and had wiped out everybody save for a few people who — I think it was a blood type issue — didn't seem to be affected in the same way." Production designer Arthur Max, who had spent several months looking at grisly crime scene and medical textbook photographs for David Fincher's *Se7en*, began the equally unenviable task of researching starvation and burn victims, in order to provide factual background for the emaciated and scarred Hemocytes Scott envisaged. "There were some very gory photographs that we looked at depicting different deficiencies and illnesses," Despretz told *SFX*. "We also went through many documentaries because Ridley told us he wanted an emaciated look, and was thinking of using CGI to give actors a skeletal appearance."

During his own research, Despretz found a medical text on skinless bodies, and studied the Nubian portraits of German photographer Leni Riefenstahl, using them as inspiration for the tribal delineations of Protosevich's earliest draft, which called for tribal markings and jewellery to adorn the bodies of the Hemocytes. The creatures had a clearly defined hierarchy: at the bottom were the caretakers, who looked after the wounded. Next were the drummers, who chant menacingly while beating out rhythms on huge drums. Then came the clerics — a melancholy group set apart by their ornate, 'religious' markings. Most numerous though were the warriors: savage, strong and terrifying. Near the top of the hierarchy, Protosevich's script went on, were two lieutenants, Christopher and Eva, governing the clerics and warriors respectively. And above all is the leader, Cortman, the legendary first test-subject of the viragene, who has led the Hemocytes since the original ten experimental subjects escaped from the facility where their fate — and mankind's — was sealed.

"In the process of working on it," says Logan, "sometimes the

Hemocytes were mutants, sometimes they spoke, sometimes they had a leader, and sometimes they were just a feral pack — we went all over the map. We spent a lot of time on them, because Ridley has such an eye for the visual and tactile world around him, and how to present that cinematically, so we wanted to figure out how these people evolved. That was the word we used with the Hemocytes: *evolution*. What would truly happen if we wanted to create this race of subterranean vampires? What would they look like? How would they live? How would they survive? And what would their relationship with Neville be?"

"The Hemocytes went through various stages of design," says Tani Kunitake. "Early on the concepts were that we wanted to see them physically degenerate, so they would look like your typical modern vampire, wearing street clothes. But that as they degenerated throughout time, they slowly lost all their pigment, and then they began to lose their moisture and dry out, so that they started to bandage themselves to keep their skin moist." Although this may have given them the appearance of traditional movie zombies, Kunitake says that Scott wanted them to move like cheetahs. "He didn't want them lumbering around like *Night of the Living Dead*," the artist explains, "he wanted them extremely fast, so they were running around like agile mummies." Above all, Scott was keen to distance the Hemocytes as far from traditional vampires as possible. "God knows I didn't want *I Am Legend* to be a 'fang movie'," the director told Paul M. Sammon. "I did want the vampires to look monstrous, but we had difficulty with making them look monstrous without humanising them. Then they started to become too human-looking, which became a huge problem." One idea which struck Kunitake as particularly intriguing was the concept of having the Hemocytes constantly surrounded by flies, "so you would hear this buzzing, and that would clue Neville in that there's a Hemocyte around."

Pre-production continued on the film under Scott's supervision, with special effects artists Alec Gillis and Tom Woodruff Jr — the talented team who had worked on *Aliens* and *Tremors* amongst many other genre pictures — engaged to work on make-up tests. In the summer of 1997, Gillis commissioned conceptual artist Miles Teves to create an image of a female Hemocyte. "Alec gave me a brief description of what the make-ups should be like," says Teves, "but it was loose, with room for interpretation. I think he said that the Hemos' were hairless, with translucent skin and eyes adapted for night vision alone." Teves says that his brief was to make the female Hemocyte "repulsive yet sexy", adding that he based his design on a young Sophia Loren. "[I] figured that her beauty and sexuality was so strong that they would shine through the layers of make-up and remain somehow attractive," he explains. "I am told that silicone test make-ups were made based on my design, as well as others. I hear that they were looking pretty darn cool."

Meanwhile, in London, CGI artists Craig Penn and Tim Zaccheo of Mill Film, the London-based special effects company co-owned by Ridley Scott and his brother Tony, were asked to begin research and development on software which would allow them to create something more complex than computer-generated Hemocytes, or views of a deserted and devastated city. "They wanted us to create a fully animated deer," Zaccheo, who has since worked on *Babe: Pig in the City* and *Gladiator*, explains. "There were things that they wanted the deer to do which you couldn't do with a real deer, like walk around the subway system." Adds Penn, "We wrote a whole new piece of software, and we came up with a pretty amazing twelve-second sequence, which Ridley loved." The scene in question, which emerged in one of the many rewrites of the script, has Neville venturing into the city to hunt wild animals for food. He draws a bead on a wild deer, only to frighten the creature away when he accidentally activates the telescreen in a disused solar-powered phone booth. As the sound scatters the deer, a frustrated Neville fires off an angry gunshot at a giant billboard, which was placed in a part of the city that meant it could only have been generated using CGI. "There was also talk of us working on some aspects of the Hemocyte designs," Zaccheo adds, "but we never got that far."

As pre-production progressed, and the original October 1997 start date came and went, rewrite after rewrite had yet to produce a script that Scott and the studio could agree on, even though every new draft often involved a major re-vamp. One version even began before Neville has encountered the Hemocytes for the first time. "For the longest time you don't even know this is the story," Despretz recalls. "It starts with Neville as a sort of crazy Jeremiah Johnson figure with a long beard, laughing and dynamiting buildings. And he doesn't understand for a while that he has competition. The story picks up at the point where he encounters what he thinks is his first fellow survivor, only to realise that it's not. And that's when he goes into hell, because once he's been spotted and identifies himself, he becomes a target. He hunts them by day, and they hunt him by night."

John Logan recalls the thinking behind this version of the script. "One of the bravest choices we made, beyond the omnipresent silence, was the idea of creating a pseudo-love interest, which was a Hemocyte woman that he captures. And by using his own blood as a serum or an antitoxin, she sort of de-evolves back to a human state. We had totally rejected the idea of any human beings, but we thought, if there's no humans, then how is this going to work? And it was Ridley who came up with the idea of capturing one of these feral, ferocious Hemocytes, and having Neville sort of experimenting on this creature, discovering that it is a woman, and finally having her transformed into a mostly human form, to be sort of a companion in the story. It worked very well." Kunitake recalls Scott describing a scene in which the female Hemocyte, having begun her transformation, reaches out to touch a painting of a sunrise on the wall of Neville's home, and burns herself on a shaft of sunlight across the painting. "A lot of these things weren't specifically written," the artist notes, "but because Ridley's approach was so extremely visual, he would add these little painterly and poetic images."

The introduction of this "pseudo love interest" went some way toward appeasing the studio, which was understandably nervous about the human presence in the film — or rather, the lack of it. Says Logan, "We went through six drafts in the space of five months, just constantly reworking. It was the most intensive work I've ever done in my life, and it was absolutely thrilling, because we were going in, reinventing, and making very brave choices. Warner Bros were very open to let us try things and experiment with material as much as possible," he adds, "but there was certainly resistance to the absolute severity of what Ridley and I did, because although it had the big action set-pieces and a wonderful sense of mood, it was sort of unrelenting. This is a man who doesn't speak for an hour, and the love interest is a woman who never quite becomes human, and feels the call of the wild from her

Hemocyte brethren. It was a very grim and extreme version of the story, because there was no happy ending, in that he doesn't find people again. He finds something of himself, and there was a glimmer of hope in terms of him finding a radio transmission being received from somewhere else, but it was a tragedy: an unrelenting, intense story of one man responding to a harsh environment."

The studio was still not ready to gamble upwards of $100 million on this version of the story, however, not least because nobody seemed to know what kind of film they were making. "People were picking the script apart," says Despretz, "and they were asking very good questions about what the picture was about, and what it was saying, and what feeling it left you with, and what the point was. They didn't want to make a film that didn't really convince everyone that the point was clear." Nor did they want to make a film that would feel inferior to either of the two earlier versions: "It was a legacy question: if this is going to be made, it has to convince everybody that this is the ultimate [version]. Everybody thought it really had to be great, and nobody was sure that it was headed that way." According to Despretz, the studio apparently saw Arnold Schwarzenegger stalking a future Los Angeles as the ultimate survivalist as being something akin to James Cameron's *The Terminator*, whereas Scott saw the film in an altogether different light. "There was always going to be action in it," he says, "but mostly it was going to be atmospheric, and in Ridley's highest ideal, it was going to be an emotional, moody, melancholy piece about memory and recollection of life. So on one hand there was an attempt to create a repetition of something, and on the other, an attempt to create something highly original."

Finally, Warner Bros "practically insisted" that Logan was removed from the project, and that original screenwriter Mark Protosevich be given another chance. "From what I heard," Protosevich says candidly, "the John Logan drafts were viewed as pretty much a disaster. The studio felt that they had gotten off track, and had lost focus, and so the next thing I knew, I was back in Ridley's office, being treated as the fair-haired boy, with them essentially saying, 'We made a terrible mistake. Please come back, all is forgiven.'" Protosevich was given Logan's scripts to read, and quickly understood the studio's reservations. "When I read them, my jaw just dropped," he says, "because I felt like everything I had done was just erased, aside from the world and the feel that I had created. I just found it incredibly dull, and rather sombre, and very pretentious. It would have been a rather dreary art movie, which just happened to have a lot of violence in it. I have a lot of respect for John Logan as a writer," he adds, "but I don't think he was well suited to this script, and I felt that whatever ambitions he may have had about it, *it did not work.*"

Scott and Protosevich spent a week and a half hammering out some of the problems of the intermediate drafts, before the writer sat down and began afresh. This version — in which a Schwarzenegger-style Neville spends much of the film alone, his dog (named Stoker, a nod to *Dracula* author Bram) having been killed early on by the feral, bloodworshipping Hemocytes — was clearly informed by some of the developments made during the Scott-Logan collaboration. "We definitely reduced the voiceover," Protosevich agrees; "the Hemocytes didn't speak, they became much more animal; and Ridley had a location that he wanted to use for the house," he says, referring to Neville's adopted home: the Los Angeles Police Department Sports and Recreational Facility. "But aside from some things that Ridley really wanted, in terms of location and specific action bits, it wasn't very much the same [as Logan's drafts]. It really was a whole new movie." This draft includes the third act described by Logan, in which Neville uses his own blood to turn a Hemocyte woman back into a human, and ends on a positive note, as Neville escapes an all-out assault on his fortress home by fleeing to an abandoned airfield, where, in the closing moments, he is surprised to see a fellow survivor — a small boy, equally surprised to see him, who shouts 'Mommy!' before running inside a hangar. Although this ending did not satisfy Protosevich, it was this draft which came the closest to being made. "They started shooting make-up tests, they finally got Arnold locked in, and I was being patted on the back as the guy who wrote the draft that got the movie virtually green-lit."

At this point, the budget became the biggest impediment to an *actual* green light. The tightening of Warner Bros' belt in the wake of costly disappointments, such as *Sphere, Batman & Robin* and the similarly post-apocalyptic *The Postman*, led studio co-chairmen Bob Daly and Terry Semel to re-evaluate all of the projects on the production slate. On 7 December 1997, *Variety* confirmed industry speculation that *I Am Legend* was among the Warner Bros projects undergoing budget downsizing in an effort to bring the cost down to eight figures. As Sylvain Despretz puts it, "In the climate of 1997, when Warner Bros had lost a lot of money on a lot of turkeys, a picture with a guy laughing in the desert was just something they felt pretty badly about." According to Tani Kunitake, the script had simply outgrown the original ambitions for the project. "It started to get bigger and bigger," he says. "First of all, it felt really small, in the script, with your regular number of villains, etc. But then Ridley's take on it was to make it a lot larger, and to have these vast underground complexes of Hemocytes that would be almost like 'anti-cathedrals,' with shafts of light coming in from above. It probably frightened them, ultimately, because the scale was so huge." Despite Ridley's lofty ambitions, however, Protosevich felt that he, not the director, was shouldering much of the blame for the budget problems. "Ridley had a couple of producers working for him that I just did not trust," he says, "and I just started to feel that I was being pushed out, and that I was getting scapegoated. I was fired again, and I heard that they were going to go to this other writer, Neal Jimenez, to do a draft of the story, and hopefully work out some of the budget stuff. The next thing I knew, Jimenez had turned in his draft, and the project was as good as dead."

Sure enough, in March 1998, *Hollywood Reporter* was among the trade publications which reported that budget concerns had caused Warner Bros to officially pull the plug on the film. The studio had apparently been reluctant to shelve the project while Ridley Scott was still involved, preferring to wait until the director quit. Eventually, he did, taking several of his *I Am Legend* collaborators — including writer John Logan, production designer Arthur Max, and conceptual artist Sylvain Despretz — and setting to work on *Gladiator*, a film whose underlying themes seemed to reflect Scott's view of *I Am Legend* as an emotional piece about memory and recollection of life, in which the protagonist is a natural born survivor who, although dead inside, is determined to soldier on to the bitter end. In addition, says Kunitake, "I think a lot of the exterior lighting schemes at the beginning of *Gladiator*, and some of the interior lighting of [Scott's next film] *Hannibal*, were highly influenced by the planning of the lighting schemes in *I Am Legend*." (Intriguingly, *Gladiator* also borrows a sequence from the *I Am Legend* script in which Anna allows maggots to clean Neville's infected leg wound, replayed in the Roman epic as a scene between Maximus and Juba.)

Although many mourned the director's departure from the seemingly stillborn project, few were more disheartened than the artists who spent many months interpreting and illustrating Scott's vision for the film. "If Ridley could have done what he wanted it would have been a terrific film," Despretz told *SFX*. "It would have been a stunning mood piece, unlike anything that anyone would have expected or had been released [before]." Today, the artist describes working on *I Am Legend* as "the most rewarding experience I've ever had in film, despite the fact that, unfortunately, it never became a picture. It was the best drawing I've ever done, and the energy was so charged up, and we were all so into it, that I still think of it as my best experience at the drawing board working on a film. Had it been made," he adds, "it probably wouldn't have been so rewarding, because there's no way that anything that would have happened afterwards would have come close to what happened during those months. It was heaven." But would it have been the hit that Warner Bros so desperately needed? Kunitake, for one, is not sure. "I don't think it would have been the hit that *Gladiator* was," he admits, "but what Ridley did with a monster in a rocket ship [in *Alien*], he would have done for vampire and zombie films. It would have been pretty spectacular."

Despite the project's apparent collapse in the spring of 1998, however, *I Am Legend* looked set for a revival as early as July of the same year, when a new producer, Steve Ruther, was put in charge of a newer, leaner, and more cost-effective version of *I Am Legend*, with Protosevich returning for yet another draft of the script. "Ruther really wanted me to come back on to get the project going again," the writer recalls. "He said, 'I've read all the drafts, and your original draft was the best one, and we want to go back to that, are you interested?' And, of course, I was — I had, and still have, tremendous affinity for the project. So I went back for a third time, with Arnold still attached, and on the understanding that what they wanted to do was make the movie not for $100 million, but maybe for $70 million.

"The other thing they wanted was a new director," Protosevich adds, "and the impression I got was that [they were after] somebody that both Ruther and Warner Bros could feel comfortable with, and who was eager to work on a big studio movie, rather than somebody who was already established, like Ridley Scott. What Warner Bros did not do with Ridley was say, 'Look, here is a script we love — we want you to direct it,' so what Ridley did was come in and change the script that they wanted to make. They didn't stop him. They let him do what he wanted, and what he did was create a script that Warner Bros *didn't* want to make." In July 1998, *Hollywood Reporter* announced that the film was back in development, with director Rob Bowman — a veteran director of science fiction television who had made his feature début with *The X-Files* movie — at the helm.

Protosevich took the opportunity to read the Jimenez draft, which he found "even more esoteric than John Logan's. [Their] drafts were like dark art films — atmospheric, meandering, internal, slow musings about how a person would react under these circumstances, with all these scenes of violent confrontation. They weren't satisfying, and they didn't feel commercial at all." Under the guidance of Ruther and in collaboration with Rob Bowman, Protosevich duly embarked on yet another new draft, re-imagining the story on a smaller scale, almost entirely without voiceover, and with many of the set-pieces taking place indoors, and in a limited number of locations. This version, dated 30 December 1998, was far more action-oriented but introduced Anna and her nephew (changed from her brother) Ethan as major characters. "I have a lot of fondness for that draft," Protosevich admits, "but for whatever reason, it never got off the ground."

The reason was simple, however: Arnold Schwarzenegger's star began to wane. Whether because his last two films for the studio, *Eraser* and *Batman & Robin*, had failed to achieve his usual box-office potential or, as Schwarzenegger himself suggested, because the elective heart surgery he underwent in late 1997 somehow made him a risky prospect for a starring role in a big budget picture, Warner Bros cooled to the idea of paying him $20 million to carry a major event movie. "I had several projects set up, including *I Am Legend*," the actor later told the *Los Angeles Times*. "All of a sudden, it became impossible. The script was too expensive. The director was too slow. Everything was wrong — when nothing was. I really could feel people kind of one inch at a time pulling back. You know, they don't return your phone calls the same way that they used to. Or all of a sudden the guy's on the phone all the time, or he's on a trip. It was like, 'Maybe now we can't sell him as an action star. Now he's not the kind of superhuman that kids think he is.'"

Schwarzenegger, who had privately expressed his fears over whether he could carry the movie by himself, particularly one with such an intellectual bent, moved on to star in *End of Days* and *The 6th Day*. "It's kind of funny when you watch those movies," Kunitake observes, "because he put a lot of his Neville character into them. There was this big birthday party in *I Am Legend*, and I think he rolled that into *The 6th Day*." Even now, many involved in the Schwarzenegger period of development find it difficult to imagine *I Am Legend* without him. "When we heard Arnie was going to be in it, none of us [in the art department] could picture him in that role," says Sylvain Despretz. "And by the time we were finished, we could not imagine anybody else." Schwarzenegger's action star status proceeded to slip further, thanks to the lacklustre performance of *End of Days* and *The 6th Day*, leaving the prospect of high-profile sequels like *Terminator 3* and the still mooted *True Lies 2* to make him bankable again.

With Schwarzenegger out of the frame, the next name linked to the project was Kurt Russell, star of *The Thing* and *Escape from New York*. However, the disastrous failure of Russell's last science fiction venture, the Warner-produced *Soldier*, arguably made him the last man on Earth the studio would cast as the last man on Earth. According to Mark Protosevich, the studio also considered reinventing the film as a vehicle for Will Smith. Re-casting the leading role has its own complications, however: according to several sources, the deal Schwarzenegger originally made with Warner Bros means that if the film is made without his participation, the studio would still have to pay him a sizeable fee — yet more negative costs to offset against the film's projected production cost.

More significant obstacles were to block the way of *I Am Legend*, not the least of which is the fact that newly-appointed Warner Bros president Alan Horne expressed his distaste for violent movies in general — and thus, presumably, violent R-rated $100 million remakes with no obvious merchandising potential. "When he took over as head of the studio, he made up a list of projects he liked and projects he didn't like, and *I Am Legend* was on the wrong list," Protosevich laments. "It's not the kind of movie he wants to spend that kind of money on." Although *I Am Legend* is still technically in development under David Heyman, producer of *Harry Potter and the Philosopher's Stone*, there has been no real movement on the project since the Bowman-Protosevich collaboration at the close of 1998. So what will it take to get the movie made? "All it will take," says Protosevich, "is someone, an actor or a director, with a lot of power and a lot of box-office clout, saying, 'This is what I want to do next.' What any project needs is a champion, and there's no one championing it right now."

Could that champion be Ridley Scott himself, now that the critical and commercial success of *Gladiator* and *Hannibal* has put him in the enviable position of being able to pick and choose projects at will? Although Scott followed those films with an adaptation of Mark Bowden's *Black Hawk Down: A Story of Modern War*, several of those who have worked with the director since the collapse of *I Am Legend* say that he continues to express an interest in reviving the project. "On the basis of my conversations with him, I would think he would not rule it out," says screenwriter John Logan. "I heard rumours that he might still be connected to it in some way," says Sylvain Despretz, who storyboarded *Black Hawk Down*. "He's not completely out of it. It's a film that a lot of people would like to see made, not the least of which Ridley himself. There's been talks about what would happen if the film was made, and whether it would be re-offered to Ridley, and probably it would."

Nevertheless, Despretz wonders about the approach the director might take if he did decide to make the film today. "I'm not sure how many of our original ideas would be kept," he says, "because you don't make a film the same way now as you would have in 1997. There are a lot of things Ridley could get away with today that he couldn't have done without [the success of] *Gladiator* and *Hannibal*. So that would automatically mean a different twist on things."

In other words, the sun may have gone down on one possible adaptation of *I Am Legend*. But, like the pitiful creatures of the novel itself, the project could one day rise from the dead... ■

Who Watches
The *Watchmen?*

How The Greatest Graphic Novel Of Them All
Confounded Hollywood

"Frankly, I didn't think it was filmable."

—Alan Moore, author of *Watchmen*

I n 1986, DC Comics began publishing *Watchmen*, a twelve-issue comic series by the British writer/artist team of Alan Moore and Dave Gibbons, which it eventually collected into a graphic novel. To say that *Watchmen* changed the face of comic books forever may be an overstatement — but only just. What it did, along with Frank Miller's Batman opus *The Dark Knight Returns*, was prove that mainstream comic books, for so long the domain of children and overgrown adolescents, had finally grown up and were ready to take on 'Literature' on an even playing field — and even, for a while, beat it at its own game.

Essentially, *Watchmen* is a literate, mature and narratively spellbinding deconstruction of that most basic of comic book staples, the superhero story. Set in New York City in an alternative 1987, the first issue opens with the murder of Edward Blake, aka 'The Comedian'. Blake formerly belonged to an outlawed group of costumed crimefighters known as 'The Crimebusters', which also included neurotic inventor Dan Dreiberg (alias 'The Night Owl'), molecular marvel Dr Jonathan Osterman ('Dr Manhattan'), mother and daughter Laurie and Sally Juspeczyk (two different incarnations of superheroine 'Miss Jupiter'), bodybuilder Nelson Gardner ('Captain Metropolis'), billionaire businessman and self-styled 'cleverest man in the world' Adrian Veidt ('Ozymandias') and Walter Kovacs (the renegade 'Rorschach', the only one of the crimefighting cadre who refused to turn in his costume when vigilantism was outlawed by the Keene Act in 1977). Blake's death sparks a wave of paranoia and nostalgia among the former super-friends, who suspect a 'costume killer' may be on the loose. But as the world heads toward a seemingly inevitable nuclear confrontation, sparked by Dr Manhattan's self-imposed exile from planet Earth, the evidence points to a larger conspiracy and eventually toward the machinations of one of their own, designed to save mankind from itself, albeit at a cost of millions of lives.

Such a synopsis hardly does justice to the scope of what Terry Gilliam later described as "the *War and Peace* of graphic novels." and which, like *The Dark Knight Returns*, looked beneath the mask of the superhero to find out what makes them tick. With its roots in seventies-era conspiracy stories, but with an ahead-of-its-time, nineties-style cynicism, Moore and Gibbons explored the vigilante aspect of the costumed hero, as well as the notion of superpowers as a curse and the blurred line between hero and villain — all using a formal four-colour, nine-panel layout. Although intended to be the last word on comic book superheroes, ironically *Watchmen* breathed new life into the genre, popularising the cynical comic book hero as a staple of superhero fiction, and leading to a succession of mostly inferior imitations which continues to this day.

As Moore himself told Danny Graydon of his Hugo Award-winning epic, "I can see that the literary content of *Watchmen* may have impressed people for whom it may have been the first modern comic that they had read. But the way that *Watchmen* works, and the reason it works, I think, is not entirely to do with its literary content... I think what made *Watchmen* work was the fact that what I was trying to do was to exploit the possibilities of comics as a medium." Comic books, he reasoned, are not literature, film or gallery art, but a different art form with a language all their own. "I realised that me and Dave [Gibbons] had somehow broken through into a whole new possibility in this language," he added; "that we could have the details in the back of the panels telling a whole backstory, and we could use them to almost programme the reader with certain symbols that would evoke a certain set of associations or an emotional effect. We were able to juxtapose what was happening in the pictures and the words to startling effect. Play with the time frame; do all of these things that you can't do in literature or films." Gibbons agreed with Moore's view that, just because comics and films are both made up of individual frames, placed sequentially in order to tell a story, it doesn't mean they are the same. "A lot of people make this parallel between comics and film, but I think it's a completely bogus comparison," he told Mark Salisbury. "A comics script looks a bit like a film script and comics art looks a bit like storyboards," he added, "but there is no sound in a comic book and no movement. Also, with a comic book the reader can backtrack, you can reach page twenty and say, 'Hey, *that's* what that was all about in that scene on page three,' and then nip back and have a look. We wanted to take advantage of that kind of difference."

Collected in graphic novel form in 1987 (two years before Tim Burton's *Batman* rewrote the rules of superhero stories on a more limited scale, but with far greater commercial success), it didn't take long for a film version of *Watchmen* to be mooted. And yet, for Moore, this was more the result of readers trying to evaluate it in terms of a medium with which they were more familiar, such as cinema. "You get people saying, 'Oh, yes, *Watchmen* is very cinematic,'" he told Danny Graydon, "when actually it's not. It's almost the exact opposite to cinematic." This did not prevent Twentieth Century Fox from asking Moore to write a screenplay based on the story and, when he declined, turning to *Batman* scribe Sam Hamm, who delivered a first draft as early as 9 September 1988 — almost a full year before *Batman*'s record-breaking opening.

Hamm, who more recently wrote *Monkeybone* for Fox, found Moore's densely plotted prose and Gibbons's even denser, elaborate artwork extremely arduous to adapt. "We felt constantly crestfallen about what we couldn't get in," he told *Entertainment Weekly*. Indeed, Hamm found it difficult even to describe the story. "Dismal cyberpunk is not quite right," he told *Starburst*'s Andy Mangels. "It's a bleak satire of humanity's foibles... It's something that nobody should be able to pull off," he added, referring to the graphic novel itself, "and it's a miracle that they did it."

It is arguably an even greater miracle that Hamm managed to distil Moore's 400-page, nine-panel-a-page strip into a workable screenplay. Yet he did, condensing the story into a *Ten Little Indians*-style murder mystery in which the surviving superheroes — collectively known in the script, though never in the comic book, as 'The Watchmen' — investigate the deaths of their former members, eventually uncovering a conspiracy leading to a conclusion which managed to be as epic in scale as Moore's (Ozymandias manufactures a fake alien invasion in order to unite the superpowers against a perceived extraterrestrial threat) without being as improbable. "I will come out and say that I didn't think the ending of the comic book worked," Hamm told Andy Mangels. "I appreciate the ideological intent of what I think Alan [Moore] was trying to do with that notion — trying to establish that it's wrong to place our faith in Nietzschean characters who are willing to take very, very draconian measures to achieve aims which may or may not be good for mankind. While I thought that the tenor of the metaphor was right," he added, "I couldn't go for the vehicle. I didn't think that the threat of some big tentacled alien critter appearing in New York was going to prevent the incipient nuclear war which was only moments away from starting. Secondly, it seemed to me that even if it did have that effect, you would have to keep doing it over and over again every six months."

Despite his more manageable ending (involving an assassination and a time paradox) and overall sparse approach to the material, Hamm knew that his 128-page script would clearly have required a monumental investment. "The joke going around was that it was $1 million a page," said Hamm, adding wryly that "that was back when $120 million meant something." Nevertheless, when Fox put the project into turnaround, Warner Bros swooped in faster than the Owlship's Rorschach rescue, quickly attaching a formidable producer, Joel Silver — whose eighties Midas touch launched the *Lethal Weapon* and *Die Hard* franchises — and a director, Terry Gilliam (*Twelve Monkeys*). "Joel told me he was sitting on $40 million and a green light," Gilliam told Ian Christie. "There was a script by Sam Hamm that had some nice things but didn't quite do the job." In fact, he told Bob McCabe, "[Hamm] had made some very clever jumps, but killed it. It made it into a movie, but what did you end up with? You ended up with these characters, but they were only shadows of the characters in an adventure. And I didn't think the book was about that." Gilliam invited his regular collaborator Charles McKeown, with whom he co-wrote *Brazil* and *The Adventures of Baron Munchausen*, to work on a new draft, but later admitted that he wasn't really happy with what they wrote. "It's really dense," he told McCabe, "and when you try to reduce it down to a couple of hours it's just like straight comic book heroes again, and it doesn't have a real meaning. All the characters needed time, and I just felt we weren't able to give them the time."

Also unhappy were the many *Watchmen* fans who sneaked a look at this second draft, credited to Gilliam, Warren Skaaren (*Batman, Beetlejuice*) and Hamm. Among the causes for concern were such seemingly unnecessary script alterations as The Comedian's reproach of Dr Manhattan, who arrives late at the scene of a terrorist attack on the Statue of Liberty, causing the public relations disaster which leads to the enforced disbanding of The Watchmen. In the first draft, The Comedian says, "Asshole! What *took* you so long?"; in the second, he says, "Manhattan, you cad! This lady's gone to pieces waiting for you!" To his credit, Gilliam and his collaborator(s) utilised portions of Rorschach's diary as voiceover to give the narrative his uniquely warped perspective, and restored several scenes from the comic books missing from Hamm's draft. But while this inevitably brought the screenplay closer to Moore's version, it arguably took it further from his *vision* and closer to Gilliam's, thereby eroding the studio's confidence in the project as another blockbuster like *Batman* (with all of the merchandising millions that might have helped offset the potentially vast production costs).

As it transpired, Silver had been over-optimistic about his fundraising abilities, having managed to raise only around $25 million for a project which, even by conservative estimates, was likely to cost north of $100 million. "It was such wonderful arrogance on [Silver's] part," Gilliam recalled. "He had just done *Die Hard 2*, which had gone way over budget, and I was fresh from [*The Adventures of Baron*] *Munchausen*, also famously over budget. We were running round Hollywood together trying to make this dark film that was going to cost a fortune and, of course, nobody wanted to do it. Joel was very upset. He'd made billions of dollars for Hollywood and he thought that at some point he'd get a chance to do what he really wanted. But it doesn't work that way: even someone like Joel doesn't get what he wants."

In fact, Gilliam may have been turned against the idea of filming *Watchmen* even before the tarnish on Silver's exuberance was revealed, having already discussed the proposed project with its creator. "[Gilliam] asked me how I would film it," Moore told Danny Graydon. "I had to tell him that, frankly, I didn't think it was filmable. I didn't design it to show off the similarities between cinema and comics, which *are* there, but, in my opinion are fairly unremarkable. It was designed to show off the things that comics could do that cinema and literature couldn't." Indeed, as Moore told *Film Threat*, "If you follow the viewpoint that comics are identical to cinema, what you end up with is films that don't move." Whether or not Moore liked Hamm's adaptation is probably a moot point, though the screenwriter confirms that they did discuss it. "Alan was very complimentary and gracious when I talked to him about it," Hamm told Andy Mangels, "but he's such a natural gentleman that I suspect even if he did have very large reservations about it, he would keep them to himself."

Whatever Moore may have felt about Hamm's attempt to adapt his story for the cinema, his feelings about *Watchmen*'s effect on the comic book medium were clear. He blamed it and Frank Miller's *The Dark Knight Returns* for ushering in an era of poor imitations in which 'realistic' superheroes (an oxymoron if ever there was one) with 'issues' were portrayed in 'grim and gritty' settings. "At the time, I found it rather depressing," he told Danny Graydon. "It was a bit like being in one of those carnival Hall of Mirrors, where you are looking at something and it's enough like it so you could see the resemblance, but then, enough unlike it, so you could see it was a travesty. For a while, that bothered me, and I felt that *Watchmen* in particular had had a deleterious effect on the industry; there was all of this joyless grimness everywhere. The only thing I was interested in *Watchmen* for, and the only thing I remain interested for, is the storytelling: the elaborate, crystalline story structure; the insanely detailed dove-tailing of imagery and words. And I kind of hoped that if people took anything from *Watchmen* it would be that. But, unfortunately, I guess it was easier to take Rorschach's brutality or the cynical, world-weary viewpoint."

Although the graphic novel continued to sell extremely well throughout the nineties, little was heard of the project until early 2001, when it emerged that the film rights to *Watchmen* now resided with producer Lawrence Gordon, an avowed comic book fan whose many production credits include *The Rocketeer, Mystery Men* and *Lara Croft: Tomb Raider.* In addition, it was revealed that writer-director Darren Aronofsky was interested in finally bringing the story to the screen. Aronofsky had burst onto the independent film-making scene in 1998 with his directorial début *Pi*, and followed it by directing the Oscar-nominated *Requiem for a Dream*, producing the science fiction submarine thriller *Below* for director David Twohy (*Pitch Black*) and earning an assignment from Warner Bros to script an adaptation of another ground-breaking comic book, Frank Miller's *Batman: Year One.* Could Aronofsky be the man to finally break the *Watchmen* deadlock?

"I think I read it in college, around 1988 or 1989," Aronofsky recalls.

"I wasn't a comic book fan as a kid. I had a small collection, but I really wasn't into superheroes — I was more into *Twilight Zone* comic books. But when I got turned onto *Watchmen* by my roommate, who was an animator and totally into comics, it just blew my mind, because here was finally a story about comic book heroes that introduced Freudian psychology — what does it take for a real man to put on tights and fight crime? And it was a great concept for me, and that's why I really got into *Watchmen* and *The Dark Knight Returns*." Aronofsky recently bought a page of original *Watchmen* artwork in an *eBay* auction, his first and only piece of comic book art. "*That's* how much of a fan I am," he laughs.

"I've entertained the idea at times that it would be something really fun to do," he says of the prospect of adapting *Watchmen* to film. "I think it's a tremendous property. It's such a great book, but it's huge in scope and I think also, now that we're post-Cold War, it's a very different dynamic in politics today. The whole conceit of the macro element of the story, the whole geo-political vision of the war between Russia and the United States, would have to be re-thought for the film." Hamm, who did not need to address these concerns in his screenplay, recently voiced similar concerns. "There's so much Cold War stuff that's gone by," he told the *Coming Attractions* website, "teens may be left scratching their heads about what's going on. There's a lot you would have to move around."

Aronofsky agrees. "I don't know how you would fix that," he says, "because the whole motivation for Ozymandias is the impending doom of the world. So I think you would have to figure out some kind of new threat that an audience of today would actually buy — that's the big invention that would have to be created." When *Watchmen* was first published, he observes, the threat of global thermonuclear war was a real one. "I remember, as a kid, going to sleep being terrified that I wouldn't wake up the next morning because of the nukes," he admits, "and that threat doesn't really live in the heads of anyone any more. The biggest threat is that the plane you're on is going to be blown up by terrorists. I guess you could create something like a Middle East meltdown, where people take sides," he suggests, "but that overall conceit of nuclear war is gone, you'd have to figure out something else. The other thing you have to remember is that in 1987, all the Rorschach conspiracy stuff — that there was this whole incredible conspiracy going on — was really a fresh idea," Aronofsky adds. "But now it's no longer cool to believe in conspiracies — it's become so 'pop', because of *JFK* and *The X-Files*, it's entered pop culture consciousness, and Rorschach's vision is not that wacky any more." In other words, he says, there are many elements of *Watchmen* that would need updating, "but the drama of it is fantastic."

"Ultimately," Aronofsky says, "it comes down to the characters in *Watchmen*, which are so well sketched, from the middle-aged and pouchy Night Owl, to the homeless, crazy, wild Rorschach and the supreme being of Dr Manhattan, to the intellect of Ozymandias — there are so many great characters with all their different egos and complexities. It's unbelievable stuff." Aronofsky admits that the writing in *Watchmen* has been influential on his own work. "I remember once a few years ago going back to read *Watchmen* and realising that I'd stolen certain lines unconsciously," he reveals. "I'd read it so many times that it just got in my head. What's the line with Rorschach, when he's in jail? 'I don't know if I'm locked in here with you or you're locked in here with me? [sic]' And Dr Manhattan in Vietnam — fucking incredible. There are so many good scenes."

Aronofsky claims not to be discouraged by the budgetary issues which led to the collapse of the Terry Gilliam-Joel Silver attempt at the project, because of the advances in technology in the intervening years. "The reality is that, back in 1987, it was a different film-making world," he says. "Fourteen years later, we're two or three *Jurassic Park* and *Toy Story* films down the road, and what you can do for a certain budget is remarkable. If Jar-Jar Binks showed us anything," he adds, "it's that you can create characters on the screen that look like live-action — he was as real as maybe some of the real actors in *Episode I*! So although $40 million probably isn't enough today, with a reasonable budget it is probably do-able. It now becomes a question of, 'Does it actually play?'"

Despite Aronofsky's interest, Dave Gibbons feels that the time may have passed to make a *Watchmen* movie. "It was most likely to happen when *Batman* was a big success," he told Ken Tucker, "but then that window was lost. To be honest, I'm not holding my breath." Gilliam is equally philosophical about his failed efforts. "In a way, I'm glad," he told *Neon*, "because it wouldn't have been up to the book." Writer-director-comics fan Kevin Smith agrees. "It reminds me how everyone wishes *Catcher in the Rye* would be made into a movie," he told *Entertainment Weekly*, "but at the same time, they're glad nobody has, since you know no one would ever be able to nail it." ■

The *Fantastic* Journey

Why Getting *The Fantastic Four* To The Big Screen Has Proved A Real Stretch For Hollywood

"I want a Fantastic Four flick and I don't want it good —
I want it Tuesday."

—producer Bernd Eichinger to Roger Corman's Concorde Pictures

Some time between Sputnik and Apollo, four relatively ordinary individuals — Reed Richards, his fiancée Susan Storm, her younger brother Johnny and their friend Benjamin Grimm — were involved in a traumatic and bizarre accident during the inaugural spaceflight of an experimental rocket designed by Richards, a brilliant inventor. Their bodies were torn apart, infused with cosmic radiation and reformed, atom by atom. Upon their return to Earth, they each began to manifest fantastic superpowers: Richards found himself able to stretch any part of his body to extraordinary lengths; Susan could turn herself and any object invisible, and create similarly see-through forcefields; the hot-headed Johnny could ignite his body into living flame, fly and control fire; and most tragically of all, Ben Grimm's body took on stone-like properties, giving him virtual invulnerability, along with superhuman strength, and the appearance of a humanoid rockery. United by their unique gifts and by their outsider status among fellow humans, the four members of this literally nuclear family don natty blue-and-white matching outfits and set out to save the world — most commonly by preventing a vengeful former colleague of Richards' named Doom from having his day.

In 1961, the above premise became the basis of the first issue of Marvel Comics' *The Fantastic Four*, the brainchild of Stan Lee and Jack Kirby, who proclaimed the title 'The World's Greatest Comic

Magazine'. For forty years, the four-colour exploits of Reed ('Mr Fantastic'), Susan ('The Invisible Girl'), Ben ('The Thing') and Johnny ('The Human Torch') — people with extraordinary powers but often everyday problems — have continued to fascinate fans around the world, a fact acknowledged in the comic when Reed and Susan finally tied the knot and The Beatles — the original fab four — could be glimpsed in the congregation. Yet the fantastic fight to bring *The Fantastic Four* to the big screen has been a battle as arduous as any the mutant marvels ever fought against the forces of Doom.

The first real attempt to develop *The Fantastic Four* as a major motion picture came as early as 1986, before *Batman* upped the ante — and the asking price — for comic-to-film adaptations. Bernd Eichinger (*The Neverending Story* and its sequels), a German-born producer for Neue Constantin Films, took an open-ended option on the rights to make a *Fantastic Four* film, on the understanding that the film entered production on or before 31 December 1992. If not, the rights would revert to Marvel Comics, which would be free to shop them around elsewhere — with a considerably higher price tag, given the intervening success of *Batman* and *Teenage Mutant Ninja Turtles*. Yet, with barely a month to go before his deal was due to expire, Eichinger pulled off a feat worthy of Mr Fantastic himself: he got the movie made.

The producer's reasoning was simple but brilliant: by making an ultra-low-budget film which was recognisably based on the comic book, Eichinger could hold onto the rights, hoping that in the meantime, he would be able to set up a big deal at a major studio. If such a deal could not be made, the producer would still be left holding the negative of a *Fantastic Four* film, which could be released at a profit. Thus, according to *Entertainment Weekly*, Eichinger approached Roger Corman's Concorde Pictures, with an offer the veteran B-movie-maker could scarcely refuse: "I want a *Fantastic Four* flick and I don't want it good — I want it Tuesday!" The deal was done, the film was cast, director Oley Sassone (*Bloodfist III: Forced to Fight*) was engaged, pre-production was rushed through, and principal photography began on 26 December — with a whole five days to spare before the deal expired.

Despite the truncated development period and four-week shooting schedule, the film fulfilled the only criterion stipulated by the Marvel-Eichinger contract: it was recognisably a *Fantastic Four* feature film.

Playing Reed Richards proved no stretch for Alex Hyde-White (*Biggles: Adventures in Time*); Rebecca Staab (*Too Hot to Handle*) was seen as Susan Storm; actor/stuntman Carl Ciarfalio (*The Incredible Hulk Returns*) donned a convincingly concrete costume to play Ben Grimm; while Jay Underwood (*The Boy Who Could Fly*) burned his scalp and almost fried his hair off, dyeing his brown locks blond to play Johnny Storm. For some of those used to low-budget independent film-making, *The Fantastic Four*'s schedule was unusually relaxed, as Alex Hyde-White explained: "I thought, a month is kind of good to get ready for an independent film. Usually it's 'Here's the offer. Are your bags packed?'" The realities of film-making Concorde-style required the budget to stretch considerably further than Sassone imagined. "The people at Concorde told me it would be a $3 million budget," the director told *Entertainment Weekly* in 1994. "It turned out to be about $1.5 million, which I might not have agreed to if I'd known."

As work on the film's complex post-production continued through 1993, Eichinger continued to pursue Plan A: shelving the movie in favour of a movie deal, much to the resentment of the cast and crew. "We busted our ass to finish the effects," complained Sassone who, along with the actors, toured comic book conventions in an effort to promote the film. Sassone preferred Plan B: releasing the film, which they fully intended to do on 19 January 1994 at a Minneapolis charity première devoted to children's causes. Suddenly, word got around that Eichinger had paid Concorde Pictures $1 million to buy back the negative of the film, in order to shelve it — permanently. "I feel very, very sorry for the actors and the director and most of the people involved in [the] movie," *Fantastic Four* co-creator Stan Lee commented. "I tend to like creative people, and here were a bunch doing their best." Like many, however, Lee felt that the characters and storyline would best be served by a big-budget blockbuster, rather than a low-budget production you could rent from Blockbuster. "I have a sentimental attachment to *The Fantastic Four*, and I was heartbroken to think it might appear only as a low-budget quickie."

Although *The Fantastic Four* has never officially been released, bootleg copies can often be found at comic conventions. Michael J. Legeros, an internet-based critic who reviewed the film for *rec.arts.- movies.reviews*, felt that it was likely to "both delight and disappoint" fans of the Fantastic Four. "With almost zero budget for EFX, the burden of proof rests squarely on the shoulders of the actors and, to their credit, they perform their parts handsomely. Only Joseph Culp is a wash — he's okay as the pre-Doctor Doom Doom, but he doesn't have much to do after getting encased in armour. Bad speeches and overgesticulating do not a character make. Too bad that the production design can't match the enthusiasm of the actors. The throne room of Castle Doom is bad, the interiors of the Baxter Building are worse, and the inside of Reed's spaceship is just plain awful. Even bad sci-fi looks better than this stuff." Overall, Legeros concluded, "Enthusiastic performers and a faithful storyline can't do much for cheap EFX and a flimsy production design."

On 25 August 1994, *Daily Variety* reported that Eichinger had signed Chris Columbus to direct a $40 million-plus *Fantastic Four* feature for Twentieth Century Fox, for whom the director had made the smash hits *Home Alone* and *Mrs Doubtfire*. Columbus, in turn, engaged avowed Fantastic Four fanatic Michael France, whose scripts for *Cliffhanger* and *Goldeneye* revived the fortunes of Sylvester Stallone and James Bond respectively, to co-write the first draft of the proposed film. "Everyone involved with the project wants the movie to have the feel of the early Jack Kirby comic," France told *Cinescape* in late 1995. "We want to have the same impact on the audience today that those comics had on kids then. Kids at the time had never seen anything like that before." Counter to the darker worldview of Tim Burton's *Batman*, France added, "We want [*The Fantastic Four* film] to be a big adventure that has some humour in it, and there's a lot of humour to be had from the interaction of the characters without getting silly. It's funny to see how they interact, especially the Thing and the Torch."

According to France, one of the most important elements, aside from the humour, was the exploration of how ordinary people come to terms with their extraordinary powers. "What we're hoping to get across in the movie is that these people react the way I think you and I would react if we had these powers forced upon us," he explained. "There's a mixture of being horrified and, once you get used to the power, learning how to integrate it into your daily life. It's something you have to get used to. The whole arena of the thing allows for a very big movie as well, involving the origin of The Fantastic Four, their encounter with Doctor Doom, and much more. The trick," he added, "is to give the audience something they haven't seen in other movies. Something that's big enough; something worthy of Doctor Doom. It's a tricky area to go into because what Doom's got to do is something that's bigger than you see in a *Die Hard* movie or even a Bond movie. It's got to be big, but it can't be so big that it becomes ridiculous."

France and Columbus worked on the script together, taking inspiration not from Tim Burton's *Batman*, but from Richard Donner's *Superman*, made a decade before it. "I know that Chris really likes the first *Superman*, and that's come up a lot in our conversations," France revealed. "I watched it again recently to look at the way they built up Clark Kent as he grows up and turns into Superman. It's really nicely done. I wouldn't say it's the model we're using," he added, "but in terms of points of reference, that's the only one that's come up." France admitted that both he and Columbus felt badly about the participants of the Concorde version, destined to remain as invisible as Susan Storm. "Chris wasn't behind the shelving of the picture," he said. "In fact, I know that he felt very badly about what happened to the guys who made that movie, being basically tricked into doing a movie just to keep the option for the studio. Not a real pleasant situation, because my understanding is that the guys involved worked really hard to make the most of their... budget." Of their own version — in which Doctor Doom threatens the world with a Johnny Storm-powered hurricane he terms the 'hypercane' — France added, "I just want the fans to know that *The Fantastic Four* is in good hands. It will be done in the spirit of the original comic. It's not going to be dismantled or deconstructed in any way."

France's comments proved somewhat optimistic, however, as the script he and Columbus delivered — and, it was widely rumoured, offered to real-life couple Dennis Quaid and Meg Ryan — was reportedly budgeted at $165 million. When Fox balked at the huge cost, Columbus jumped ship in favour of *Stepmom* and, later, *Bicentennial Man*, although he remained on board as producer, along with Eichinger. Peter Segal (*Tommy Boy*, *My Fellow Americans*) was the next name to be stencilled on the director's chair, while *Daily Variety* reported that the *Fantastic Four* film had been halted in pre-production due to budget problems and was undergoing extensive remodelling, courtesy of screenwriter Philip Morton (*Fire Down Below*). "We had budgetary concerns," Columbus admitted to *Cinescape*. "You have four characters who have these intense super-powers. One person is invisible, which is fairly easy to do. But when you combine that with a guy who bursts into flames plus can fly, and a guy who can stretch nearly any part of his body nearly a mile and an eight-foot character made out of concrete and rock — well, it gets to be a budgetary nightmare. We're trying to find a way to do it that's not complete animation. It's really daunting."

In 1997, after completing their third draft of the *Silver Surfer* script (see chapter 13), the screenwriting partnership of Rudy Gaines and John Rice were offered the opportunity to write a new *Fantastic Four* script, but declined. "In retrospect, it might have been possible to do," Gaines recalls. "Chris Columbus had just done a whack at it and was possibly going to direct it, but apparently they could literally count the number of words he had changed in his rewrite. Although his name was the only one on the script, I think he had just done a rewrite of somebody else's draft." Nevertheless, being fans of *The Fantastic Four*, Gaines and Rice took the opportunity to read the script. "It was possibly one of the worst scripts I had read in my life," says Gaines. "I remember reading it and thinking, 'Wow!' It was unmitigatingly bad."

Then, early in 1998, *Variety* reported that Sam Hamm, who scripted *Batman* and *Watchmen* (see chapter 11), had begun yet another draft. "The Fantastic Four are generally a sunnier bunch than Batman," Hamm told *Cinescape*. "The notion of comic characters having to deal with petty real-life issues in addition to alien invasions and supervillains who want to take over the world is what gave them so much flavour. And that's really what we tried to capture in [the script]." In addition, he said, "The fun of doing a team story is that it's really about an extended dysfunctional family." What set alarm bells ringing among Fantastic Four fans, however, was that executive producer Avi Arad — who became chief creative officer of Marvel following its takeover by his company, Toy Biz — appeared to want to take Hamm's "dysfunctional family" spin on *The Fantastic Four* even further. "It's probably the biggest sitcom of all time," he told *Entertainment Weekly*, later adding: "*X-Men* is about dark secrets. *Fantastic Four* is... a comedy. It's about famous heroes. They appear on talk shows. They are celebrities."

Although Fox extended its option on the rights to the property in early 1999, the studio's strategy was to wait until the release of its other Marvel super-team movie, *X-Men*, before making a firm commitment to the *Fantastic Four* film. Nevertheless, the producers made an offer to director Raja Gosnell (*Big Momma's House*), who had lobbied for the position vacated by Peter Segal. "I worked really hard to get a meeting on it," Gosnell, Columbus's former editor, told the *Los Angeles Times* in August 2000. "I really wanted to do a big action comedy thrill-ride like *Men in Black*." In the same article, newly-appointed Fox co-chairman Tom Rothman suggested that, following the success of *X-Men*, which Bryan Singer (*The Usual Suspects*) had managed to make for $75 million and went on to earn $300 million world-wide, *The Fantastic Four* could be in production by the end of the year. "We expect and hope to make [*The Fantastic Four*] pretty soon," Rothman commented, admitting that "if *X-Men* hadn't worked, we may have reconsidered."

Despite the success of *X-Men*, however, several months passed without any movement on the *Fantastic Four* project. "It's in the future," Gosnell told *Cinescape* in January 2001. "It's such a big project that we're really taking the time to get it right." Although Columbus remains on board as producer, despite the expiration of his production deal with Fox and his directing duties on *Harry Potter and the Philosopher's Stone*, he remains unconvinced that Fox will be able to bring the *Fantastic Four* film in for less than nine figures. "Bringing this one to the screen is a budgeting nightmare," he reiterated to the *Calgary Sun*. "One estimate was as high as $280 million because every time the four characters walk into a scene, it will cost upwards of $100,000."

While Fox continued its efforts to bring down the potential cost of the film, proposed director Raja Gosnell — who once described his proposed take on the *Fantastic Four* film as "more comedic, not as dark and less angst-ridden than *X-Men*" — moved on, accepting Warner Bros' offer to direct a live action *Scooby Doo* movie. Then, in April 2001, *Daily Variety* confirmed widespread rumours that Peyton Reed, director of the teen hit *Bring It On*, had replaced Gosnell and was looking for a new screenwriter to bring the story to life. "He has just the right sensibilities," commented Avi Arad. "He has a great sense of comedy, and we are very excited about him." Although the fact that Fox chose to sign a new director rather than wait for Gosnell to finish the *Scooby Doo* feature showed they were still eager to move forward, it remained to be seen whether the aptly-named Reed — who was reported to be working with comic artist Alex Ross to create conceptual designs for the film — could solve the budget problems of previous drafts. In the meantime, the outlook for a live-action Fantastic Four film continued to look grim... ∎

The *Silver* Screen

Silver Surfer Goes To Tinsel Town

"There was a script before ours, and it had Surfer in the company of a twelve-year-old girl who was like a street prostitute. When we read it, we were like, 'My God, what were these people thinking?'"

—*Silver Surfer* co-screenwriter Rudy Gaines

I n 1990, two students at the computer graphics department of the University of Southern California's (USC) cinema and television faculty, Erik Fleming and his partner, known only as 'RL', got it into their heads to create a short film based on one of Marvel Comics' most popular and enduring characters, the Silver Surfer. The idea was to prove to Marvel figurehead Stan Lee, who had created the Surfer with artist Jack Kirby back in 1966, that special effects had caught up with the twenty-four year-old comic book creation, and that it was now possible to render the silvery, surfboard-riding superhero on film.

Making his first appearance with a three-issue story arc beginning in *The Fantastic Four* #48, the Surfer proved so popular that he had his own title by 1968, written by Stan Lee and drawn by John Buscema, detailing the character's origin. According to Lee, the Surfer began life as a scientist named Norrin Radd, who is living a peaceful existence on his home planet, Zenn-La, when planet-eating alien Galactus pays a visit. Radd stands up to the galactic glutton, who agrees to spare Zenn-La if Radd will become his minion. Radd takes the deal and Galactus imbues him with cosmic energy, transforming him into the solar flare-surfing Silver Surfer, scouting the far reaches of the cosmos for worlds which Galactus can devour. The Surfer continued to make guest appearances in other Marvel titles and he actually proved more popular as a supporting character: the stand-alone series did not last, and Silver Surfer would not enjoy his own title again until 1982, with a Stan Lee-John Byrne one-shot. This was followed in 1987 by a regular title which proved more successful, spanning more than 100 issues, under various writers and artists, including Steve Englehart, Jim Starlin, George Perez and J. M. DeMatteis.

"We were both big Silver Surfer fans since we were kids," Fleming explained to the website *Comics2Film*, "so we were talking about how great a Silver Surfer movie would be. And we came up with all these ideas, and the only way you could do it is to computer-animate it." A short film entitled *Sexy Robot* convinced Fleming and RL that the Silicon Graphics computer in the basement of the USC's computer graphics department would be able to render the chrome-like figure on film. Although computer animation had previously been used in Disney's *Tron* and *The Last Starfighter*, and to create the water tentacle in *The Abyss*, the emergent technology had yet to be exploited to create a humanoid form, which was unsurprisingly extremely complex to computer-animate.

Fleming and RL found Marvel representatives, including Lee, staunchly sceptical about the possibility. "We went and talked with Marvel comics... back in '90-'91," Fleming recalled. "They said it could not be done. They said they'd looked into it. They'd actually talked to [George] Lucas. They'd met with [Industrial Light and Magic] and everyone said there's no possible way to do the Silver Surfer." Fleming learned that various film-makers had attempted different methods of bringing the Surfer to life, including a reverse photographic process by which an actor was painted with a black oil, on to which was mapped silvery light — a method not dissimilar to that used for the lightsabers in *Star Wars*. "There were all kinds of tricks that they tried, and nothing ever worked," Fleming observed. "They all looked like crap. And obviously you're not going to put a guy in a silver body stocking... "

Fleming and RL remained convinced, however, that they could succeed where others failed, and somehow convinced Marvel and Bernd Eichinger's Neue Constantin Films — the German production company which had acquired the rights to the Silver Surfer along with another Lee-Kirby creation, The Fantastic Four (see chapter 12) — to let them try it their way. By the time Fleming and RL met with the Constantin representatives who could give their blessing to the project, the pair had commissioned a clay model of the Silver Surfer, digitised it into a computer as a wire-frame figure with the assistance of USC computer graphics expert Steven Robiner, and rendered it in silver, convincing Marvel and Constantin to give them a shot. "They gave us permission to do it, [but] both companies said, 'You're wasting your time. Don't do this. It can't be done.' So we went ahead and did it anyway, because we just love the Silver Surfer."

Initially, the trio planned to produce a simple special effects test in which the Silver Surfer would cruise into a live action background on his surfboard, turn, and fly out of frame. But, when various local companies offered to donate equipment to the project, it began to expand in scope, developing a narrative element provided by fellow student and fledgling screenwriter Jeff Eastin, who wrote a five-page script. "In terms of the narrative elements, we were really trying to sell them on how this could be a high-concept, studio, superhero kids movie," Fleming explained, "like Richard Donner's *Superman*." Eastin's script begins with an alarm being sounded at a SETI-style space tracking facility, as various scientists and a military general are surprised by a fast-moving blip streaking towards the Earth at light speed. The unidentified flying object decelerates as it reaches the atmosphere and enters Earth orbit. Meanwhile, a bespectacled boy is being chased down a street by a gang of teenage youths, who are evidently aiming to steal the GI Joe action figure the boy holds. Having backed him against a wire fence, the gang advances menacingly, until they see the boy's eyes widen as he spots something behind them. A silvery shape is reflected in the lenses of his glasses, and the gang turns to see the quicksilver-like figure of the Silver Surfer, standing with one foot on the pavement and the other resting on his hovering surfboard. The gang panics and runs, and the Surfer stoops to pick up the action figure which the boy has dropped, imbuing it with cosmic energy and transforming it into a miniature version of himself. He hands the figure back to the wide-eyed boy, who smiles back at the Surfer as he rides the board along the street and up into the sky, leaving behind a trail which hangs in the air for a few moments even after the Surfer has disappeared in a flash of light.

Unfortunately, the initial testing phase of the project had taken so long that, by the time the trio were ready to begin filming, James Cameron's *Terminator 2: Judgment Day* had been released into cinemas, featuring the chrome-like figure of the T-1000. Although this proved that their theories about the possibility of rendering lifelike humanoid figures with quicksilver-like bodies were correct, it arguably made their film redundant as a special effects test reel, since one could now point to *Terminator 2* to show how Silver Surfer might appear on film. Not to be discouraged, Fleming and his fellow film-makers decided to acknowledge that Cameron had beaten them to the screen by changing the GI Joe action figure in the original script to an Arnold Schwarzenegger doll from *Terminator 2*, and continued working on the project which, by now, had swallowed two years of their lives.

A greater obstacle was still to come, however. By the time Fleming, RL and Robiner were ready to begin shooting the live-action elements of what had, by now, evolved into a short film, they had all graduated from USC and the equipment, which was to be loaned to them on the understanding that the project was a student film, was suddenly withdrawn. "We got right up to the day we were going to shoot it, and we got caught," Fleming admitted. "The camera company called USC to verify we were film students, and nailed us." The trio approached USC's head of production and begged to be allowed to continue; much to their surprise, they were, although the project would now become the property of the USC. Although they had originally envisaged using a prototype of the motion capture method, whereby an actor's movements are recorded by computer and then reinterpreted digitally to create a fully-rendered three-dimensional entity, the fledgling film-makers eventually decided to animate the figure using Silicon Graphics workstations which, at the time, were unutterably slow, taking six hours to render a single frame and four days to create the tiniest movement. "All the way up to the very end it looked like total crap," Fleming said. "We were like, 'I can't believe we wasted two years of our lives!' [But] somehow, in the last week, it just all came together. The animation smoothed out; the movement looked real."

When, in 1993, USC began screening the five-minute short film, entitled simply *The Silver Surfer*, Fleming, RL and Robiner suddenly found themselves the talk of the town, invited to studios and agencies eager to grill them about their efforts. "I don't think they were ever gonna give us big movies," Fleming admitted, "but they just wanted to know how the hell we did it." Much of the interest was focussed on the character of the Silver Surfer himself, however, and when the studios discovered that Fleming and his fellow film-makers did not own the rights to the character, their interest evaporated like a vapour trail. "Overnight, we just got totally dropped," Fleming said. "So we ended up doing what some people warned us [about] — we ended up making a million dollar commercial for free for Marvel and Constantin." Nevertheless, the short film served to raise the profile of each of the film-makers involved in the project: Erik Fleming went on to direct several low budget features, including *Cyber Bandits*, *Tyrone* and *My Brother the Pig*; RL worked on several major CGI projects; Steven Robiner worked in the visual effects department of Renny Harlin's *The Long Kiss Goodnight*, as well as providing effects for Fleming's films; and screenwriter Jeff Eastin, meanwhile, collaborated with Fleming on an unproduced spy comedy which came to the attention of James Cameron, who promptly hired him to write *True Lies 2*.

While their careers blossomed, however, the crew behind the live action Silver Surfer short were not rewarded as they had hoped to be: by being allowed to work on the Silver Surfer movie being developed at Constantin Films under its deal with Twentieth Century Fox. By the mid-nineties, despite rumours that writer-director Quentin Tarantino was interested in bringing the Silver Surfer — whose image appears on Tim Roth's wall in *Reservoir Dogs* — to the silver screen, Constantin's Bernd Eichinger commissioned a more accessible screenwriter, John Turman (*The Crow: Stairway to Heaven*), to write the first draft of the script, dated 24 August 1995. According to an anonymous Coming Attractions correspondent who read the Turman draft, the story began like the short film, before having the title character shot out of the sky by paranoid military personnel who consider him a hostile alien force — a correct assumption, as it turns out. Drained of his powers, the Surfer is hidden from the government forces by a SETI researcher and a blind girl named Alicia Masters, who are unaware that his hidden agenda is to ready the planet Earth for destruction by Galactus.

When this script — the cover of which bore the lame tag-line 'Aliens Don't Surf' — failed to ignite Fox's interest, Bernd Eichinger brought in Richard Jeffries, who scripted *Scarecrows* and *The Vagrant*, to write another draft. This attracted the interest of Bombay-born, Australian-raised director Geoffrey Wright, who had given Russell Crowe his feature début in *Romper Stomper*, followed by the Surfer-sounding picture *Metal Skin*. Rejecting Jeffries's draft, however, Eichinger approached the screenwriting partnership of Rudy Gaines and John Rice, who had written an unproduced adaptation of *The Stars My Destination* (see chapter 1) for the producer. "John and I were in Cannes at the film festival and ran into Bernd Eichinger, and he asked us if we wanted to take a crack at Silver Surfer," Gaines recalls. "But we had been in the sci-fi realm a little bit — we'd written a few drafts of *The Stars My Destination* and another film called *The Calling*, which is a little bit sci-fi — and weren't sure we wanted to stay there." Nevertheless, he adds, "he got about four bottles of wine into us, and the next thing we knew we were flying to Munich."

Gaines and Rice had both been fans of the Silver Surfer as teenagers, not least because he was an anti-hero in a world of super-heroes. As Gaines explains, "For me that was interesting, because you've got to take this guy and at some point start pulling for him to win. So that was the key — trying to find a way to get us to really like Silver Surfer, instead of just being a cool dude on a silver surfboard that does sunflares and dooms entire planets. We wanted to find a way into his character." After researching countless *Silver Surfer* comics, Gaines and Rice came up with a story which, they felt, succeeded where the previous scriptwriter had failed. "There was a script before ours," Gaines recalls, "and it had Surfer in the company of a twelve year-old girl who was a street prostitute, like Jodie Foster in *Taxi Driver*, or something. When we read it, we were like, 'My God, what were these people thinking? This is a comic book hero!'"

The Gaines and Rice story opens as the Silver Surfer streaks down to the surface of a muddy alien planet populated by humanoid creatures known as Cynoxians. "Essentially the idea was that the opening sequence sets up how the Silver Surfer works: he comes down and scans the planet for lifeforms, which are all down there firing stuff up at him, but of course he's untouchable. And Galactus reads that scan from his ship somewhere out there in the cosmos, and Surfer then returns to Galactus' ship. And what Galactus says is, 'This is the last world' — basically he's eaten his way across this particular galaxy — 'so go find another galaxy. There's a milky one out there, I believe... ' So Surfer streaks off to the Milky Way and eventually finds Earth, while Galactus goes down and starts doing horrible things to the planet he's just left. So that sets us up that Surfer's not the best of guys — he's cool and all that, but look what he's doing!

"So then we had him come streaking into Australia," Gaines continues, "which is known for its waves and its surfers; dives into the ocean on his silver board, and comes up on this wave of water right there next to an Australian surfer, which was kind of cool. He's basically ripping across the world looking for a population centre, because Australia's not a very populated country. He ends up in New York City, and does this scan thing which screws up computers and traffic lights, and he essentially says to Galactus, 'Here's your next spot.' So he's just doomed the world in the first ten pages!" Since the writers knew that no actor would want to spend the entire film enveloped in chrome computer graphics — nor would Fox want to finance such an expensive project — they needed a way to bring him down to Earth and return him to human form.

"The way we brought him to Earth was to have a super-secret scientific project going on in the Bronx, which was all about harnessing the sun's power in a pretty spectacular way. They were going to shoot up a vacuum beam from Earth which was literally going to fly the length of space towards the sun, collect the solar flares, and suck them down into these massive batteries that could then power an entire city. So after Surfer condemns the Earth, he is heading off to find other galaxies, when he gets caught in this vacuum beam, which starts stripping his powers away. The batteries are about to overload, and one of the scientists says, 'There's some element caught in our beam that goes way beyond solar power!'" Just as the overloaded batteries are about to blow a hole in New York, however, the Silver Surfer manages to surf out of the beam, and falls to Earth, his powers drained.

"He and his board come crashing down," Gaines explains, "next to this woman named Kat, who is working as a waitress but really wants to be a cellist for the New York Philharmonic, of all things. She's got this big audition coming up, so she's been practising the cello and here comes this man into her life. But most of his powers are gone — the silver [energy] having been sucked away from him — so he essentially becomes Norrin Radd again. He survives the fall and escapes the hospital, and he puts Kat in a kind of tractor beam — an invisible, silvery force that keeps her trapped so that she has to help him." Alerting Galactus to his situation, he is told to locate the source of the beam which drained his powers and destroy it before Galactus arrives, in case it should pose a threat. "So essentially Surfer's stuck on Earth until he destroys that ray, so he and this Kat gal try to this energy ray thing in the Bronx, even though Kat — who's a real New York gal — says, 'There's nothing in the Bronx!'"

Radd begins to fall under Kat's spell, and the longer he remains away from Galactus' influence, the more he begins to recover his conscience and his humanity — or rather, its Zenn-La equivalent. "If you're going to spend your eternal life going from galaxy to galaxy condemning everybody you meet to death, you've kind of got to give up on your humanity," says Gaines. "You can't remember where you came from, or that you've got a soul, because that all gets squashed in order to be this silver guy. So, essentially, the story becomes the Surfer realising (a) that life is worth something on these planets — they're not just things for Galactus to eat; and (b), because he is among humans, and because he is starting to fall in love with Kat, he starts to remember that he was once Norrin Radd. And we had some flashbacks built into the script where we see him as Radd on his own planet, standing up to this mighty being, Galactus, who says, 'I'll turn you into Silver Surfer, you'll become my minion, I'll spare your planet.' I believe that's the way it was in the comic book, but I can't say for sure."

The Gaines-Rice draft also brought in a military element, the 'United States Alien Force,' which has been dormant since the UFO crash in Roswell, New Mexico. "So you get a general who is crazy to get in on the action and make sure that what happened really wasn't a silver guy who fell to Earth," Gaines continues, "but of course there's hospital video camera footage of him blasting up the place to get out of hospital. So suddenly you've got these army types rolling into

Manhattan in their Humvees. They get a military satellite flying over, which has some kind of sensor beam that can sense the temperatures of everybody down there on the surface. Everybody on Earth is 98.6 degrees, but the Silver Surfer runs a little colder by about twenty degrees — he's about seventy-six. As soon as they nail down this guy who's seventy-six [degrees], they can figure out where he's going at any moment, so Surfer really can't escape. And we used that to build our love story," he adds. "When Surfer figures out why the military guys know where he is all the time, he does some hand-ray thing that shows the beam that's focussed on him from somewhere way on high. Then he realises that in order to raise his temperature, he has to kiss Kat. And she's like, 'Wait a minute, what are you doing?' And he explains to her, and she says, 'Is that the only way you could do it?' He replies, 'No, but you'd have to remove your clothing.' So essentially he leads them into the back of a taxi, and kisses her, and you see her eyes flutter (it's a nice long kiss) and suddenly you see the beam disappear as he raises his temperature to 98.6."

In the early stages of the script, the Surfer used Kat to contact Galactus. "At some point when Surfer has lost the rest of his powers, he contacts Galactus to tell him he hasn't destroyed the weapon yet, and to do this he has to use Kat's energy," Gaines says. "He puts his hands on either side of Kat, and her eyes roll back in her head and go dead black, and the voice of Galactus starts speaking through her. And as I recall, Galactus says, 'What are you doing? There's a mortal presence I sense there. Kill her... ' And Surfer says 'I can't,' because he's starting to have second thoughts. Galactus replies, 'Look, I'm coming to this planet, and if I don't, I know where there's a planet where I can get plenty of things to eat,' meaning Surfer's home world. So Surfer has to make a choice between Earth and his home, and we've seen from the flashbacks what his planet is like, the humanity there."

Gaines and Rice felt that their script had not only captured the heart of the Silver Surfer, but done so in such a way that would make a highly commercial feature film. "We did three drafts," Gaines recalls, "and I know the story was there, and the script generally read very, very well. The action sequences were great, the characters were great, and we slayed the main dragon, which was to make him a character you were really pulling for, as opposed to a guy who was here to destroy the Earth. That was the biggest nut to crack in terms of that script as far as I was concerned." Gaines also feels that he and Rice had managed to bring in elements of character development, which are often lacking in films about visiting aliens. "Generally there's not a tremendous amount of conflict or emotional stuff to put into alien characters in sci-fi movies," he explains. "But in our take on Silver Surfer, we start out with this Surfer as sort of a bad seed, and we watch the journey, as he becomes humanised, and essentially becomes Norrin Radd again.

"We thought we had it nailed, and I think they were very happy with the draft," he adds, "but I think they were worried about it getting too expensive." One of the reasons was that the script had included versions of other Marvel characters — The Punisher and Ardeena — which would both require full CGI rendering. "Surfer, of course, was CGI in the beginning, and Galactus coming to Earth in the end was CGI, but The Punisher and Ardeena were all CGI, so they were freaking out about the cost. We had a big set piece down in the New York subway, where a train's rolling along, and here comes Ardeena melting her way down to the train, and here comes The Punisher like a metal dog, clamping onto the back of the train and pulling it to a stop and eating his way through the train... that was pretty expensive." Although Gaines was willing to take The Punisher and Ardeena out of the script, his writing partner was not. "As I recall," he says, "John and I got in rather a heated debate about that. My feeling was we could have taken them out of there, because in terms of the thrust of the story, all they were was another threat. But my partner was rather bull-headed about not taking any of that stuff out, and I think perhaps consequently it was just too expensive a movie for them to pull the trigger on."

Gaines and Rice also found that director Geoffrey Wright, still technically attached to the project, did not like their take on the story. "That was an interesting dynamic," Gaines explains, "because I don't think he wanted us on the project. He felt like Bernd Eichinger went over his head. But the way Fox and Constantin saw it was that we were bigger than Geoffrey Wright, because he had never really done a big movie. I think if the script had reached a point where they could go out and get one of the big sci-fi directors, they were gonna do that. That was the feeling I got, and I think when they picked us, [Wright] saw the handwriting on the wall. We had several miserable meetings with him, and it was clear that he was not happy about us being there." Gaines recalls having many meetings with Constantin, Fox and even Stan Lee, but when Wright jumped ship, the project moved over to the studio's children's division, Fox Family (later Fox Animation) and evolved into a thirteen-episode animated series.

While Marvel underwent its collapse and rebirth, Fox renewed its option to distribute the *Silver Surfer* movie for at least another two years. Then, in July 1999, *Daily Variety* reported that screenwriter Andrew Kevin Walker — who scripted *Se7en*, *8mm* and *Sleepy Hollow* — had been hired to start over on the script, with a story said to be set entirely in space. Since then, despite the success of the *X-Men* feature film and rumours of a new Batman, *Silver Surfer* has yet to ride into cinemas. "It was sort of frustrating for us because they never gave us a shot at it," Erik Fleming, whose decade-old, five-minute short film represents the only live-action incarnation of the Silver Surfer, told *Comics2Film*. "Our dream was to take a Val Kilmer or a Liam Neeson or somebody like that and have him play Silver Surfer, [and] literally capture everything that the actor does. He plays it off a set and you've got him wired up, and in post you turn him into the Silver Surfer. But every facial movement, every expression is the actor. And the voice is the actor and it's all that actor's performance. So you're not replacing [them] with computer animation." Instead, Fleming stated, "these scripts were like, he comes to Earth, he loses his silver skin, and he's walking around human the whole movie, and in the end he gets his skin back and flies away."

Fleming has high hopes for Walker's draft — "He might crack it because he's a great writer" — but still hopes that Fox will come to its senses and hire him to turn his short into a feature. "My dream is to make a film that breaks me out so I can have a crack at Silver Surfer, [and] that it'll still be sitting there," he stated. "But it's just too big of a movie to give to an unknown." Today, Fleming realises that he might have been better to use the technology displayed in his short film to create his own character, instead of a property owned by Marvel Comics and already optioned for feature films by Constantin and Fox. "In retrospect we might have done that," he admitted. "But I honestly would say that it would not have come out as good if it wasn't the Silver Surfer. We were so driven by our passion of wanting to bring that character to life." Hopefully, an executive at Fox or Constantin will one day share his enthusiasm. ■

The Death Of
Superman Lives

How A Billion-Dollar Franchise Failed To Take Flight

"Who is Warner Bros going to back — the guy who made
Clerks, or the guy who made them half a billion
dollars on *Batman*?"

—*Superman Lives* screenwriter Kevin Smith

O n 1 May 1998, the production offices of *Superman Lives* were quietly closed by Warner Bros, the studio behind four *Batman* blockbusters and whose parent company, Time-Warner, owns DC Comics, the imprint that had launched Superman almost exactly six decades earlier. For the previous five years, the studio had — not quietly, but with steely determination — been pursuing its plan to produce the first of what it hoped would be a new series of Superman feature films, reviving the rather cheesy concept of the Man of Steel with the same efficiency with which Tim Burton's first *Batman* film had erased memories of the Adam West-Burt Ward *Batman* of the sixties. Alas, it was not to be.

Somehow, Time-Warner's takeover of DC Comics had left its movie-making subsidiary, Warner Bros, without the rights to make movies based on one of its flagship characters. This situation was remedied when, in 1993, Warner Bros purchased those rights from former film mogul Alexander Salkind who, with his son Ilya, had produced four *Superman* films between 1978 and 1987, each starring Christopher Reeve as the eponymous hero. Warner Bros announced its acquisition with suitable fanfare, taking out full-page advertisements for *Superman: The New Movie* in the trade press, depicting a shining gold 'S' symbol familiar to millions of Superman's fans. The future looked bright for what the studio considered its next billion-dollar franchise.

Although it was several years since the underwhelming perform-ance of the over-earnest *Superman IV: The Quest for Peace* sent the for-merly super-powered film series to the Fortress of Franchise Solitude, the studio was bullish about its new property, not least because inter-est in the fifty-something superhero had not waned in the wake of the series' demise. The same year, 1993, saw the publication of *Superman #75*, the culmination of a best-selling mini-series, quickly collected under the title *The Death of Superman*, in which the supposedly inde-structible son of Krypton meets his end at the hands of Doomsday, a monstrous supervillain contrived by writer Dan Jurgens for one pur-pose: to kill Kal-El, alias Superman. Gaining the kind of national news-paper coverage which had not been seen in the US since funny paper favourite L'il Abner got married in 1952, *The Death of Superman* — ironically — revived the fortunes of one of the few superheroes who still considered wearing his underpants over his tights to be the height of crimefighting fashion. DC took the bold step of retiring its *Superman* titles for six months, publishing in their place the intriguing *World Without A Superman* series, which explored what life — ours and the DC Universe — would have been like without Jerry Seinfeld's favourite super-guy. Then came *Superman Reborn*, an inevitable but effective revival of both the character and the fortunes of DC's monthly titles.

Warner Bros wasted no time in capitalising on Superman's new-found comic book success, launching a weekly prime-time television series enti-tled *Lois & Clark: The New Adventures of Superman*, and assigning *Batman* producer Jon Peters the role of bringing the Man of Steel back into cinemas. Peters, in turn, approached Warner Bros script doctor and screenwriter Jonathan Lemkin to script Superman's next big-screen adventure. "I think based on the action of *Lethal Weapon 4*, some of the more supernatural elements of *Devil's Advocate* and the fantasy elements of *Demolition Man*, everyone felt comfortable with going forward with me as the writer of *Superman Reborn*," he told *Cinescape*, referring to other scripts he had worked on for the studio. Lemkin was equally com-fortable working with Peters. "He knows this genre," he said of the *Batman* producer. "The brilliant thing about John is that he comes up with fifteen ideas in any sentence. He is a constant fount of ideas, and probably has more ideas in a single day than most producers have in a year."

Major toy companies, which effectively had as much power to decide Superman's fate as Doomsday, insisted on seeing a draft before the deadline for Toy Fair, the industry's annual trade show. Lemkin told *Entertainment Weekly* that he was asked simply to "write a great movie", ideally based on *The Death of Superman* and its follow-ups. "Let's face it, I've been entrusted with this corporate asset, and it's a very different process than any other script I've ever worked on," he told *Cinescape*. "This is a *huge* corporate asset, and if you look at the marketing that can come from this, it's phenomenal. So they're being very careful with what we do." Lemkin was keenly aware of the difficulties facing him. "How do you bring Superman into the nineties and keep him fresh? The good thing about Superman is that he wants to do the right thing. He's *not* a conflicted hero, which is its own genre and can be a wonderful thing. There's something about Superman that's great in terms of his attitude of stepping into the breach, come what may." The difference between Superman and Batman, he observed, is that the former is an alien, while the latter is human. "[Superman] demands fantasy elements that Batman doesn't. I think that's much more exciting, and I feel that the result should be sort of like crossing Batman with *Star Wars*. Superman versus humans is not an interesting match. That's like me versus a slug — who cares?" Thus, he added, "In any good Superman movie, the fate of the whole planet should be at stake... You've got to have villains whose powers and abilities *demand* that Superman — and only Superman — can be the one who stops them. Their powers have to tax Superman to the limit. That's the only way to make the movie exciting and a dramatic challenge."

Taking the comic books *The Death of Superman*, *World Without A Superman* and *Superman Reborn* as a "stepping-off point," Lemkin opened his script with a defeated Superman in his death throes, and went on to tell the story not of his rebirth but of the birth of his successor, who is born after Superman impregnates Lois Lane with his spirit. Maturing faster than a speeding bullet, the new superhero saves the universe before he is out of short tights. "[Superman] literally dies as he professes his love to [Lois]," Lemkin revealed, "and his life force jumps between them. Superman dies and Lois later finds out that she's pregnant — immaculately. She gives birth to a child who grows twenty-one years in three weeks, and is, essentially, the resurrected

Superman." Resisting the lightweight format of *Lois & Clark*, and taking a cue from the first two *Batman* blockbusters, Lemkin's story was littered with nightmarish images which director Tim Burton — who was not yet involved — would probably have loved. The studio, however, felt that some story elements trod the same path as those of *Batman Forever*, "and some of the underlying themes were close," as Lemkin put it. "That concerned them, and they decided to go a whole new way."

Gregory Poirier, who had scripted the worthy drama *Rosewood* for producer Peters, was next up to bat. Poirier chose not to lighten the script, adding Kal-El's existential woes about being an outsider alienated on Earth, but wrote in a popular comic book villain — the mad alien machine creature, Brainiac — who attempts to defeat Superman with the aid of a monster with Kryptonite for blood. At the script's end, almost certainly at Peters' request, Superman has exchanged his trademark blue-and-red caped costume for a sleek new bat-style black ensemble, which might have had die-hard Supes fans getting their tights in a twist, but certainly would have looked cooler on screen than Christopher Reeve's overstuffed underpants. Poirier's script reportedly received a warm welcome from Warner executives, and he was somewhat surprised to learn that comic book fan-turned-indie movie icon Kevin Smith — whose 1997 comedy *Chasing Amy* dealt with two comics creators and who now writes for DC and Marvel in his spare time — had been engaged to pen a new version.

Smith began by reading Poirier's draft, and promptly told the studio exactly what he thought of it. "I said I thought it was terrible," he admitted to *Entertainment Weekly*. "Poirier didn't get the Superman mythos." Fearing, probably with some justification, that Smith — who co-owns a New Jersey comic book store — spoke for millions of Superman fans, Warner Bros and Jon Peters encouraged him to start over, albeit with certain caveats. "There's certain rules you gotta follow if you're gonna accept the big studio dime," Smith told Elston Gunn for the website *Aint It Cool News*, adding that his script, entitled *Superman Lives*, "wouldn't necessarily be the version of Superman I would've done if they were just like, 'Just write a Superman movie.' There were a lot of parameters I had to work with, you know: the death of Superman was a major parameter they wanted me to use in that storyline; Brainiac as the villain was something they were intent on. When I had to work closer with Jon Peters on the project, he had all sorts of weird parameters. Like, 'I don't wanna see him in the suit and I don't want to see him fly and I want him to fight a giant spider in the third act,'" Smith revealed. "Shit, where I'm like, 'What?! A giant spider? Are you crazy?!'" Nevertheless, Smith accepted the terms, realising that he was not being hired for his vision but to execute a pre-ordained idea of what a new Superman film should be like: "'Here are all of the ingredients; do this.' So I couldn't go in there and be, like, 'No, I wanna do this thing. I want to do my version,' because you're accepting the job of translating all their ideas into one flick."

Smith pitched his outline to Peters in August 1996 and immediately got the go-ahead to turn in his first draft, which he did the following month. In Smith's story, the energy-sucking extraterrestrial Brainiac is in space with his faithful robot L-Ron (a typically sly reference to Scientology founder and sci-fi author L. Ron Hubbard) when he is contacted by Lex Luthor, who summons them to Earth to rid the world of the superhero formerly known as Kal-El. Discovering that Superman's superpowers are derived from the sun, Luthor and Brainiac block the sun's rays, thus diminishing his powers and allowing Doomsday to defeat the suddenly vulnerable Man of Steel. Littering the script with playful or ironic references to the superhero's past, and assuming that his lover Lois Lane has already figured out that Superman's secret identity is her *Daily Planet* colleague Clark Kent, Smith further displays his fan knowledge by incorporating fellow DC Comics characters Deadshot and Batman in cameo roles (the latter giving a moving eulogy at his fallen friend's funeral), as well as such *Superman* staples as *Planet* photographer Jimmy Olsen and his venerable boss Perry White. Although details of Superman's new look are sketchy — Smith admitted "Superman, um, '90s style" is as far as he got — the script accounted for audiences *not* believing a man can fly by depicting Superman in flight as a red-and-blue blur accompanied by a sonic boom, thus neatly avoiding the sometimes wobbly blue-screen effects of the previous *Superman* film series.

Warner Bros was reportedly delighted with Smith's upbeat take on the material, although studio executives were less impressed with his loose-lipped comments in the press. "I was quoted as saying, 'The

Warner Bros executives are the most anxious group of motherfuck-ers I've ever met in my life.'" Smith told the UK's *Premiere* magazine. "That was based on the fact they called constantly while I was doing Superman — three, four times a day. It was almost a joke." But Smith said that he wasn't referring to Warner Bros executives, "I was talk-ing about the executives at Jon Peters' company, and I was kind of misquoted, but an exec is an exec. I don't think it was a real person-al attack," he added. "They *are* a group of anxious motherfuckers." Smith endured what he called "a degree of silent treatment for about a week, where everybody tried to figure out how insulted they were," before being asked to write a second draft, which he delivered on 27 March 1997, and which Smith claimed Warner Bros liked even more than the first.

Nevertheless, according to one source close to the production, a succession of directors were turning down the film at this stage, for a variety of reasons. One of them was maverick Texan Robert Rodriguez (*From Dusk Till Dawn*), who chose to make *The Faculty* instead. "I real-ly, really liked Kevin Smith's script, but I had just moved back to Texas," Rodriguez told *Cinescape*, adding that, at the time he was offered the project, he was exhausted after a whirlwind succession of events. "The day after I wrapped *From Dusk Till Dawn*, they premièred *Desperado*. My book came out that next week. Then two weeks later, my first child was born. Then Christmas. Then *From Dusk Till Dawn* opened, like, two weeks later. I mean, it was great, [but] of course, I totally crashed and burned after that." Although Rodriguez knew that the Superman movie could give him a *bona fide* blockbuster, he ultimately chose to take a break, before filming *The Faculty*. "I knew it would be a big movie and have big [McDonald's] Happy Meals and stuff," he said of *Superman Lives*, "but I also knew it would be like that no matter who made it."

One shortlisted director who did accept Warner Bros' offer, much to the studio's surprise, was Tim Burton, who had made one of 1997's costliest flops, *Mars Attacks!*, but had worked well with Peters on the hugely successful *Batman* franchise. "At the time," Kevin Smith later told the screenwriting magazine *Fade In*, "I think his signing on had more to do with *Mars Attacks!* going right into the crapper and him needing a sure-fire hit." In addition to Burton, the script also met with a favourable response from actor Nicolas Cage, who was fast cementing his status as an A-list star, thanks to *The Rock*, *Con Air* and an Academy Award for *Leaving Las Vegas*. Cage, a long-time comic book fan who had previously been linked with a screen adaptation of Marvel's Iron Man character, explained his decision to step into the cape by pointing out that he had made films in many genres, but "the one genre that I haven't really done is the biggest of them all, which is the comic book genre. The bottom line is that I don't want to do only what is [typically] regarded as the 'important' movies," he added. "I believe that a movie like *Leaving Las Vegas* has an important value, and I believe that a movie based on Superman has an important value as well... because it's going to affect children around the world. With Tim Burton," the actor continued, "hopefully we're going to bring a lot to it and totally reconceive the character. The death of Superman and his resurrection will be a part of the story, but I have other points that I want to address that haven't really been examined before. Superman is an American myth. Like the English have Shakespeare, America has Batman, Superman and Mickey Mouse." Many Superman fans reacted negatively to this unusual casting choice, however, causing Burton to point out that fans had been similarly unhappy when he cast Michael Keaton as Batman. Besides, as Kevin Smith later told *Premiere*, "I think Nic is such a great actor that you would forget that he doesn't look like the classic Superman. I think his performance would have been tremendous."

With Cage on board, another recent Oscar winner, Kevin Spacey, reportedly expressed an interest in playing Lex Luthor, while comic actors Jim Carrey and Chris Rock were rumoured to be eyeing the Brainiac and Jimmy Olsen roles respectively. Jack Nicholson, who had played the Joker in Burton's *Batman*, was also mentioned in connection with the Brainiac role, while Sandra Bullock was widely reported to be the studio's first choice to play Lois Lane. Needless to say, all this might have been wishful thinking, either on the part of Superman fans or the studio itself. Yet surprising rumour turned to even more surprising fact when Burton and Cage both signed lucrative pay-or-play deals — meaning that they got paid whether the film was made or not — worth $5 million and a staggering *$20 million* respectively. Offices on the Warner lot were set up and *Superman*

Lives officially entered pre-production in the summer of 1997.

Then, it transpired, Burton decided he didn't like Smith's story so much as he liked the idea of making a Superman movie. "The studio was happy with what I was doing," Smith told *Empire* magazine, "[but] then Tim Burton got involved, and when he signed his pay or play deal he turned around and said he wanted to do *his* version of Superman. So who is Warner Brothers going to back — the guy who made *Clerks*, or the guy who made them half a billion dollars on *Batman*?" Besides, Smith told *Premiere*, "What are they gonna do — piss Tim off cause they wanna hold onto my script? I didn't make the studio a billion dollars over the course of my career. Tim did. So that was that." Nevertheless, Smith was smarting, admitting to *Entertainment Weekly* that he was "under the impression that Burton would at least have the courtesy to sit down with me. He didn't."

Instead, Burton brought in screenwriter number four, Wesley Strick (*The Saint*), to reimagine the film in the director's own trademark style. "As soon as Tim was hired by Warner Bros he brought me in, owing to a prior, pleasant collaboration," Strick recalls, referring to his production rewrite on *Batman Returns*. Strick was given the Kevin Smith draft, which he read "with eager anticipation and a rising sense of bafflement. First, everywhere Superman went, he was accompanied/shadowed by someone/something called The Eradicator, who seemed to have more lines and more things to do than Superman," he says. "The villain, Brainiac, had a comic sidekick called L-Ron, who similarly took up as much script space as Brainiac and wasn't all that funny. Brainiac's evil plot was to launch a disk into space that would blot out the sun, necessitating the use of his own energy-production — a plot device I'd seen not long before on *The Simpsons* [with] Mr Burns doing the Brainiac role. Lastly, the script was crammed with so much techno-jargon, there were whole pages that were — to me — nearly impenetrable. I had no idea how Tim reacted," he adds, "but at our first meeting he made it clear that he wanted to jettison the Smith draft." According to Strick, neither the studio nor Jon Peters was comfortable with this, despite the fact that both acknowledged that Smith's script was problematic. But although there were aspects of it they wanted to preserve, Strick says Burton was adamant that he wanted a new tone and a fresh approach. Ultimately, a compromise was reached: Strick could start over with a page one rewrite, so long as the 'death of Superman' theme remained.

As Strick recalls, "After going down to the comic book store and purchasing *World Without A Superman*, a collection that comprised the 'death' and its traumatic and ultimately triumphant aftermath, I started, belatedly, to make sense of some of Kevin Smith's constructs — particularly the bothersome and boring Eradicator. Still determined that our Superman not play like a buddy movie, but seeing the need for the felled Superman to return to life through the ministrations of some sympathetic, off-planet intelligence, I created an entity I called 'K', a sort of sprite who would flit around as a digital light-effect, representing the spirit and heritage of Krypton. Tim liked the concept, but was concerned that 'K' might be a bit too 'Tinkerbell'... and, ultimately, the clock ran out before we were able to solve this." Nevertheless, the screenwriter adds, "We did take pains to characterise Clark/Superman as an alien, painfully conscious of his profoundly 'outsider' status and not always in control of his powers — think 'extraterrestrial Scissorhands.' Plus, after 'K' revives Superman in the Fortress of Solitude, [Superman] returns in a peculiar Kal-El persona — freaking out Lois, Metropolis and himself before reverting to the more familiar and comfortable Clark/Superman schism. Tim and I both relished the fact that our hero wasn't merely split down the middle like most Burton heroes, but was for a time a tri-furcated personality. And we doubled the theme by having Brainiac invade the body of Lex Luthor at story's midpoint, creating an amusing schizo/scary mega-villain we dubbed Lexiac." Strick's storyline also revealed that Brainiac was created by Superman's father Jor-El, making him the great scientist's 'first born,' whose primacy and birthright was supplanted by Kal-El, thus explaining Brainiac's quest for vengeance when, years later, he encounters Kal-El/Superman on Earth. "Tim and I would meet at least once a week at his apartment," Strick adds. "We'd talk, [and] he'd make wonderful sketches of our characters on napkins. As things progressed, he moved over to an office on the Warner lot, surrounded by concept art that was growing increasingly bizarre, detailed and inspiring."

Heading up Burton's design team was production designer Rick Heinrichs, who had produced the director's early shorts, *Frankenweenie* and *Vincent*, and worked in some capacity on almost every one of Burton's films since. "Tim first spoke to me about the project in the spring of 1997, right after I finished *The Big Lebowski*," Heinrichs recalls. "I was excited by his take on the Man of Steel, which felt appropriate to the character and yet within the *oeuvre* of Tim's other work." Other members of the team included John Dexter (*Mars Attacks!*), Jacques Ray (*The Fifth Element*), Harold Beckler (*Minority Report*), Jack Johnson (*The Shadow*), James Carson (*Ed Wood, Mars Attacks!*), Bill Boes (*Alien Resurrection, Monkeybone*) and Sylvain Despretz (*The Fifth Element, Alien Resurrection*). "The phase we were working on was very preliminary," says Despretz. "We got the Kevin Smith script, but we were told not to read it, because they knew he wasn't going to stay on the movie. So we used Kevin Smith's script as a guide to the sets we might be doing, and we waited and waited for the new script to come in, but it never did."

Nevertheless, like Heinrichs, Despretz feels that Burton was the perfect choice to handle a Superman movie. "His take on it was quite interesting," he says. "To Tim, it wasn't a simple heroic story, and I think the casting of Nicolas Cage was quite good because he wasn't a square-jawed hero. He wanted to show a very vulnerable side of Superman, similar to the way Jesus was portrayed in Martin Scorsese's *The Last Temptation of Christ*, so what you saw was a reluctant Messiah. It was the story of a man struggling with the burden of extraordinary powers." Cage evidently relished this approach, telling *Premiere* that the film's vision of the Man of Steel would be as "a freak, but a beautiful freak in that he really cares about people. I wouldn't be afraid to talk about his loneliness and his feeling like an alien, never fitting in and so always compulsively needing to do heroic acts so people would like him and he would feel loved."

One of Sylvain Despretz's most dramatic conceptual illustrations depicts the lantern-jawed Kryptonian in a stylish black moulded bodysuit — *sans* underpants, red or otherwise — with a stylised silver 'S' in relief on his chest. That look was designed by Jim Carson, and was just one of many different costume concepts which were put forward. "The types of designs that we were being asked to create had little or nothing to do with DC Comics' approach over the years," Despretz told *SFX* in 2000. "They were looking at the comic books and saying, 'We can't have him wear that — it looks ridiculous.'" Instead, Despretz recalls today, "They were trying to create something with a nice body mould, similar to the style of the Batman suits, but that had that 'S' thing. Something sleeker, more in tune with the Y2K look." Would Burton's radical new approach have pleased the fans? "I think, by and large, yes," says Heinrichs. "The only point in creating a new version of something is to bring a fresh eye to it, to attempt to re-grasp the essential interpretation of one of our society's iconic cultural myths. Real Superman fans know how much of the original comic was about a conflicted hero facing some rather daunting choices brought on by urgent crises. Oh, and he happens to possess extraordinary physical powers that he wields with ease, but not much understanding."

Not that Burton was technically in charge of the film at this stage, its direction being dictated, as always, by Peters and his Warner Bros bosses, who, in turn, were being guided by the toy companies and promotional partners who would make the production viable. "Jon Peters was in constant contact with toy companies, whose deals would help offset the picture's huge expense," says Wesley Strick. "[Peters] would occasionally call me to demand that Superman use a certain sort of jet-pack — when he'd temporarily lost his flying ability — or that Brainiac float above the Earth in a 'Skull Ship' which he'd reach via a shuttle that must have a particular design. Though this could be annoying," Strick admits, "it wasn't especially difficult to incorporate these items. And Jon, though occasionally confusing and intrusive, was no more so than many other producers I've encountered over my years in Hollywood." At least one member of the art department does not agree with Strick's sentiments, however. "Peters was basically running the show like a star producer," says Despretz. "He would come down yelling and saying, 'This is the way I want it,' and make the most ridiculous observations. He used to bring kids in, who would point at drawings on the wall and rate them, like they were evaluating the toy possibilities." According to Despretz, the studio was apparently looking not so much for actual conceptual designs, but for drawings that could reassure the toy companies that their multi-million dollar investments would be wisely made. "This was how the movie was being designed. It was basically a toy show."

On one occasion, Peters reportedly visited the art department working on designs for Brainiac's 'skull ship'. "He got really worked up about a *National Geographic* issue that had a holographic skull on the cover," Despretz recalls, "and he flung out his arms and said, 'This is it! This is what I want! I want a skull!'" We laughed about it for months." Another time, the karate-mad producer allegedly asked production designer Rick Heinrichs if he would stand still while Peters wrestled him to the ground. "It was just sheer, humiliating madness," Despretz says. "I found out later that Tim Burton was in Hell. He mentioned several times that it was the worst time of his life, because he really had no desire to be in this predicament, but he'd just done *Mars Attacks!*, which didn't work very well, and he needed a big film."

While Strick toiled on the script, now retitled *Superman Reborn*, the art department continued to turn out drawing after drawing, based on the few elements they knew would be included in the new draft: Superman himself; the new 'S' logo; numerous versions of Brainiac's skull ship; exteriors and interiors of the planet Krypton; the Kryptonians; the Fortress of Solitude; the city of Metropolis; and the film's chief antagonist, Brainiac. "I still have a sketch from Tim Burton describing what he wanted," Despretz says of the latter. "It was pretty crude, graphically. He looked like a cone, with a round ball on top with something that looked like an emaciated skull inside. Imagine you take Merlin's hat, and you stick a fishbowl on top, with a skull in it — that was Brainiac."

Meanwhile, Burton scouted city locations which could double for Metropolis, eventually deciding that Pittsburgh — famous as a steel-producing city and home to the Steelers football team — would be the ideal home for the Man of Steel. "[Burton's] Metropolis was not Gotham redundant," Heinrichs says. "Its character was not derived from the same sort of reference used to create what that 'urbanscape' became." Says Strick, "What excited Tim was that, in contrast to the two Batman films which he associated with darkness and night, Superman was going to be a superhero adventure set primarily in day-light — in sunlight, even. He saw it as, ideally, a more 'American' and mainstream fable — this was the challenge. And Nic Cage, whom we sat with several times, seemed to share our concept." With each successive draft, however, the budget rocketed alarmingly — according to several reports, to between $140 million and $190 million. "It's not like building a house," Warner Bros president of production Lorenzo di Bonaventura explained to *Entertainment Weekly*. "You're creating a world where a guy flies around, something new where it takes a lot of time between when you create a scene and when [Industrial Light & Magic] puts a price tag on it."

Then, in 1998, shortly after the cancellation of the by now ratings-starved *Lois & Clark*, the studio began to experience caped fear. Less than a year later, following the disastrous performance of such ambitious science fiction fare as *Sphere* and *The Postman*, Warner Bros co-chairman Terry Semel announced that, in the future, the studio would be eschewing expensive 'event' movies in favour of mid-priced films. With a proposed budget that was always going to be in excess of $100 million, *Superman Lives* had already become one of the first casualties. "We didn't have a script we loved, and the budget was too high," Semel's partner, Bob Daly, explained. "When the budget started getting out of control, that's when we decided to pull the plug."

"Our script was strong and getting stronger when the plug was pulled," laments Wesley Strick. "Evidently the execs had finally accommodated themselves to a Burton Superman — stages were reserved, scenery was built, locations were scouted — when Terry Semel read my draft and, so I'm told, reacted violently against it. At that point the team did an about-face and it fell to Tim — somewhat sheepishly and sweetly — to invite me to his apartment one last time, to tell me the news. The Warner Bros 'team' was never completely comfortable with our script," he adds. "I wasn't quite sure what their specific problems were but I think the level of nervousness and second-guessing over so valuable a franchise as Superman would have made it impossible for them to feel completely comfortable with any version."

Nevertheless, with the commercial disappointment of *Batman & Robin*, the fourth entry in the *Batman* franchise — which grossed less than half of the first *Batman*, released almost a decade earlier — the cancellation, or at least postponement, of another comic book block-buster with a bloated budget seemed, with hindsight, to have been a wise move. By this time, however, the studio had already spent a reported $30 million developing the *Superman* movie, and ultimately engaged a fifth screenwriter, Dan Gilroy (*Freejack*), in an effort to bring the spiralling budget back down to Earth. "We know we're getting close," Di Bonaventura told *Entertainment Weekly* at the time, "but we're not there yet. The creative process is imprecise at best, but over the last two or three months we've accelerated in a good way. But we had hoped to accelerate that way six months ago."

After the studio's closure of the *Superman Lives* production offices, regular visitors to Warner Bros' official website, *supermanlives.com*, were greeted with the following announcement: "Out of commitment to Superman's worldwide legacy and countless fans, and to the potential of creating a Superman story that will push the narrative envelope, Warner Bros has decided to postpone the start of production on its Superman movie. Warner Bros feels that, at this time, the script does not yet do full justice to the potential of the film and of the character, one of the most popular superheroes in history. The project, which had been tentatively scheduled to begin principal photography later this summer, remains in active development, and the studio stated that Nicolas Cage, director Tim Burton, producer Jon Peters and screenwriter Dan Gilroy all remain firmly committed to the project. Warner Bros intends to aggressively continue developing the Superman project until it satisfies the highest standards of everyone involved."

The film's laid-off crewmembers responded by organising an unofficial "wake" to commemorate the death of *Superman Lives*, their invitations cheekily depicting a sketch of Superman lying in a coffin — an image straight out of *The Death of Superman* comic book. While Warner Bros considered its options, Peters chose to play out his giant spider fantasies with another would-be 'event' movie for Warner Bros, *Wild Wild West*. Nicolas Cage, despite having earned $20 million for little more than lending his name to the stillborn project, was reportedly upset to learn of the film's demise secondhand, and revived his interest in a rival comic book property, *The Iron Man*. Burton, meanwhile, left Metropolis for *Sleepy Hollow* and the *Planet of the Apes* $5 million richer. "I 'made' the movie, only I didn't film it," Burton later told the website *Mr Showbiz*. "You'd have to ask Warner Bros why. It was going to be expensive, and they were a little sensitive that they had screwed up the *Batman* franchise. Corporate decisions are all fear-based decisions," he added. "They were afraid."

Nevertheless, *Superman Lives*, like its title character, refused to die. "We have a mandate to make event pictures," Lorenzo Di

Bonaventura told *Entertainment Weekly*, "but do you need four a summer? No. Do you need two or three? Probably. So hopefully, we'll make five [mid-priced films] as well as *Superman*." Certainly, Warner Bros continued to develop the project after 1998, albeit with a much lower profile than previously. For a time, Oliver Stone expressed an interest in the project, before ceding the director's chair to Ralph Zondag (*Dinosaur*). "We are now meeting with many, many directors," Peters commented to *Cinescape Online*. "We're looking at a lot of different people. Everybody wants to do it." William Wisher — who previously scripted the screen adaptation of another well-loved comic book character, Judge Dredd — was drafted in to write yet another version, which was then reportedly scrapped in favour of an entirely new seventeen-page treatment by comics writer Keith Giffen, whose story included his own popular creation: Lobo, a marauding intergalactic mercenary who might be more than a match for the Man of Steel. Then, in April 2001, *Hollywood Reporter* revealed that Oscar-nominated screenwriter Paul Attanasio (*Quiz Show*, *Donnie Brasco*) had been commissioned to write a brand new draft, receiving a staggering $1.7 million for his trouble. "Attanasio will sift through the three or four *Superman* scripts previously written during its five-year development at the studio," the report said, "but he will focus on his own, original take on material based on the death and rebirth of the Man of Steel."

No wonder Kevin Smith has questioned just how much of his *Superman Lives* storyline has survived. "If they stick to the formula using *The Death of Superman* storyline with Brainiac as the villain, that's about the only similarities it may have," he told the website *Ain't It Cool News*. Besides, as Smith admitted to *Empire*, "Working on *Superman Lives* was fun to do, and for a while it looked like it was going to happen. It was fun while it lasted, and — Lord knows — I made a lot of money and learned a few things about the business. But ultimately, nothing was really yielded from it." According to Di Bonaventura, all of the writers "have contributed creative elements that continue to be part of the overall mix."

As, presumably, have artists like Rick Heinrichs and Sylvain Despretz. As Heinrichs says, "The collapse of the project in the spring of 1998 was a great disappointment to all of us who had not only invested so much of our time, but felt excellent about what we had accomplished up to that point, and excited by the prospects for film production and final product." With hindsight, Despretz is inclined to agree. "At the time, I would have said it wasn't going to be great," he told *SFX*, "but as it stands, hearing myself describe it for the first time in ages, I would say, in fact, yes — I am now sure it would have been a brilliant show, and a landmark movie." Adds Heinrichs, who has since worked with Burton on *Sleepy Hollow* and *Planet of the Apes*, "While I am not holding my breath in anticipation, it seems unlikely that Warner Bros will keep Superman in the deep freeze forever. Let's hope they see fit to make the movie someday and that they seek out Tim Burton to direct it," he says. "They would have a hit and a revived franchise."

Henrichs may get his wish. Lorenzo Di Bonaventura, who has since helped to revive Warner Bros' fortunes thanks to the success of *The Matrix*, has admitted that he'd be "shocked" if the studio, having spent six years and $30 million developing the Superman project, decided not to actively pursue it. "Superman is popular at our stores," he told *Entertainment Weekly*. "It's a good product we're hoping to tap into." Nevertheless, despite the appointment of the new screenwriter at further expense, and the début of *Smallville*, a new small-screen outing for the character, the studio may yet consider that taking a $30 million flier on the film is less risky than spending a further nine figure sum actually *making* it.

In other words, at this point, only Warner Bros can decide whether or not *Superman Lives*. ∎

The Six Million Dollar Movie

The Bionic Man Almost Gets A Big Screen Makeover

"Getting the job was fun, but having to actually do it
was really tough."

—*The Six Million Dollar Man* screenwriter Kevin Smith

"**S**teve Austin, astronaut. A man barely alive. Gentlemen, we
can rebuild him. We have the technology. We have the capability to make the world's first Bionic man. Steve Austin will
be that man. Better than he was before. Better. Stronger. Faster." With
these words, a television phenomenon was born, leading to over 100
hour-long episodes, a spin-off show, three made-for-television reunion
movies, at least six million dollars' worth of merchandising tie-ins, and
— very nearly — a big-screen adaptation.

Loosely based on Martin Caidin's novel *Cyborg* (which could be
seen as a twentieth century Frankenstein story), *The Six Million Dollar
Man* was centred on a NASA test pilot, Colonel Steve Austin (Lee
Majors), who suffers catastrophic injuries when his experimental high-
atmosphere aircraft crashes. His damaged legs, arms, left eye and hearing are replaced by atomic-powered equivalents, using top secret organ
and limb replacement technology known as 'Bionics'. Having spent the
titular $6 million on his new body parts — back when $6 million was a
lot of money — the Office of Strategic Investigations (OSI), the government agency which rebuilt him, is eager to get its money's worth from
their man. Austin is soon pressed into service on all manner of top
secret assignments, under the supervision of OSI agent Oscar Goldman
(Richard Anderson) and Dr Rudy Wells (Martin Balsam in the pilot
film, then Alan Oppenheimer, and later Martin E. Brooks).

Premièring on America's ABC network in 1973, *The Six Million Dollar Man* quickly captured the imagination of prime time audiences, who marvelled at the weekly adventures of a hero with superhuman strength, telescopic vision and the ability to run faster and jump higher than any man on Earth, yet who did not feel the urge to wear his underpants outside his tights. A somewhat reluctant hero, whom circumstance had dealt a single crushing blow before offering him a second chance, Steve Austin was a true icon for the seventies, an era in which suicidal stuntmen like Evel Knievel were revered for their superhuman feats and post-Watergate America was more than aware of the government's nefarious network of agencies working behind the scenes of the military-industrial complex. More importantly, perhaps, 'Bionics' — a word which seemed to enter the national vocabulary within weeks of the show's first US broadcast — seemed to offer a thrilling, yet thrillingly plausible, vision of future technological advances in the medical world. Many people already wore artificial pacemakers and, some day, we might all be able to replace our bodies' failing organs and limbs with Bionic equivalents, giving us all a chance to be "better, stronger, faster" — just like our hero, Steve Austin. And perhaps most importantly of all, the star of the show was dating America's number one pin-up girl, *Charlie's Angels* star Farrah Fawcett, who made three appearances in the show.

The Six Million Dollar Man amassed 103 episodes and spawned one hugely successful sister series, *The Bionic Woman* — which starred Lindsay Wagner as Bionically-enhanced Jaime Sommers — as well as an idea for another, *The Bionic Boy*, which was swiftly discarded when non-Bionic children began emulating the heroics of their TV counterpart. "Many, many kids —*adults*, actually — have come to me, who have jumped off the barn door and broken their legs," says Majors. "The parents didn't mind them watching because it wasn't real violence — nobody got killed." When *The Six Million Dollar Man* finally came to an end in 1978, the idea to continue the Bionic adventures refused to die — much like Steve Austin himself. "I believed there were more stories, but I moved onto other things," says Richard Anderson. "But I always felt there was more to it, and when the time presented itself in 1988, ten years later, it happened quite by accident."

According to Anderson, he and Lee Majors found themselves

guests at a charity event in London and decided to continue their European visit with a trip to France. "One day, Lee said, 'Richard, I'm going for a run,'" Anderson recalls. "So I went on a bicycle and I saw him [and] caught up with him. We were coming to a winding road, and very slowly I'm pedalling, and he's loping along, and I said, 'Steve, what about one more mission?' And he says, 'No, Oscar... ' And we went into it. Then we said, 'Wait a minute, this might really [work].'" When Anderson returned to the US, he contacted Universal, who held the rights, and suggested reuniting the Bionic team for a made-for-television movie. "I helped Universal go through the motions, and interfaced with the network, and got all the principals, and we made the first one, which was successful," he says, referring to 1987's *Return of the Six Million Dollar Man and the Bionic Woman*. Two more TV movies followed: 1989's *Bionic Showdown* and 1994's *Bionic Ever After*, which Anderson executive produced.

"The first one was kind of interesting and it was kind of fun," says Lindsay Wagner, who was initially reluctant to return to the role that made her famous. "I had grown so much that I was wanting even more out of the stories than I did before, and I didn't really get it. Universal were willing to do them, but it was tough," she adds. "They basically turned out to be just capers — somehow they weren't able to get to do stories which to me were meaningful." Overall, she says that the quality of the reunion movies did not live up to that of the TV show, and she probably would not consider doing another. "Certainly not if they were going to do something in that vein. I never say 'never' to just about anything, but they would have to come up with one heck of a meaningful story for me to ever consider it again." Wagner initially held out on the third TV movie, stating that she would not reprise the Jaime Sommers role unless she and Steve Austin were finally allowed to get married. "You've got to give that to the public," she explains. "You can't just drag them around, the two of us in wheelchairs, and people still waiting for the two of us old fogies to get married. These folk have been with us, and loved us, and we've had this wonderful relationship with them, and they should have the satisfaction of that. Plus, what's it saying about these two who can't get off their own situations and commit to each other? Or jump level and stop having this unrequited stuff?" Ultimately, Wagner got her way, the world's first

Bionic marriage taking place in 1994. "I think that might be the end of that," commented Majors.

But *The Six Million Dollar Man* was not yet ready to retire. When television supplanted cinema as chief supplier of entertainment to the masses, the power base in Hollywood shifted from cinema to television. Increasingly, attempts were made to translate classic US television shows into films, with *Star Trek: The Motion Picture* arguably being the most risky and ambitious. The idea of mining television series as subject matter for movies was too good to ignore. There were, after all, two obvious advantages: one, the property had the kind of built-in audience awareness which publicity spending could not buy; two, the studio's television arm almost certainly owned the rights to the property. By the early 1990s, most of the studio production heads had their background in television, and show after show began to hit cinemas, feeding on the nation's nostalgia for the heyday of television. The results were a mixed blessing: *The Addams Family*, *The Fugitive* and *Mission: Impossible* were all gigantic hits; *Lost in Space*, *The Beverly Hillbillies* and *Car 54, Where Are You?* were equally emphatic flops. But the studios were always willing to re-run the risk of giving yet another TV show its day on the big screen.

Wagner, for one, thinks it is high time that *The Six Million Dollar man* followed other successful seventies TV shows into the multiplex, if only so it could benefit from the kind of special effects Universal would not pay for in a mere TV movie. "They tried to do the [TV movies] in the old style of the special effects, which in the seventies was the cutting edge, [but] today is laughable. Today, the special effects are so extraordinary and advanced, and the audiences expect them, and without Universal taking it to the feature level and putting the money into it as they would a feature, we can't do that. That was actually the very first problem that I had with the remakes: how are you going to do this today? How are you possibly going to get away with it today?" Wagner feels that the only reason the reunion movies were able to pull off the seventies-style special effects — for example, the classic Bionic paradox of using slow motion to depict high speed — is that the audience remembered them that way. "People love Jaime and Steve, and they will accept it because they remember the same kind of stuff on [the show]."

It was whilst post-producing the third TV movie, *Bionic Ever After*, that Richard Anderson had the idea for a big-screen outing for the Bionic man. He had a poster made up, pitched the idea to Universal's motion picture division and was met with an enthusiastic response from producer Jim Jacks, who wasted no time setting the wheels in motion. Comic book fan and self-confessed TV junkie Kevin Smith, who was also tapped to write film scripts for *Superman Lives* (see chapter 14) and *Daredevil*, was working on his second feature, *Mallrats*, when he was offered the chance to write a *Six Million Dollar Man* movie. "Jim Jacks, the producer, was really good friends with the guy who plays Oscar Goldman," Smith explained to *Ain't It Cool*'s Elston Gunn, referring to Richard Anderson. "He had the rights to *Six Million Dollar Man* and he wanted to make it into a movie. We went out to lunch one day and I told him, 'I'd love to write it.' I was a huge fan and had all the toys and such, so I pitched my idea for the story and he said, 'That's great. Let's do it.'" Jacks, who later produced *The Jackal* and *The Mummy* for Universal, accompanied Smith as he pitched the story outline to Universal executive Nina Jacobson. "She dug it," Smith said, "and I was hired and sent off to go."

So far, so good. But Smith soon had cause to remember the old adage about being careful what you wish for. "Getting the job was fun, but having to actually do it was really tough," he admitted. "It took me a year to turn in a first draft because I was working on other stuff." Like getting over writer's block. "I would get up and some days I'd be like, 'Fuck, I don't know what Steve Austin does today. I have no interest right now.' So, I finally did get around to doing it," he added. "I approached it like a comic book and turned in my draft." Smith's script opens with a break-in at OSI headquarters, and the theft of experimental medical replacement technology known as 'Bionics'. The script then introduces Colonel Steve Austin, a test pilot and astronaut who is about to fly one last mission before retiring from his glittering career, for a quiet life with fiancée Jaime Sommers. The mission goes disastrously wrong, however: Austin's aircraft crashes — "I can't hold her! She's breaking up! She's breaking up!" he calls out desperately, in a snatch of dialogue faithfully retained from the TV opening credits — leaving Austin barely alive, having lost both legs, an arm and an eye. OSI, however, can rebuild him. They have the technology. They have the capability...

Sage, the ruthless woman in charge of OSI, convinces Austin to have his missing parts replaced by Bionics, but during the operation — overseen by Dr Rudy Wells and Sage's subordinate, Oscar Goldman — Sage orders the removal and replacement of his good arm and good eye with Bionic equivalents. Austin is given other enhancements: the badly burned skin on his face is replaced with a sophisticated substance allowing him to morph its shape and colour at will; the skin on the rest of his body is replaced by a bulletproof dermal coating; even his brain is improved by the addition of sophisticated cybertechnology, allowing him to download information instantaneously from a variety of sources. What Austin doesn't know is that he has also been fitted with a failsafe mechanism, allowing OSI to deactivate and even reprogramme him, if there should ever be a reason to do so.

Having grown accustomed to his superhuman strength and physical prowess, Austin is despatched after the Bionics thieves. It emerges that the culprit is Klatch, an early experiment in Bionics who has since gone insane, and is now intent on taking over the world with an army of cyborgs built from human corpses with Bionic parts. Austin is furious that he was never told about Klatch, but the failsafe mechanism means he has no choice but to go after him. After being reunited with Jaime, who was told he had been killed in the crash, Austin follows Klatch to his tropical island lair, where he is taken prisoner, He soon learns that the madman intends to take over the world with the help of a superweapon which can turn oxygen to carbon. As Klatch launches an attack on Washington DC, Austin escapes and battles it out with the android army, only to discover that Jaime has fallen into Klatch's clutches... "It's actually not played for laughs," Smith told New Jersey radio station WHTG-FM shortly after delivering his first draft in September 1996. "It's kind of serious. It's close to *Mission: Impossible* in theme and tone — revamped, but more faithful to the show."

By the time Smith's draft was done, however, *The Six Million Dollar Man*'s chief advocate, Nina Jacobson, had — in true Bionic style — been replaced, by Kevin Misher. "Universal was in a very bad period," Smith told the UK's *Premiere* magazine. "They had switched execs three times. The people I had pitched my story to were gone, [and] when I turned in my story they were like, 'Wait a second, in your story you said there was a Bionic man before Steve.' And I said, 'Yeah, that was the story I was supposed to do.' And they said, 'Then Steve loses his specialness.' 'Specialness? Really?' And so they were like, 'We don't want to make a movie where there was one before Steve.' So they shelved it." In addition, as Smith told Elston Gunn, Misher felt that the script read like a comic book. "And I said, 'Does it? Awesome!' He didn't like that. Him saying it was too much like a comic book... I think he meant as an insult, but I felt it was a compliment." Smith was not invited to write another draft, although he claimed to be satisfied with the script he had written. "When I was finally done with it, I really did like it," he said. "I didn't try to push the edges of the envelope technologically, like inventing shit where they had to craft shots. It was really kind of retro in its 'low-tech' approach."

In the wake of Smith's departure, Universal retained its commitment to the project, which passed into the hands of producer Lawrence Gordon (*Predator*, *Die Hard*). Rumours were rife that *Buffy the Vampire Slayer* creator Joss Whedon was being courted to write another version, but this was never confirmed. By 1999, would-be producer Richard Anderson confirmed to *Dreamwatch* that John Pogue (*US Marshals*) had been working on a new draft. "I hesitate saying too much," he said, "because it's been in development for a long time. But we're at a point where we have a really extraordinarily good script. It's really exciting — [made] for the big screen — and we're in motion to get underway. We have scenes to shape; budgetary considerations." As well as acting as executive producer for Gordon and Lauritt Levin, Anderson confirmed that he had been invited to reprise the Oscar Goldman role, but that "everything else is up for grabs."

Majors, for his part, is under no illusions that he would be offered a major role in any big screen version of the series. "I don't think age would let me do it," he says. "I wouldn't mind doing another reunion movie, that's what I thought Richard was doing. But I have no idea what he is up to. It may be something on his own; maybe a younger version or something. [It] may not include me." Nevertheless, he adds, "If it's a younger guy, maybe I'll get an assistant's job!" Majors is not surprised to learn that Anderson has been offered the chance to reprise the Oscar Goldman role on the big screen. "Oscar's Oscar," he says. "He can't be replaced. He looks the same. The [new] guy better be strong." But who might the studio have in mind for "the new guy"? At one time, the Hollywood rumour mill suggested that Harrison Ford — who had starred in the successful TV-to-cinema translation of *The Fugitive* — might be paid rather more than $6 million to play the inflation-friendly *Six* Billion *Dollar Man*, but this was almost certainly wishful thinking on the part of Bionic fans. Kevin Smith claims not to know who Universal might have considered for the title role while he was writing his script, but said, "That was the period where all they talked about was Matthew McConaughey."

Little more was heard of the project as the new millennium dawned, although on 5 April 2000 it was widely reported that *Shanghai Noon* co-writers Miles Millar and Al Gough were working on a new draft. "They're making it into a comedy and I think the Farrelly brothers are involved," Kevin Smith had told Elston Gunn, referring to the directors of *There's Something About Mary* and *Me, Myself & Irene*. In June, Peter and Bobby Farrelly confirmed their interest to *Entertainment Weekly*, suggesting that Chris Rock (*Lethal Weapon 4*, *Down to Earth*) was considering playing the title role in an entirely new take on the character. "There's this billion-dollar-man battle at an airport, where six of our one-billion [dollar] guys get blown to smithereens," Bobby Farrelly said of the proposed story. "Of course the government reassembles them into one great big six billion dollar man — but they get some parts wrong. Chris Rock would play the not-so-genius baggage guy who gets vaporised in the explosion. When he wakes up (from death), his head is on a six billion dollar body."

Despite the somewhat bizarre — and quite possibly apocryphal — direction the project seems to have taken of late, the film's would-be executive producer and co-star Richard Anderson still claims to be actively involved. "The studio is interested in the franchise," he says. "It doesn't go away, and there must be a reason. [People] in their twenties, thirties and forties remember the show with the same enthusiasm I have." Contrary to reports of a comedy version, Anderson reveals that John Pogue's draft has been fine-tuned, ostensibly to make it more of an adventure movie than an action film. "'High adventure' to me is characterisation, rather than 'action', which is just one fight after another. We're trying to layer our movie. Within the constrictions of what we can do," he adds, "the only thing that I've tried to do in my work is to be thoughtful. I have high hopes for this." ■

Do Panic!

The Movie-Maker's Guide To The Hitchhiker's Guide To The Galaxy

"[Like] trying to grill a steak by having a succession
of people coming into the room and breathing on it."

—Douglas Adams's description of trying to make *The Hitchhiker's Guide to the Galaxy*
movie in Hollywood

*T*he *Hitchhiker's Guide to the Galaxy* is one of the most remarkable and certainly one of the most successful books ever to come out of the great publishing companies of Earth. It is about the size of a paperback book, within which any of over 150 pages can be summoned almost instantly, simply by flicking through it. It comes in a plastic-coated paper cover, upon which the words 'The Hitchhiker's Guide to the Galaxy by Douglas Adams' are printed in large, friendly letters. This is not its story. It is, however, the story of a film — based on the hugely successful book, which itself was based on a moderately successful radio series — which might very well have been made, had the prospect of such a mind-manglingly expensive motion picture not proved so improbable to a bunch of ape-descended Hollywood executives who almost certainly *still* think digital watches are a pretty neat idea.

Famously conceived by a drunken Douglas Adams in a field in Innsbruck, the first *Hitchhiker's* radio series was broadcast by the BBC in 1978, quickly garnering a legion of fans, who dusted off their barely-used radio receivers and eagerly tuned in to a weekly radio series with an enthusiasm rarely seen since the advent of television. What they heard was a bizarre, comedic and peculiarly English science fiction story about Arthur Dent, an ordinary ape-descended life form (human) to whom extraordinary things happen. Firstly, he is surprised when his house (suburban) gets knocked down to make way for a new bypass. Surprise turns to astonishment when, mere moments later, his planet (Earth) gets blown up to make way for an interstellar equivalent. But astonishment cannot adequately describe what he feels when his old friend Ford Prefect reveals himself to be a roving reporter from a small planet somewhere in the vicinity of Betelgeuse and not an out-of-work actor from Guildford, as he usually claimed.

Ford flags down a passing spaceship and rescues Arthur from Earth — which, much to Arthur's indignation, boils away into space — and thus begins a galaxy-trotting adventure during which Arthur will be read poetry by aliens, be picked up by a ship powered by improbability, witness the end of the universe from the vantage point of a fancy restaurant, and possibly learn the Ultimate Answer to Life, the Universe and Everything. Along the way he will meet a two-headed President named Zaphod Beeblebrox, an ancient planet-sculptor named Slartibartfast, a rock star named after an Islington estate agent, a bovine being that wants to be eaten, a paranoid android (*Radiohead* fans take note) named Marvin, and a girl named Trillian (née Tricia McMillan), whom he met at a party once and completely failed to get off with.

As early as 1979, Adams had been approached by a Hollywood producer interested in making a film based on the radio series — interested enough to offer Adams $50,000 for the film rights. What the unnamed producer seemed to want, however, was less a film true to the spirit of *The Hitchhiker's Guide* and more like *Star Wars* with jokes. "We seemed to be talking about different things," Adams told Neil Gaiman, author of *Don't Panic — Douglas Adams & The Hitchhiker's Guide to the Galaxy*, "and one thing after another seemed not quite right." Adams realised that the only reason he was going along with the idea was the money, "and that, as the sole reason, was not good enough (although I had to get rather drunk in order to believe that). I'm sometimes accused of only being in it for the money," he added. "I always knew there was a lot of money to be made out of the film, but when that was the whole thing prompting me to do it... I didn't want to do it. People should remember that." Adams did not regret his decision to turn down the offer. "I was quite pleased with myself for not doing it, in the end," he said. "But I knew that we were doing it for TV anyway at that time."

The BBC-produced television series reunited much of the original radio cast, though they were squeezed into space-age costumes very different from the open-necked shirts and slacks they had worn as vocal actors (apart from Simon Jones as Arthur Dent, who had always worn his dressing-gown to the radio sessions anyway). A resounding success in Britain, the series garnered excellent reviews, new fans and several awards. It was, arguably, too successful, since its popularity seemed to go to everyone's head — especially Zaphod Beeblebrox, who had two heads to begin with — and led to a major falling out between Adams and producer Alan Bell, which scuppered the prospect of a second series.

By this time, *The Hitchhiker's Guide* had already suffered one attempt — "thank heaven, abortive", in Adams's view — to bring it to US screens: ABC Television's proposed version of the BBC series (which had itself proved surprisingly popular when broadcast in America). "It was like every horror story you have ever heard," Adams said of the project. "They weren't really interested in how good it was going to be, they just wanted to do lots of special effects, and they also wanted not to have to pay for them." Thankfully, when the network learned that the cost of the pilot episode would be $2.2 million — rather more, given the punitive exchange rates of the time, than thirty Altarian dollars a day — it abandoned the project, with Adams having only spent a single week hanging around the production office, during which time he was paid four times as much as he had been to write the entire series for radio.

ABC had evidently become interested in a television production of *Hitchhiker's* due to the level of sales in the US not of the first book, which struggled somewhat to find an audience of the size it had enjoyed in the UK, but of the sequel, *The Restaurant at the End of the Universe*, which had made the US bestseller lists. Adams claimed to have no more of an idea why it suddenly became successful than an olive knows how to mix a Pan Galactic Gargle Blaster, but he was pleased with the royalty cheques — or rather *checks* — he received as a result. He was also pleased — or, more accurately, relieved — that ABC's proposed series did not go ahead, since he would not have been involved with the script process and felt that the series would have lost much in translation. "One is told at every level of the entertainment industry that the American audience does not like or understand English humour," he said. "We are told that at every level except that of the audience, who, as far as I can see, love it. It's everybody else, the people whose job it is to tell you what the audiences like; but the people I meet [in the UK], and in the US, who are fans, are very much the same type of people." According to Adams, even the Americans did not want *The Hitchhiker's Guide* Americanised. Audiences in the US, he suggested, were routinely treated as idiots by television programme makers, "and when you've been treated as an idiot for so long you tend to respond that way. But when given something with a bit more substance they tend to breathe a deep sigh of relief and say 'Thank God for that!'"

While the idea of a Hollywood-produced version of *The Hitchhiker's Guide* television series went away, plans for the *Hitchhiker's* film were quietly revived at the suggestion of Adams's friend Terry Jones, a founder member of the *Monty Python's Flying Circus* team, to whose final series Adams had contributed. By 1981, Jones was a respected scriptwriter and director, having co-written and co-directed *Monty Python and the Holy Grail* and *Life of Brian*, and decided to approach Adams with the idea of collaborating on a British *Hitchhiker's* feature film. Adams, who had by then seen the series through its radio, theatre, novel, record and television incarnations, declined to adapt the story a sixth time — "I didn't want to drag it through another medium," he explained, "I was in danger of becoming my own word processor." Adams suggested the creation of an entirely new story, consistent with what had gone before for the sake of the legion of *Hitchhiker's* fans, but self-contained enough to welcome newcomers. "And that began to be a terrible conundrum," Adams admitted, "and in the end Terry and I said, 'It would be nice to do a film together... but let's start from scratch, and not make it *Hitchhiker's*.'" Although nothing came of this proposed collaboration, Jones would later write a novelisation of Adams's computer game, *Starship Titanic*.

Instead, in 1982, Adams went to California with John Lloyd, his co-writer on some episodes of the original *Hitchhiker's* radio series, to write their book *The Meaning of Liff*. It was there that Adams met with Hollywood producers Michael Gross and Joe Medjuck. Former members of *National Lampoon* — a kind of American version of *Monty Python* but with more jokes about tits and bums — Gross and Medjuck were working for producer-director Ivan Reitman, who had scored successes with *Meatballs* and *Stripes*, two comedies starring *Saturday Night Live* alumnus Bill Murray. Columbia Pictures optioned the book for Reitman, signed Adams as co-producer and paid him a mind-mangling amount of money, so large that even Zaphod Beeblebrox could not conceivably have left it in a cab. Whether enthused by the prospect of a *Hitchhiker's* film, or humbled by the sheer size of the advance Columbia Pictures had paid him, Adams moved to Los Angeles to begin working on the script which, he discovered, was like trying to pour a quart of Pan Galactic Gargle Blaster mix into a pint pot.

"The material just doesn't want to be organised," he said later, noting that if the film was 100 minutes in duration, and the first twenty-five minutes dealt with the destruction of the Earth, the remainder of the story would have to be told in seventy-five minutes, which was, of course, impossible. "*Hitchhiker's* by its very nature has always been twisty and turny, and going off in every direction. A film demands a certain shape and discipline that the material just isn't inclined to fit into." At least with radio and television, he noted, he had three hours to play with.

Yet even if Adams could have overcome the problems inherent in adapting three hours of radio material to an hour and a half of film, he and Reitman were in constant disagreement over the direction the script was taking. "It really didn't work out," Adams told *The Onion*, "because once we got down to it, Ivan and I didn't really see eye to eye. In fact, it turned out he hadn't actually read the book before he bought it. He'd merely read the sales figures." After Adams turned in various drafts — which, he admitted, "fell between two stools — they didn't please me, and they didn't please [him]" — Reitman apparently had another, unnamed screenwriter tackle the adaptation, which Adams described as "the worst script I'd ever read. Unfortunately," he added, "it [had] my name on it, and the other writer's, whereas I did not contribute a single comma to it." Adams's discovery that this script which bore his name had been widely circulated was, he said, "rather distressing [since] everyone assumes I wrote it and am therefore a terrible screenwriter." In any event, after an interminable development period — described by Adams as like "trying to grill a steak by having a succession of people coming into the room and breathing on it" — Reitman eventually passed on the project. "I think it really wasn't his cup of tea," Adams explained, "so he wanted to make something rather different. Eventually, we agreed to differ and went our respective ways, and by this time the ownership had passed from him [back] to Columbia, and he went on to make a movie called *Ghostbusters*, so you can imagine how irritated I was by that."

The project remained at Columbia Pictures for several years, during which time the studio continued to renew the option, without ever actively developing the film. Then, in the early nineties, Adams was introduced to Michael Nesmith, a former member of sixties pop group The Monkees. Becoming one of Adams's closest friends, he expressed interest in producing *The Hitchhiker's Guide to the Galaxy* movie in partnership with the author, who would adapt his own story for the screen. Adams even went as far as naming his dream cast for the project: Simon Jones and Stephen Moore reprising their original roles as Arthur Dent and (the voice of) Marvin respectively, Jeff Goldblum as Ford, Michael Keaton as Zaphod, Sean Connery as Slartibartfast and Amanda Donohoe as Trillian. "We had a very good time working on it for quite a while, but I just think Hollywood at that point saw the thing as old," Adams told *The Onion*. "It's been around the block. And basically, what I was being told an awful lot was essentially that science-fiction comedy will not work as a movie, and here's why not — if it could work, somebody would have done it already."

Indeed, for years, accepted wisdom in Hollywood was that science fiction comedy was about as popular as the proverbial fart in a spacesuit. However, the success of Barry Sonnenfeld's *Men in Black*, released in the US in July 1997, proved otherwise. "Suddenly, somebody [had] done it already," Adams noted. "And suddenly, a comedy science-fiction movie that was very much in the same vein as *Hitchhiker's* became one of the most successful movies ever made. So, that kind of changed the landscape a little bit. Suddenly, people kind of wanted it." By this time, however, Nesmith and Adams had dismissed the idea of making the film together. "In the end, we hadn't gotten it to take, so we parted company very good friends, and still are."

Then, in November 1997, when Adams and one-time proposed *Hitchhiker's* feature director Terry Jones conducted a major book tour promoting the novelisation of *Starship Titanic*, Adams revealed that the project had been revived, and that an announcement was imminent. Sure enough, on 6 January 1998, *Daily Variety* reported that Disney affiliate Hollywood Pictures had acquired the film rights to *The Hitchhiker's Guide to the Galaxy*, and that director Jay Roach (*Austin Powers: International Man of Mystery*) was due to direct the film, which would enter production in 1999 for a summer 2000 release. "He's a very interesting fellow," Adams said of Disney's proposed director. "I've now spent quite a lot of time talking to him. The key to the whole thing, in many ways, was when I met Jay Roach, because I hit it off very well with him, and thought, 'Here's a very bright, intelligent guy.'" Bright and intelligent enough to want to keep Adams closely involved with the project, as the writer had been with the development of the radio series, back in 1978. "When I was making the original radio series, it was unheard of to do what I did, because I'd [only] written it," Adams pointed out. "But I kind of inserted myself in the whole production process. The producer/-director was a little surprised by this, but in the end took it in very good grace... I had a huge amount to do with the way the programme developed, and that's exactly what Jay wants me to do on this movie. So I felt, 'Great, here's somebody I can do business with.'"

Despite his initial reservations about having *The Hitchhiker's Guide to the Galaxy* adapted to celluloid — the only medium it has yet to conquer — Adams admitted that the film's on-again, off-again status was frustrating. "Nevertheless," he told *The Onion*, "I feel extremely buoyed by the fact that one can make a much, much, much better movie out of it now than one could have fifteen years ago. That's in technical terms; in terms of how it will look and how it will work. Obviously, the real quality of the picture is in the writing, and the acting, and the directing, and so on and so forth, and those skills have neither risen nor sunk in fifteen years. But at least one substantial area, in how it can be made to look, has improved a great deal." Indeed, Adams was so committed to the project that he packed his towel and moved to Los Angeles in order to be closer to the development process. Shortly thereafter, he confirmed that the storyline of the *Hitchhiker's* movie would encompass only the events of the first novel, but that sequels based on the subsequent books would follow if the film were successful. "Somebody said, and I think quite accurately, that the best source material for a movie is a short story," Adams told *The Onion*. "Which effectively means, yes, it's going to be the first book. Having said that, whenever I sit down and do another version of *Hitchhiker*, it highly contradicts whichever version went before. The best thing I can say about the movie is that it will be specifically contradicting the first book."

By early 1999, Disney had closed the doors of Hollywood Pictures after a string of underperforming releases, and the rights to the *Hitchhiker's* film had been passed on to another of the studio's subsidiaries, Caravan Pictures. However, during a lecture at Carnegie Mellon University in April of that year, Adams revealed that the film was not exactly on the fast track and that the original release date of summer 2000 would probably be pushed back by at least six months. He also admitted that Simon Jones was no longer a possibility for the role of Arthur Dent, and confirmed that British actor and comedian Hugh Laurie was favourite for the role, despite the fact that, although a familiar face to millions in Britain thanks to shows like *Blackadder* and *Jeeves and Wooster*, he was virtually unknown to cinema audiences in the US. All that changed with the release of *Stuart Little*, which became the biggest hit of the 1999/2000 Christmas season and turned its male lead, a somewhat bewildered Hugh Laurie, into a box-office star. Roach subsequently told the UK's Teletext service that Laurie was still Adams's "favourite choice" for the role of Arthur Dent, but added: "Casting for the movie will be international. We would cast Ford Prefect as an American. Zaphod Beeblebrox could be Jim Carrey or Bruce Willis. Someone big."

Unfortunately, Disney evidently wanted "someone big" to rewrite the script, and decided that Josh Friedman (*Chain Reaction*) was the perfect writer to take it on. Delivered to Disney in March 2000, and leaked to the internet three millionths of a second later, Friedman's draft truncated the story into two hours, preserved the overall plotline of Arthur Dent's part in Zaphod's quest for "The Ultimate Answer to the Ultimate Question. Wait... Actually... the Ultimate Question to the Ultimate Answer. Never mind", added in an uncomfortable romance between Arthur and Trillian, a nonsensical night club scene presumably included to tie up some loose ends, and some gigantic space battles with "large black spider-shaped battle machines" and "Vogon launching hives", doubtless designed to sell a few toys. Somehow, in the course of all this, Friedman managed to suck out most of *Hitchhiker's* humour.

Perhaps understandably, Friedman's script was greeted by *Hitchhiker's* fans with much the same appreciation as might be afforded to a new collection of Vogon love poetry. "A terribly disjointed, incomprehensible, and frustrating mess that was never as humorous or fun as it was aiming to be," one veteran internet-based script reviewer wrote, admitting that they had not read the book. "I really wanted to enjoy the screenplay," the critic continued. "But despite its sporadic wit I never became involved in the comedy and never cared what happened next." Another internet-based reviewer, who *had* read the book, was no more impressed: "I can safely say that this is the worst adaptation from book to screenplay that I've read/heard/seen in my entire life. Everything that makes [*Hitchhiker's*] enjoyable is completely stripped away... From a *HHGTTG* fan perspective, it captures almost nothing from the books. From a movie fan perspective, it's an incomprehensible, difficult to read/sit through screenplay that cries out for many rewrites to come."

Adams was sufficiently moved by the hostile on-line reaction to the leaked script to comment on the Friedman draft, describing it to the website Slashdot.org as "a version of the screenplay that got leaked, and which people didn't like very much. There is a whole story to be told about that script and the role it played in the politics of the development process," he added, "but now is not the time and maybe there won't ever be a time." In any event, Friedman was asked to take a hike and, once again, Adams himself was invited to take on the role of screenwriter, delivering a new draft three months later. "I finished and delivered this new draft last week," he told the website *slashdot.org* on 21 June 2000, "and it's suddenly really working in a way that no previous version really did. It's a very hard circle to square," he added, "that it should on the one hand be true to the spirit of *Hitchhiker*, and that on the other hand it should work as a structured movie with a beginning, a middle, and an end, and character motivation and so on. Well, I think we've finally got there, after all these years."

Adams also expressed his belief that the story's peculiar Englishness was one of the aspects of the book that made it difficult to translate in Hollywood terms. "Arthur may not seem like much of a hero to Americans," he said. "He doesn't have stock options, he doesn't have anything to exchange high fives about round a water-cooler. But to the English, he is a hero. Terrible things happen to him, he complains about it a bit — quite articulately, so we can really feel it along with him — then calms down and has a cup of tea. My kind of guy!" Adams explained that his latest draft had encapsulated Arthur Dent's essential qualities — whether Americans like it or not. "I think that Arthur's non-heroic heroism is now absolutely preserved," he said, "and I'm pleased with the way he works out." Roach evidently agreed; within a few days, Adams had posted a brief but heartfelt message to *douglasadams.com*: "Jay loves it." Disney, however, did not, placing the film into the Hollywood equivalent of the Total Perspective Vortex: turnaround. "The studios see it as an obscure *Monty Python* in space," said Adams, noting that foreign investment was being sought to cover the huge production costs for the film. Roach was equally philosophical. "It's quirky and expensive and it's hard to sell," he admitted to *Entertainment Weekly*. "It's a risk, but *Austin Powers* was rejected at every studio before New Line took it."

The success of Roach's *Meet the Parents*, which opened in October 2000, appeared to revive interest in the *Hitchhiker's* film, but by March of the following year, rumours spread that Roach had quit the project over budget disagreements, and that *Hitchhiker's* had a new guide in the shape of French film-maker Michel Gondry, director of the Charlie Kaufman-scripted *Human Nature*. Not so, said Roach, "unless there's an elaborate conspiracy I'm not aware of. I'm currently working with Douglas on new strategies and approaches for how to get the movie made," he told *Inside.com* and *SFX Network*. "It's a tricky balance between faithfulness to his original, wonderfully out-there material, and the studio's need to justify the budget." Roach, who had recently signed a production deal with Twentieth Century Fox but continued to develop *The Hitchhiker's Guide to the Galaxy* at Disney, also denied that the budget had hit or even surpassed the $100 million mark. "The budget was never set at $120 million, or even estimated at that," he stated. "[It's] closer to $80 million."

It is a sad irony that, after twenty years in the Hollywood system, the *Hitchhiker's* film was at its closest to production when Douglas Adams died suddenly of a heart attack in May 2001, shortly before his fiftieth birthday. In June, Roach admitted that this was "a tragedy for the project", adding, "It's a little bit up in the air because we were all looking forward to doing it with Douglas... [but] we're still fighting for it." Meanwhile, Adams's literary agent Ed Victor announced the publication of a posthumous volume, collecting the author's unpublished work, including the screenplay Adams had spent so many years writing, and rewriting.

Until his death, the fact that *The Hitchhiker's Guide to the Galaxy* continued to draw interest, whether it be from fans or Hollywood studios, mystified Adams. "All I know is that I worked very hard at it, and I worried very much about it," he told *The Onion*. "And if ever there was an easy way of doing something, I would find a much harder way to do it. And I suspect that the amount that people have found it [enjoyable] is not unrelated to the amount of work I put into it. That's a simplistic thing to say, but it's the best I can come up with." ∎

Thunderbirds Aren't Go

Why The Live Action *Thunderbirds* Movie Came With Strings Attached

"We really have enough creative people on the crew, so we can't take on another person."

—unnamed *Thunderbirds* film producer to series co-creator Gerry Anderson

"*Five... four... three... two... one... Thunderbirds are go!*" For anyone growing up in Britain in the sixties, these words signalled the beginning of an hour of adventure, excitement, narrowly averted disaster and funny walks, courtesy of Gerry and Sylvia Anderson's *Thunderbirds*, easily the most successful of the Andersons' numerous sixties sci-fi series, which included *Supercar*, *Fireball XL5*, *Stingray*, *Captain Scarlet and the Mysterons* and *Joe 90*.

Filmed in something called 'Supermarionation' — the Andersons' self-styled puppetry technique, combining marionettes and miniature models — the hugely popular series was set in the year 2065, and centred around a secret organisation known as International Rescue, whose *raison d'être* is to keep a constant vigil for danger anywhere in the world, and swoop to advert disaster where possible. The organisation, which operates from a secret base on an island somewhere in the South Pacific, is overseen by former astronaut and self-made millionaire Jeff Tracy. His five sons — Scott, Virgil, Alan, Gordon and John (named after the first five American astronauts in space) — act as field operatives, each in charge of one of the five futuristic rescue craft known as the *Thunderbirds*. Scott, Jeff's eldest son, flies *Thunderbird 1*, a 7,000 mph, swing-wing, rocket-powered flying machine with Vertical Take-Off and Landing (VTOL) capabilities; Virgil pilots *Thunderbird 2*, a huge green aircraft which ferries pods containing a wide variety of sophisticated vehicles — including *The*

Mole, a mobile drill, and *The Thunderizer*, a laser cannon — to danger zones; former racing driver Alan Tracy pilots the orange spacecraft *Thunderbird 3*; while youngest son Gordon is Virgil's co-pilot, and also commands the yellow submarine *Thunderbird 4*, conveyed to disaster areas by *Thunderbird 2*; finally, John mans the space station *Thunderbird 5*, from which vantage point he can detect disaster before it happens.

Although the year 2065 has more than its fair share of natural disasters, an equal number are man-made, usually at the hands of The Hood, a tyrannical villain with mysterious hypnotic powers who seeks to destroy International Rescue — after first learning the secrets of its *Thunderbirds* craft. Assisting the brothers are a diverse assortment of supporting characters: Brains, the bespectacled genius whose scientific skills are in direct contrast to his social skills; Lady Penelope Creighton-Ward, International Rescue's rich, elegant and glamorous London agent, who is chauffeured around in her pink, gadget laden six-wheel Rolls Royce (registration number FAB 1) by Parker, a Cockney ex-criminal whose nefarious skills are often called upon to help the Tracy brothers out of a sticky situation; Kyrano, Jeff Tracy's loyal manservant, whose fraternal relationship to The Hood renders him vulnerable to the villain's hypnotic powers; and finally, Tin-Tin, Kyrano's daughter, an electronics expert who works with Brains.

When *Thunderbirds* concluded in 1966 after thirty-two hour-long episodes, International Rescue was not yet ready to shut its doors, and the Tracy brothers subsequently starred in two two-hour feature films written by Gerry and Sylvia Anderson: *Thunderbirds Are Go!* in 1966, and *Thunderbird 6* two years later. The Andersons eventually left the puppets behind, however, in favour of live-action series such as *Space:1999*, whose cast — including Martin Landau and his real-life wife (and *Mission: Impossible* co-star) Barbara Bain — was often accused of acting that was more wooden than the *Thunderbirds* puppets. Despite a return to puppetry with the 1983 sci-fi series *Terrahawks*, Anderson never repeated the success of *Thunderbirds*, which spawned a Japanese-made cartoon update, *Thunderbirds 2086*, in 1986, while the original series continued to enjoy periodical revivals as each new generation of children discovered the joys of Supermarionation — most notably in 1991, when repeats of the show achieved unprecedented ratings and a Tracy Island playset became one of the fastest-selling toys in history;

and 2000, when the first DVD releases appeared.

More frustrating for Gerry Anderson — now an MBE and, in his seventies, still taking an active interest in the television industry — was the fact that, when *Thunderbirds* was first mooted as a big budget feature film in the early nineties, the show's creator was offered no role in its development. Small wonder that Anderson sounds bitter when he speaks about the project. "I was approached for the possibility of my being a consultant on the picture," he told *SFX*, "and I met the producer, who wrote to me after a couple of days, saying, 'Lovely to meet you Gerry, but you know we really have enough creative people on the crew, so we can't take on another person,' which I thought was about the biggest insult that could be made. They come to me because I made the show and invented it, and the moment we talk about going into production, they talk about a writer — and, worse, an American writer... who was immediately sent to London to watch all the episodes because he hadn't seen the show." The writer in question was *Chicken Run* scriptwriter Karey Kirkpatrick, who takes a unique view of Anderson's objections to him. "My heart goes out to any writer or creator who's being pushed aside," he says, "but if I look at *Thunderbirds*, I could look at it the other way around — where does this British guy get off writing about five American brothers and their American father in a show that's patterned after *Bonanza*, a quintessential American Western? The only two British characters in the whole piece are Lady Penelope and Parker, and it really tries to be American. So it's like, isn't turnabout fair play?"

Kirkpatrick got his break in Hollywood co-writing a 'spec' script for Disney, which, although unproduced, led to credits on *The Rescuers Down Under*, the direct-to-video sequel *Honey, We Shrunk Ourselves* and *James and the Giant Peach*. After working briefly on an unproduced Disney project entitled *Me and My Shadow*, Kirkpatrick wrote a script for Interscope, a US subsidiary of PolyGram, which bought out ITC Entertainment in 1995 for $165 million, thereby acquiring the entire catalogue of Gerry and Sylvia Anderson creations. Of all of them, *Thunderbirds* was the one which PolyGram saw as having feature film potential. Their belief was shared by PolyGram-owned production company Working Title, which inherited the project from Interscope and began seriously developing it in 1997, initially as a computer animated film in the style of *Toy Story*, but later as a live-action, puppet-free production.

Kirkpatrick is the first to admit that he had not heard of *Thunderbirds* when he was first approached to write the feature film adaptation of the classic series. "Interscope called me into a meeting and said, 'We have something we think you'd be really right for,'" the writer recalls. "They said, 'Do you know the *Thunderbirds?*' And I said, 'Yeah, as a kid I loved them,' because I thought they were talking about the American formation flying team! So when they started talking about Lady Penelope and Parker and Supermarionation, I had to come clean and say, 'Okay, stop. I have *no idea* what you're talking about.' I thought, 'That's it, I may as well leave now,' but they said, 'No, that's good, because we need somebody to develop the movie who doesn't know it all.' I think they thought it was good that I wasn't British, and that I wasn't a devotee."

In other words, the things that made Kirkpatrick unsuitable in Gerry Anderson's eyes — his nationality and his ignorance of the series — were the very things that Interscope was looking for: a Hollywood writer who would not allow his reverence for the original show to interfere with his creation of a blockbuster. "Movie executives really don't care if the film stays true to the show," Kirkpatrick told *SFX*, "because in their eyes, it [has] to play in the American market, and subsequently at the world-wide box-office." Thus, the writer was given a copy of a story treatment written by British director Peter Hewitt (*Bill and Ted's Bogus Journey*) and a video cassette of the original pilot episode, and returned the following day with some story ideas. Within a couple of months, Kirkpatrick was in London, developing the script with Hewitt while the latter was in pre-production on *The Borrowers*.

Hewitt had first heard about the *Thunderbirds* film through Scott Kroopf, who had produced *Bill and Ted's Bogus Journey*, and had pursued the project ever since. "I kept my tabs on *Thunderbirds* for years, since the early nineties," he says, "but it was tied up in all sorts of legal problems for ages, and I remember that at one point [*Teenage Mutant Ninja Turtles* director] Steve Barron was interested." Hewitt had been a fan of *Thunderbirds* since the age of four, "and it had the same appeal then as it does as an idea for a movie now — this highly successful astronaut billionaire with his five handsome sons, living in a luxurious sort of 'floating Batcave' in the middle of the South Pacific. I think what kept my interest," he adds, "was a fondness for fifties- and sixties-style futurism." Hewitt pitched his idea to PolyGram president Michael Kuhn in 1996, finished a treatment soon afterwards and then began work on the script. "But that's when Tim Bevan offered me *The Borrowers*, so I met with a bunch of writers to carry on with the script I'd started, and me and Karey Kirkpatrick really hit it off. So I went off to do *The Borrowers* while he did the first draft of *Thunderbirds*."

As part of his research, Kirkpatrick dutifully sat down and watched all thirty-two episodes of the original series, and went to the British Film Institute library to immerse himself in *Thunderbirds* lore. "Pete [Hewitt] and I were thinking, 'There's a lot of really, really rich stuff in here,'" Kirkpatrick noted in 1998, adding that he and Hewitt were being "very diligent about staying as true to the series as we can, while still making it an exciting action movie." That was not to say that there were not aspects of the series which Kirkpatrick knew would have to be altered. "There are some frustrating things in there when you're a writer trying to create a movie for an audience that's a tad more savvy," he admitted. "Like, it's a top secret organisation, and yet the brothers turn up and show their faces to everyone at the rescues. When they leave, they go, 'Now remember, this is secret. Don't talk.' That's not very clever. So it was part of my job, figuring out ways to keep their identities hidden and to really play up the fact that Jeff Tracy's this billionaire who owns an island and has five rich playboy sons that the world thinks are these John F. Kennedy Jr types, born with silver spoons in their mouths, who don't do anything. Nobody knows who International Rescue are. Even the US President doesn't know who they are or where their secret base is."

According to Kirkpatrick, the 150-page first draft of *Thunderbirds* would probably have cost more than *Titanic*. During subsequent rewrites, however, Kirkpatrick and Hewitt managed to reduce both the scale of the story and the extent of the special effects, without diminishing the movie's appeal as an action-adventure. The third draft, dated 24 October 1997, is set in the year 2026, and concerns a plot by The Hood to steal the Earth's atmosphere on behalf of archvillain Thaddeus Stone, who is dying after twenty years of self-imposed exile on his failed Moon colony. As Hewitt explains, "We took the idea that [because] Jeff Tracy was always so secretive about the technology, the worst thing that could happen to International Rescue would be that somebody steals the technology to destroy the world. So it was taking his worst fear and using it in the most dramatic way. We had a bad guy who lived on the Moon, who had constructed a machine that would suck the atmosphere off the Earth and turn the Moon into a little world for him to live on. But the final power source that he needed for the machine was the one that Brains had invented for Tracy Island, so his agenda was to find Tracy Island and steal the power core, and then destroy the world." Says Kirkpatrick, "That whole Moon plot was all Pete's idea, and I thought that was really clever. And together we came up with this really interesting character called Thaddeus Stone, who talked with a computerised voice, like Stephen Hawking, and wore an exoskeleton because his muscles had atrophied after being on the Moon, so he moves like a puppet."

The story opens as a dozen scientists are abducted from Washington's newly opened World Science Center by The Hood; the building promptly explodes, burying the President under tons of rubble — only to be rescued at the last minute by *The Mole*. "What we tried to do was have a series of events that felt unconnected," says Hewitt, "so you were introduced to International Rescue doing what they do, and then it turns out that they're are all small parts of the bad guy's plan, and it all fits together. So it began with the kidnap of twelve top scientists who were all then taken to the Moon, and they were all going to be forced to work together to achieve his mad dream." A few disasters later — including an experimental atomic-powered airliner, the Skythrust, crashing into the face of Big Ben — Thaddeus Stone's dastardly plan is thwarted, the world is saved, and even Brains finds romance. "It was an absolutely unruly piece of storytelling," says Kirkpatrick, "because I had these objectives: we had to see the *Thunderbird* craft in action, so we needed set pieces in space, underwater, and on the ground; and Pete wanted to see Tracy Island, and Lady Penelope in FAB 1... There was just a whole list of things that I had to accomplish."

Eventually, even Kirkpatrick felt that the scope of the script was overambitious, especially as the intention was to create a franchise which would have room in sequels for the ideas squeezed out of the first film. "The story was so big and so unruly, I said to Pete, 'I know you're not going to like this, but we have a sort of convoluted plot here; maybe we should simplify it, so that the villain is [just] The Hood. He's trying to steal International Rescue's secrets and reveal their identities, because there's this group of nefarious characters, and he'll get a lot of money if he brings this to them, [so] they can perform their dastardly deeds without International Rescue showing up. And I made this whole case, because my point was that structurally, the threat was not direct. So I came up with something really simple, and Pete said, 'You know what? You're right. This feels really right.' And then we pitched it to Tim Bevan, and he said, '*What!?* The Moon/atmosphere-sucking thing is the best thing you've got!' But it was clear it was going to be hugely expensive."

One positive effect of Kirkpatrick's efforts to tone down the action in the script was to place a greater emphasis on character. "The subplot, or character plot, was Alan being a bit of a loose cannon and deciding to quit the organisation because his father's always yelling at him," Hewitt recalls. "In the opening scene he takes an enormous risk and doesn't communicate properly with Scott — I think Scott told him to abandon a certain part of the rescue and Alan thinks he can do it, and he does. But when he gets back to the island and he's being torn off a strip by his father, he says, 'But it worked!' And you get the sense that this is always happening. Jeff's side of it was, 'You have to follow instructions, you have to report back to Scott, he's in charge out there.' I think that was my favourite scene — the one where Alan quits — because it was really quite moving and dramatic. But the film is also about Jeff realising that International Rescue isn't a series of cool machines, it's his sons working together and their talents, and he learns that through them. So there was some very lofty character stuff in there, too, because we had to do the film as though these were real people."

One of the difficulties faced by Hewitt and Kirkpatrick in turning the premise of the series into a potential blockbuster was giving the five brothers — effectively five leading roles — equal status in the story. "If you talk to Gerry Anderson," says Hewitt, "he'll tell you he never knew what to do with John, so he just shoved him up into space the whole time. So we did the same thing — we just threw him up in space — but we tried to make him pretty weird and interesting, a bit quirky and very good at languages, so he had some interesting character traits. But it was Alan's movie, primarily, [because of] the rivalry between him and Scott, and the trouble between him and his father. But there were suggestions of romance between Jeff and Penelope, and the bad guy and Jeff had a past... It had some great stuff in it, like The Hood and Lady Penelope having a fist fight, and it turns out she's a real dirty fighter! You're expecting her to be this Lara Croft-type Ninja, but she's not — she's just a real slugger. I really liked that." Adds Kirkpatrick, "There was another scene in there which Pete really loved, which had a high speed sightseeing train with a glass top, that went around the whole country in an hour, stopping at all the major landmarks. And when it crashed, it had this state-of-the-art crash protection system which is that the whole thing filled with gel, so you'd be suspended, and within seven seconds, it all slowly dissipated. So you'd be breathless for seven seconds, and then you'd be okay. But that sequence had to be cut. I think we used [the idea] in FAB 1 instead."

One of Hewitt's more intriguing ideas was to avoid the trend towards increasingly sophisticated special effects in favour of a sixties-friendly, low-tech approach very much in tune with the *Thunderbirds* television series. "In terms of design," Hewitt explains, "we took a lot from the show and also from [British sci-fi comic strip series] *Dan Dare*, in that it was a push-button, switch-pulling technology. It wasn't run by computers; it was guys with very colourful and enormous machines, using brute strength to fly them around the world with a multitude of different, highly expensive pods." Kirkpatrick saw this 'retro' vision of the future was the perfect way to capture the spirit of the series. "The charm of the show is that it was made in 1965 and its view of the future is 'atomic energy is good' and so on," he told *SFX*. "I remember in one of the first drafts I wrote, somebody picked up this cellphone, because I would try to use little things, and Pete would correct me and say, 'No, everything has got to be big. With big buttons.'" In contrast to most contemporary science fiction, in which the future is depicted as slick, minimalist and miniaturised, "everything in *Thunderbirds* has big switches and big knobs. It's got to be big, bright and colourful machinery. Where other things are high-tech, *Thunderbirds* is designed to be low-tech. I really bought into that angle," Kirkpatrick enthused. "I thought, 'That is what will make this film unique — a big colourful version of the future.'"

Despite Gerry Anderson's fears that an American writer would not be able to duplicate the quirky charm of the television *Thunderbirds*, Kirkpatrick's knowing script, based on Hewitt's story, expertly meshes fundamental elements of the original series with contemporary action-adventures, so that those familiar with International Rescue's long history would feel that the film captured the spirit of *Thunderbirds*, while newcomers would not feel they had missed anything by not having seen the sixties series on which it was based. When Brains says to Scott, "It w-w-worked on paper," referring to an impromptu spaceflight by *Thunderbird 2*, he could easily have been referring to Kirkpatrick's script.

Gerry Anderson, meanwhile, was excluded from the development process, and had little idea of the direction the *Thunderbirds* film was taking. Nevertheless, he told *SFX*, "I knew quite a lot of people who were working on it and all [I know] is what they told me. I know they spent a lot of money, [and] they did a lot of design work, a lot of which I've seen, because some of the people who were on the film have since come to me asking if I wanted to use their services... [But] frankly I didn't think much of them." One look at the colour pre-production sketches prepared by Hewitt's design team suggests that Anderson's view could be more like sour grapes than objective opinion, since the concepts — by Adam Brockbank, Julian Caldo, Temple Clark, Jane Clark and Joe Nimick III — are clearly inspired extrapolations of the original craft, adopting the basic colouring and shape but bringing them into the 'future'. "I was really disappointed to hear that Gerry Anderson didn't like the designs," says Kirkpatrick. "I thought Pete and his team did a great job."

In these artists' renderings, *Thunderbird 1* is a sleek silver swing-wing aircraft with a red nose cone, and the green and frog-like *Thunderbird 2* is slightly more detailed than its predecessor, with extra aerofoils and jet intakes. The bright red *Thunderbird 3* takes the original's shape, refines it, but also adds extra technology, while the yellow *Thunderbird 4* submersible is broken into two separable stages: a rear section with fins and the primary thrusters, and an opening front section containing the cockpit and various exterior underwater apparatus. The orange and white *Thunderbird 5* is typically unaerodynamic, being built for outer space, and is covered with communications antennae and solar panels. "The idea was that when you look at them, if you know *Thunderbirds*, you'd go, 'Wow, that's *Thunderbird 2*,'" says Hewitt. "But then when you look at the original *Thunderbird 2*, having seen the new one, it looks like a Model 'T' Ford. The new designs make the old ones look old-fashioned." The artists' designs were scanned into a computer, and Peter Chiang — visual effects supervisor for Hewitt's *The Borrowers* — produced a short CGI sequence of each of the *Thunderbird* aircraft flying, and *Thunderbird 4* plunging into the water. "They looked terrific," enthuses Hewitt.

Costume designs were more radical, with each of the Tracy brothers being given flight-suits, spacesuits and uniforms more in keeping with the times. But in all the sketches featuring International Rescue personnel, the faces of the characters betrayed no hint about the casting of the film. Nevertheless, rumours were rife in UK, most notably in the British tabloids, which claimed at various times that such real-life sibling actors as the Baldwins (Alec, Stephen, William and Daniel) and McGanns (Paul, Mark, Stephen and Joe) would portray the Tracy brothers (or the majority of them at least). Dismissing talk of the Baldwin brothers as "absolute rubbish," *Thunderbirds* co-creator Sylvia Anderson told *SFX*, "If you look at the Tracy brothers, they don't look alike, do they? And we have some lovely young actors now who could really do a good job . . . I would do a huge casting session," she added. "I'd do a campaign to find people who would be absolutely right." Gerry Anderson also felt that unknown actors were the answer. "It's a very difficult picture to cast," he noted, "because how many leads are there? There's Lady Penelope, there's Parker, there's Jeff Tracy, there's the five brothers, there's Brains. Normally you'd spend $20 million on Tom Cruise and that's your lot. I think if the film's ever made," he added, "frankly I would go for, in the main, unknowns. In that way, you could get five Tracy brothers who you could believe were brothers." The producers, however, were not ready to gamble tens of millions of dollars on unknowns. "We did some preliminary searches for the Tracy brothers," Kirkpatrick reveals. "I wrote the part of Gordon for Steve Zahn, who was incredible in *That Thing You Do!* and *Out of Sight*. And when they were shooting *Saving Private Ryan* [in England], Pete went and met with Matt Damon, who had just done *Good Will Hunting*, which hadn't come out yet. They talked to him about playing Alan, and he was interested, but the studio said, 'No, we want Leonardo DiCaprio.' And of course, within a year, *Good Will Hunting* came out, and they approached Matt Damon again, and he was booked."

Although actresses as varied as Joanna Lumley and Liz Hurley were reportedly shortlisted to play Lady Penelope, Gerry and Sylvia Anderson both share the belief that British actress Kristin Scott Thomas — no stranger to Working Title films, following her supporting role in *Four Weddings and a Funeral* — might be the best choice. "She's fun, but she's class," noted Sylvia. "She could make the thing work." Agreed Gerry, "Somebody like her could be good." Indeed, in

January 1998, *Variety* went as far as to report that Thomas was "inching toward committing to star as Lady Penelope in Working Title Films' *Thunderbirds*, a feature version of the cult British comic book and TV series." "Well, that was true," Hewitt now reveals. "She was going to be Lady Penelope, and Pete Postlethwaite was going to be Parker. And Tim [Bevan] knows Rowan Atkinson from the various movies they've done together, and he was talking to Rowan about being Brains... We never got into official pre-production," he adds, "but we did meet people who were interested in being in the movie, and if we'd got that cast together it would have been great."

One of the more outlandish suggestions made by the producers was that, in order to create a more socially realistic *Thunderbirds*, one of the Tracy brothers should be black. "That would be rather difficult to explain," Sylvia Anderson commented dryly. Nevertheless, says Hewitt, "That's true as well — it definitely came up, as these things do, I suppose." (Kirkpatrick says that this was in response to the success of *Men in Black*, and the producers' desire to put Will Smith in the cast.) Despite such left-field suggestions, however, Sylvia Anderson felt that Bevan and Hewitt were well suited to bringing the *Thunderbirds* to the big screen. "I met the two of them when they were at the studio," she recalled, "and... I thought, 'Yes, these are the right people.' At that time they were starting to do the script and they'd started to build [models]. I went over to California and I saw some of the shots they'd done, and part of the script. When the script was done they were going to ask me to take a look at it. And then the takeover happened with PolyGram," she added, referring to Universal's 1998 acquisition of the company, "and it got lost, really."

According to Hewitt, however, the takeover was not the sole reason for the project's collapse. "The other problem was that we had come up with a script and done all the designs, and we were in the early stages of pre-production, and then PolyGram would read the script and we'd end up having a conversation about whether *Thunderbirds: The Movie* should be made at all, because the show was totally unknown in America. And my thinking was, 'Didn't we have this conversation two years ago?' So they would have to take a punt on *Thunderbirds* as a new idea, which *I* think is a good idea, but to an American, you can see the concerns. And you don't spend $70 to $90 million on a movie unless you're pretty certain it's going to work."

It was these doubts which led to Kirkpatrick's departure from the project. "The way I left *Thunderbirds* was not a pleasant experience," he says, "because I basically had to tell myself I was fired. I was in a meeting with Pete, Tim Bevan, [producers] David Barron and Debra Hayward, where nobody would look me in the eye and tell me I was off the project. We were all sitting there and I walked in, and it was very awkward because clearly the people from Working Title didn't know I was going to be there, and the meeting was to say, 'We think we should get another writer.'" Hewitt and Kirkpatrick had just spent an intensive week polishing the fourth draft so that it could be sent out to actors. But during that week, PolyGram head of production, Michael Kuhn, read the script and declared that it was still missing the 'big idea'. "I thought this was a ridiculous waste of money," Kirkpatrick says, "because we spent the last two drafts polishing *this* idea, so if it was missing the big idea, that's something you solve in an outline. So Pete was saying, 'I think we should send it to this actor or that actor,' and there were lots of cagey looks back and forth, and 'Uh, well, we don't think so, Pete.' And he was like, 'Why not? I think it's really good.' And they said, 'We need to talk.' And I knew instantly, so I had to say, 'Pete, I'm off the picture. That's what they can't quite seem to say. So I'm going to leave the room now, because they want to talk about *writers*, not actors.' And later, Pete and David Barron called and said, 'I would like to apologise on behalf of my *country*.' There were no hard feelings though," Kirkpatrick says gallantly. "I was the first writer on it, and on a movie like this, there was no way I was going to be the only writer."

Working Title subsequently brought in two other writers (one of which was Debra Hayward's husband, Will), who tightened the script. But by this time, even Hewitt had begun to have his doubts about their approach: "Towards the end I was beginning to think that the outer space stuff was the wrong way to go, and had been done, by then, in *Independence Day* and *Armageddon*. I felt we should be trying to do a story more about the organisation — that there was enough [of a story] there, without having to invent a bad guy and his a big machine that's going to destroy the Earth." Ultimately, perhaps, it came down to the fact that the financiers wanted a Jerry Bruckheimer-style approach, whereas Hewitt's style was more akin to Gerry Anderson's. Whatever the reason, Hewitt left the project to make the comedy films *Whatever Happened to Harold Smith?* and, bizarrely enough, (the entirely unrelated) *Thunderpants*. Kirkpatrick, who admits that working with Working Title was the closest to a Hollywood experience he has ever encountered in England, says he saw the handwriting on the wall the weekend after *The Borrowers*, the company's most expensive production, opened to disappointing box-office. "Working Title were very reverential to Pete because he was in the middle of making *The Borrowers*, which they were very hot on," Kirkpatrick explains. "They had huge expectations for that film. And I can tell you, the weekend after *The Borrowers* opened and under-performed, the temperature in the room got so icy cold. And I think that's why they said, 'Wait a minute, what are we doing here? We're about to do this again on something which is a really big risk.'"

Looking back, it is astonishing to see how close the *Thunderbirds* movie came to production before collapsing under the weight of its own budget. "I think they're planning to start shooting this summer, in July," Kirkpatrick had stated confidently in early 1998, noting that the fourth draft — entitled *Thunderbirds: International Rescue* — was the one most likely to be greenlit. Indeed, in February of that year, a London-based production company was engaged by PolyGram Filmed Entertainment to provide concepts for a series of specially-shot 'teaser' trailers, showing International Rescue in action. One such concept depicted *Thunderbird 4* rescuing a small boy who drifts out to sea in a fishing boat; another showed *Thunderbird 3* retrieving a wrench lost by an astronaut working on the Hubble space telescope; a third had *Thunderbird 2* rescuing a cat from a tree. Each of these concepts was designed to focus on the human effect of International Rescue: for instance, in the midst of an earthquake, a child's lost toy is retrieved as part of a bigger rescue effort by *Thunderbird 2*. A second wave of proposed 'teasers' focussed on news footage of each of the five *Thunderbirds* at work, while a third dealt with a pressure group's insistence that the government come clean about its knowledge of the International Rescue organisation. According to the script, 1999 was the prospective release date, with a variety of suggested taglines including 'Stand By

For Action', 'In 1999 Thunderbirds Are Go', 'Cleared for Launch in 1999', '1999 Means No More 911', 'No Risk Too Great, No Rescue Too Small' and 'Protecting the World Since 1999'.

When, in March 1999, Universal renewed its agreement with Tim Bevan and Eric Fellner's Working Title partnership, under which the pair were given the power to greenlight up to five pictures under $25 million, *Variety* noted that, "More expensive projects, such as the upcoming *Thunderbirds*, will have to be specifically approved by Universal." By the time Century 21 arrived, however, Bevan and Fellner seemed to imply that *Thunderbirds* did not figure in Working Title's future plans. "We don't make big action movies," Fellner told *Empire*, while Bevan explained the company's strategy: "We've learned along the way that if we keep the negative costs down, and have some success, then they are going to let us make more oddball projects... We're doing four, five movies at the moment, and the combined negative cost is less than the average cost of a Hollywood movie, so we've got five shots to put out there." Invited to comment for this book about *Thunderbirds*, Bevan was more succinct: "At the present time," he wrote in April 2001, "there is nothing to report on that project."

Today, Peter Hewitt counts himself among the many *Thunderbirds* fans who hope that the proposed film will eventually be the subject of a Universal rescue. "I hope they make it," he says. "I hope that Tim [Bevan]'s still working on it and is still interested in making it. It was great to *nearly* do it, and I think it would have been spot on for all the fans... I could have guaranteed a really great *Thunderbirds* movie for all the fans, and I like to think it would have got a bigger audience too. But I suppose from the point of view of the people who are paying for it, to spend that kind of money on it, they have to be more sure than that." Gerry Anderson, who recently oversaw a CGI-assisted revamp of *Captain Scarlet* for Carlton (the new owners of the ITC catalogue), told *SFX* that, whilst the film rights currently reside with Universal "they may well revert to [Carlton]... and if so, then I think a new series of *Thunderbirds* is on the cards. As an individual," he added, "I think there's no doubt [Carlton] will get the rights back and I believe there's no doubt there will be a new series and a new feature film."

In the meantime, *Thunderbirds* fans everywhere stand by for action. ■

Lost In Space

How *Dead Star* Disappeared Into A Black Hole, Only To Re-Emerge As *Supernova*

"All Hell Is About To Break Loose."

—tagline on the *Supernova* poster

"I t just started off troubled and stayed that way," said co-screenwriter William Malone of MGM's $65 million science fiction thriller *Supernova*, which began life as a 'spec' screenplay Malone wrote under the title *Dead Star*. With five screenwriters (three credited), at least as many directors (none credited), numerous potential lawsuits, and a production history more mysterious and intriguing than anything in the film, *Supernova* may represent the most troubled production of any science fiction film in history.

Released in January 2000, *Supernova* was credited to a director named 'Thomas Lee' — a twenty-first century equivalent of 'Alan Smithee', the pseudonymous name slapped on the credits of dozens of films and TV shows when the real director demands his name be removed. The credited director *should* be Walter Hill, co-producer of the *Alien* series and director of *48HRS.* and *Last Man Standing*. But when *Supernova* disappeared into an acrimonious black hole, Hill jumped ship, and after two more directors (including Francis Ford Coppola) came aboard, it was decided to give credit to the non-existent Mr Lee.

Despite Malone's claim that the film "started off troubled", its conception was, in reality, far less painful than its birth. In 1990, Malone pitched the project to independent producer Ash Shah (*Double Dragon*) of Imperial Entertainment. Then titled *Dead Star*, the film was conceived as a modestly-budgeted, futuristic rescue movie from the team behind Malone's earlier film, the low-budget sci-fi/horror hybrid *Titan Find* (aka

Creature). "I had this idea to take the movie *Dead Calm* and make it a sci-ence fiction picture," Malone explains. "So the original script was about the first spaceship able to use two-dimensional drive, which discovered artefacts from an alien civilisation and was going to bring them back when a whole bunch of things happen. One of the things the crew pick up is a portal to Death, which is a place you can actually go to." The portal, situated on a distant world named Daveros, is actually a sophisticated alien machine known as the 'Thanatron'. "It was capable of reanimating the living and opening a gate to the world of the dead (specifically Hell)," Malone explained. "Over-eager astronauts set the corrosive (to the mind) machine into motion and unwittingly release Satan aboard their ship."

Shah liked *Dead Star* and gave Malone the go-ahead to engage H. R. Giger to produce a series of pre-production sketches, to help secure financing for the film, budgeted at five to six million dollars. As Giger later wrote, "[Malone] had written the story himself, a sort of *Hellraiser* in space, the premise of which is that mankind encounters an alien machine capable of literally taking him to Hell. He had already done some designs for it but he left the actual Prince of Darkness of the Cosmos to me." Says Malone, "[Giger] was going to design the devil, and he came up with some brilliant sketches. I spent ten days at his home in Switzerland, and he was just incredible. It was very cool working with him."

Malone admits he found it difficult keeping the artist's imagination from running away with him. "Amidst the hordes of paintings stacked against black walls, fibreglass *Alien* creatures, and strange furniture, the ideas were flying fast and furious," he recalled. "Quite often Giger would come up with so many great notions that I would have to slow him down so that some of them didn't get lost in the moment." Back in Los Angeles, Malone continued to receive a wide variety of drawings by fax. "Among the things he designed was the 'Shard', the key device to the 'Thanatron', capable of raising the dead; the 'Thanatron' itself, looking like a bundle of decaying organ pipes; and most notably a multifaced Satan with its cloak of living souls. [He also] did two full colour paintings for the production which were used for trade advertisements."

Indeed, although Giger was paid for his concepts, receiving the sum of 10,000 Swiss francs, he heard nothing more until May 1995, when a reproduction of one of his *Dead Star* conceptual paintings turned up in an Imperial Entertainment promotional booklet for a film entitled

Supernova. The image was accompanied by a synopsis of the story which, according to Giger, suggested "a much simplified version of the script which attracted me to the project," without the "heavy supernatural elements of the original." Although Giger was billed as "conceptual designer", Malone's name was absent from the credits, and the artist was given to wonder what direction the film was taking. "If the film finally gets made," he wrote, "I will be curious to see if anything besides my name has been retained. Will the film go *Supernova* or arrive a *Dead Star*? Will I turn out to be the lucky one, or will it be Bill Malone?"

As it turned out, neither of them were lucky. "There was a lot of heat about [the script]," says Malone, "but nobody would step up to the plate and make it. After that, I lost track of it until I heard that United Artists had bought it. They brought in a lot of other writers to work on the picture," he adds, referring to credited co-screenwriters David Campbell Wilson (*Tomorrow Never Dies*) and Daniel Chuba, and uncredited contributors Cathy Rabin and Thomas Wheeler, "and then it sort of mutated into something else." As Chuba explained to *Cinefantastique*, "Bill Malone is an excellent writer and did some great work on it. We liked where it was headed and suggested some significant changes." Chuba himself wrote four successive drafts of the script, which was then perceived as a potential directorial début for Jamie Dixon, one of Chuba's partners in Hammerhead Films, a special effects company whose credits include *Batman Returns*, *Spawn* and *Titanic*.

By the fourth draft, however, the script's budget meant that Dixon's involvement as director was no longer considered feasible. "We were clearly over the $20 million mark no matter how we sliced it," Chuba explained. "That was the zone in which Jamie could direct the picture. There was no sense putting the pressure on him and having his career live or die on this film. It could become a story of a first-time director being given too much rope. So he moved into the producer role with me." According to Chuba, United Artists' absorption into MGM might have left the film in limbo for several months had UA president Lindsay Doran not been such an advocate: "She never saw this as another *Armageddon* or *Lost in Space*. She got the throw-back to earlier science fiction — a thinking man's science fiction, like *Planet of the Apes* or *The Twilight Zone*."

Doran, however, felt that the script still needed work, and brought in David Campbell Wilson to write a new draft. "It's hard being rejected,"

Chuba subsequently admitted. "You have two choices: fight with them and gauge their resolve — do they know what they want, or are they just grasping? Or, being new at this, you could say, 'It's their money. Their movie. They've done this before. They made a good case. Let's see where it goes.'" Chuba evidently chose discretion as the better part of valour, staying on as producer as Wilson rewrote the script yet again. "We didn't feel we were making artistic compromises," Chuba said. "In some ways they were making the film more castable. It was a pretty tight little scary movie, but it wasn't character driven. They wanted the characters more fully rendered, and David Wilson came in and did that."

After reportedly considering former MGM executive Joe Nimzicki to direct, the studio found a more suitable candidate in Australian Geoffrey Wright (*Romper Stomper*). Reporting in early 1997 that the film was due to enter production as early as the summer, *Dreamwatch* stated that *Supernova* was "centered on Jack Conner and Dr Erin Rider, commander and chief medical officer of the deep space medical rescue ship, the *Nova 17* — essentially an emergency room in space. When the ship picks up a distress call from many light years away, the only way to attempt an effective rescue is to squeeze through two-dimensional space, flattening the entire ship and its crew and slicing through three-dimensional space like a razor. Appearing on the other side of the galaxy, the crew find the brooding hulk of the *Imperion*, an ageing cargo vessel, about to be sucked into a black hole formed by the collapse of a star. The sole survivor of the sinking ship, Anton Mason, comes aboard the *Nova 17* with a terrifying story about what transpired on his own vessel. But can Mason be trusted, or is he hiding a secret more horrible even than the hellish story he tells?"

As pre-production continued through late 1997 and into 1998, the story underwent as many mutations as the Flubber-like substance found on the *Imperion* — renamed *Nightingale 229* in the filmed version. A mere five weeks before principal photography was due to commence, Wright quit the project over a script dispute, leaving the film hanging in the balance. "We liked his sensibility," a diplomatic Dan Chuba told *Cinefantastique*, "but suffice to say, at the end of the day, his vision of the film was not the version the studio wanted to do. He was very aggressive about the way he wanted to shoot it," he added, noting that one of Wright's more outlandish suggestions was to shoot the entire film in zero gravity. With a potential Screen Actors Guild strike threatening to shut down production, MGM executive Jeff Kleeman — encouraged by actor James Spader (*Crash*), already cast in the leading role — signed Walter Hill to take over. "Jeff deserves credit for putting a coalition together to get Walter Hill," Chuba noted. "He got us all to agree to that, and see the merits. Otherwise, it could have gone down in flames." As Hill told *Cinefantastique*, "It was kind of unusual. Very simply, they called me and I read the script. Obviously, I wouldn't have done it if I hadn't liked the story, but at the same time I felt it could be told in a really different way. So I gave them my version and said if we could do that, I'd be willing."

To those working on the film, part of Hill's rationale in changing the direction of the film from an exercise in X-rated horror to a PG-13 psychological thriller seemed to be to distance it from his own earlier production, *Alien*. Despite the fact that he had described *Supernova*'s story as "spaceship gets an emergency call from a mysterious circumstance and in the process of investigating the emergency finds themselves enmeshed in a desperate, life-and-death situation", he insisted that it was "kind of the opposite of *Alien*" due to the intelligence of its chief antagonist: "The *Alien*... kind of monster is incredibly frightening because it was the lowest of all possible life forms. It only wanted to eat and reproduce — it had no other ambitions." In *Supernova*, however, "the stranger on board the ship is at the opposite end of the spectrum; you're dealing with an intelligence that's probably far beyond the powers of human beings."

Hill also sought to bring the film's 'backstory' into the present, so that past events which the audience learns about during the course of the film in earlier drafts would, instead, be experienced first-hand by the crew of the *Nightingale 229*. "The way they had set it up before, most of the key players in the cast knew about the backstory and therefore it was being explained to the audience," Hill explained. "It seems to me all they did was sit around and talk about it. I said in one of the meetings, 'I don't want to make a movie about what happened ten years ago.'" Hill and Chuba worked on yet another version of the story, giving pages of notes to David Wilson who, according to Chuba, "tirelessly and enthusiastically took our new direction and did another draft of the script with five weeks to go", while Cathy Rabin was drafted in to flesh out the characters.

With sets already built and almost all of the cast in place, however, such eleventh-hour tinkering put the crew — including production designer Marek Doborowolski (*The Craft*), creature designer Patrick

Tatopoulos (*Independence Day*, *Godzilla*) and Digital Domain-based visual effects supervisor Mark Stetson (*The Fifth Element*) — under added pressure. However, as Tatopoulos explained, "I showed up with my concepts [prepared] for Geoffrey, and I stepped into the room and right then I could tell what I did before wouldn't be right for Walter... Geoffrey is a young, long-hair, rebel kind of guy. Walter has all this experience in the business. He's a different character altogether, and part of my work as a designer is understanding the director." Despite the looming start date, Hill ordered sets to be redesigned and rebuilt, for more room to play out the story, and threw out almost all of the storyboards, leading Stetson to call in *The Fifth Element*'s conceptual illustrator Sylvain Despretz. "He called me in and said, 'We have a problem — this film is a complete disaster,'" Despretz recalls. "He asked me to come in to try to unify the design with the work of visual effects. They were in such disarray that they'd agree to anything, so at that point Mark kept some of the artists he wanted to keep, hired his own group and basically took over the office."

Production finally commenced on 13 April 1998, with Angela Bassett (*Strange Days*), Robert Forster (*Jackie Brown*), Lou Diamond Phillips (*The First Power*), Peter Facinelli (*Honest*) and Robin Tunney (*End of Days*) joining Spader on board the *Nightingale 229*. MGM, however, continued to balk at the number of effects shots Hill requested, and cut fully half of them. "The full-blown stage of the [alien] creature was shot, but never shown in the final cut," Tatopoulos told *Fangoria*, noting that Troy (Peter Facinell) was originally intended to transform into a hairless, sleek-skinned, blue-veined and red-eyed creature. "The monster was working real well when we shot it," Tatopoulos added, "but the studio turned around and said, 'We don't recognise the actor and we don't want to go there.' This was way after designs were done and approved by everyone. That was the big frustration. People would have loved our final stage of the creature. When it was taken out of the movie, it didn't make sense."

But MGM had only just begun remaking the movie in its own preferred image, much to the frustration of the film-makers. Out went a complex effects sequence in which Spader performs a nail-biting zero-gravity rescue inside a giant bubble of water. Out too went a sophisticated, remotely-operated medical robot in favour of a shuffling humanoid android, dressed in a flying costume, and described by one critic as "a cross between Kryten in *Red Dwarf* and Woody Allen in *Sleeper*." Finally, out went Walter Hill, who spent fourteen weeks in the editing room and ten weeks supervising special effects before jumping ship over yet another dispute with the studio. "Walter's vision for the film was different from the studio," a tactful David Wilson told *Premiere* at the time. "It's a shame that couldn't be resolved during production."

A disastrous test screening followed Hill's departure. MGM called in director Jack Sholder (*The Hidden*) to re-edit Hill's footage, and tested the film again. "I'm told a lot of what I did stayed in," Sholder commented to *Fangoria*. "I don't think much remained of [Walter's edit]. We pretty much re-cut every scene in the movie." Sholder also reinstated footage showing Robert Forster's character being grotesquely distended during hyperdrive. "His body was extending everywhere," Tatopoulos explained. "He had a costume, and different stages of the suit, and CGI would blend [them] together." Hill cut almost all of the sequence, evidently feeling that it did not work. "I disagreed with that," Sholder added. "Hill also said there was no way Forster's character could live [through the accident], which I did not agree with either." Sholder also altered two other significant scenes, including the ending, in which Peter Facinelli's character comes back to life after a massive explosion. "That always seemed laughable to me, and I planned to reshoot it," Sholder explained. "It never seemed to bother any of our test audiences, though." Sholder also attempted to salvage the ridiculous robot, by adding some dialogue in post-production to explain the robot's bizarre appearance and shuffling gait: "The Captain's big on twentieth century cultural artefacts, so we did him up as a World War One fighter pilot. We call him 'Fly Boy.' The story is that he crashed and burned, that's where he got his limp." As Sholder explained, "It looked and moved so stupidly, so I introduced it with a line implying that the crew made it look foolish to provide comic relief on board. In this way, I hoped to imply that the film-makers were in on the joke."

When Sholder's version tested badly, MGM allegedly met with Hill to discuss his proposal for $5 million worth of re-shoots. Unwilling to throw good money after bad, the studio balked and Hill walked. One by one, potential release dates disappeared into a black hole, until MGM board member Francis Ford Coppola was called upon to intervene, spending a further $1 million on a re-edit of his own. "I hope that my experience in the film industry has helped improve the picture and rectified some of the problems that losing a director caused," he said in a statement. One of Coppola's major contributions was a bizarre attempt to accentuate the romantic relationship between James Spader and Angela Bassett by digitally placing their heads on the naked bodies of Peter Facinelli and Robin Tunney in their zero-gravity love scene — despite the fact that Bassett is black and Tunney is white. "I suppose this gives new meaning to the term 'colourisation'," Sholder said wryly.

In the event, Coppola's cut did not test any better than the Hill and Sholder cuts; neither did it secure the hoped-for PG-13 rating, and the film was re-cut yet again. Finally, with no pre-release screenings and little publicity — even the final press materials feature only two direct quotations, both from chief science consultant Dr Jacklyn R. Green — *Supernova* was released in the US on 17 January 2000, almost two years late. Opening at a dismal $6.7 million, the film went onto gross just $14 million overall — not even a quarter of its production cost, even without prints and advertising. The critics were similarly unimpressed, with *Entertainment Weekly* describing it as "a frustrating jumble of logic leaps, impenetrable technobabble, rote action, and not one distinctive F/X piece." This latter remark was particularly surprising, given that journalists at a Digital Domain press junket in February 1999 were shown almost forty minutes of what one attendee described as "absolutely cutting edge, moving-camera effects shots", while Digital Domain spokesman Bob Hoffman told *Premiere*, "We delivered our work on *Supernova* on time and on budget. More important, we're really proud of the work we did."

With the credited director as imaginary as the premise of the film and Walter Hill's silence guaranteed as part of his severance deal with MGM, the full story behind *Supernova* may never be known. However, while the director's commentary track on the *Supernova* DVD is understandably missing, the deleted scenes included on the disc shed some light on what was lost, among them an intriguing sequence showing what looks like a giant baby. "It was a regressing character, where [Lou Diamond Phillips's character] turns back into a foetus, but his body stays [the size of] an adult," Patrick Tatopoulos revealed. "It was cool, but it got cut. I guess the studio didn't want a full-blown make-up effects film. They tried to make it more of a hip, sexy movie in space, while Walter wanted to do something more grotesque, strange and ultimately disturbing."

Indeed, a more grotesque, strange and ultimately disturbing story than the making of *Supernova* is hard to imagine. ∎

Island Of Lost Souls

The Strange And Terrible Story Behind Richard Stanley's *The Island Of Dr. Moreau*

"I look about me at my fellow men, and I go in fear. I see faces keen and bright, others dull or dangerous, others unsteady, insincere; none have the calm authority of a reasonable soul."

—from *The Island of Doctor Moreau* by H. G. Wells

I t can scarcely be said that any of the horror stories to come out of Hollywood in the past century come close to matching the real-life horror of the making of *The Island of Dr. Moreau*. For Richard Stanley, writer-director of the cult horror films *Hardware* and *Dust Devil*, it was a nightmare that began with a dream. Stanley had been virtually a lifelong fan of H. G. Wells's classic novel, in which a ship-wrecked sailor washes up on a South Sea island only to find it populated by ghastly human/animal hybrids created by early genetic genius Moreau. But the director felt that neither of the previous cinematic adaptations — *The Island of Lost Souls*, Erle Kenton's subversive 1933 adaptation starring Charles Laughton, and Don Taylor's execrable 1977 version with Burt Lancaster and Michael York — had done justice to Wells's prophetic fable which, originally published in 1896, was first banned for being blasphemous and later repudiated by its own author. Accordingly, Stanley set out to try his own hand at turning one of his favourite books into a screenplay worthy of both its subject matter and its illustrious history. He succeeded.

While still embroiled in legal and political wrangles over his second feature, *Dust Devil*, which had foundered on the rocks when British independent Palace Pictures had gone down in stormy financial waters in 1990, Stanley completed a screenplay that, over the next four years, would become one of the hottest talent-magnets in Hollywood.

Firstly, Oscar-winner Marlon Brando agreed to take the title role, his commitment to the project seemingly as much due to his liking for Stanley as for the script itself. Brando fan Val Kilmer, revelling in his newly-minted box-office status following the success of *Batman Forever*, was next up to bat, taking the role of Edward Prendick, the shipwrecked civil rights lawyer who becomes the first outsider to discover the horrific nature of Moreau's work on the island. Kilmer was followed by an impressively credible and eclectic supporting cast: *Northern Exposure* star Rob Morrow in his first major film role; Fairuza Balk (*Things To Do In Denver When You're Dead*); Ron Perlman (*The City of Lost Children*); Hammer *femme fatale* Barbara Steele; and Stanley film veteran William Hootkins (*Hardware*).

For Stanley and New Line, the film's financiers, all the ingredients seemed perfect. And yet, just as Dr Moreau's genetic experiments had succeeded only in creating life, not humanity, so the beautiful creature Stanley and his fellow believers had envisioned began to change, shedding the man who had devoted four years of his life to the project after only four *days*, and rapidly mutating into a lumbering, artless, soulless vegetable that it might have been kinder to destroy. As Moreau himself might have asked as he stood among the ruins of his experiments, "What went wrong?"

According to Stanley, the problems with *The Island of Dr. Moreau* were evident long before even a single frame of film had been shot. Just weeks before shooting was scheduled to begin in Queensland, Australia, Stanley was suddenly informed that Kilmer, who had just been served with divorce papers by wife Joanne Whalley-Kilmer, wanted his commitment to the project — and therefore his role, the film's lead — reduced by forty per cent. "He really put me in an impossible situation," Stanley recalls bitterly. "You spend years loving a book and then somebody says 'Well, chop [these scenes].' I said 'You're crazy, I can't do it, I'm not going to lose them.' And that all helped to push me down the plank towards the point where they shoved me off."

Faced with having to reduce his leading man's screen time by an impossible degree or lose his star altogether, Stanley hit upon the idea of switching Kilmer's role with Morrow, who had been cast as Montgomery, Moreau's assistant on the island, a part not only some forty per cent smaller than that of Prendick but arguably more suited to Kilmer's personality. In his place, Rob Morrow would be moved into the role of Prendick. "It was a vain triage suggestion that didn't save me," Stanley explains, "based on the presumption that if Kilmer walked out, it would be perceived as my fault. Essentially, I had to find a way of keeping Val on board. I couldn't have him walk, because if he did, he would have probably collapsed the project. And that would have been the end of me anyway." Kilmer agreed to the compromise, but the famously difficult actor — who had previously clashed with *Tombstone* director George P. Cosmatos and whom *Batman Forever* director Joel Schumacher called "childish and impossible" — was still not satisfied and he resolutely refused to give his time to even the most perfunctory rehearsal. "His line was always just, 'Be there for me and I'll give you the moment'," Stanley says, "but a lot of the other cast members *need* to rehearse to know what they're doing."

The problem was exacerbated by the scheduling of the shoot itself, which allowed no time for even a table reading of the script. "It was all stitched up in such a way that there was no available time," Stanley recalls. "Brando wasn't due to arrive until later, so people would turn up on set, and that would be the first time you'd meet them. The first time I'd seen Fairuza [Balk] in a number of months was in the middle of a hurricane on a beach at Cape Tribulation, and it was like, 'Hi, how are you doing? Action!'" Worse still, Kilmer himself failed to materialise at all for the first two days of shooting, a stunt apparently so typical of the actor that an agent at Creative Artists Agency, which represents both Kilmer and Stanley, allegedly told the director that "every Kilmer project loses the first two days". On the third day, when Kilmer did finally show, it was clear that not only did he not know his lines, he did not even appear to know which scene he was supposed to be in. Although one actor on the set recalls that Kilmer recited "lines written for other characters, in other scenes," Stanley remembers it different-ly: "He'd do [the lines], but he'd throw it all away.

"So there you are," says Stanley, recalling those first, shipbound scenes, "tossing around in the sea; nobody else in the cast knows what's coming and everyone's trapped in this situation where the best you can do is stick multiple cameras on it — which are all kind of stat-ic — and see what happens. Of course," he continues, "the moment you roll, it [becomes] rushes, [but it's] the equivalent of raw, unrehearsed material, with everyone stumbling into each other and Val saying any-thing. No one knows how to respond to it and everyone's confused. And this fairly miserable material filters back to Los Angeles, [where] everyone watches it and says, 'What's going on here? They're not doing the script!'" As a result, Stanley received a message on the fourth day of shooting saying that he was officially "relieved of his duties." The proj-ect he had spent four years of his life perfecting had been taken away from him, a victim of the very talent his script had attracted in the first place. "That doesn't matter," says Stanley. "The script is just a lure. They don't actually want or need a script to shoot the movie, they need it to draw the talent. Once the talent's on board, the script gets thrown over your shoulder and it's time to do something completely different."

Did Stanley get the feeling that Kilmer was deliberately trying to sabotage the shoot? "Possibly. I think maybe Val does it the whole time, that [he] might always automatically throw his weight around the first few days. I've heard very few reports from *Heat* or *The Doors* — I'm not sure how he responded to Michael Mann or Oliver Stone — but I understand it was much the same with *Tombstone* and [others]." Stanley suggests, however, that if Val had behaved in a similar fash-ion with a more prominent or powerful director, things would prob-ably have been different. "I mean, I'm not sure anyone would have fired Oliver Stone after three days, so I can't help feeling it's more the company's fault than Val's. I feel that I would have been able to contain Val had I had the support of the company behind me. I'm not convinced that New Line ever really understood the script, and I'm not sure anyone ever really tried." Although Stanley shouldered the blame, New Line head Michael De Luca publicly blamed himself. "I didn't give [Kilmer] a strong director," he admitted, "and that was my fault." Stanley also blames De Luca, but for different reasons. "Mike was the one that insisted that I go out to sea on the first day," he explains. "[But] the weather was extremely bad, [the wind] aver-aging thirty or forty knots, and we were tied to a stinking, creaking freighter which gave us no ability to move the camera. It was terribly hard to actually get a shot under those conditions."

Soon after Stanley left the production, Rob Morrow also moved on, escaping to the safety of a commitment elsewhere. "One of the reasons that Rob left was [that he'd] done his homework," says Stanley. "[He had] read the Wells novel and the script, and was prepared to try quite hard. In the pathetic rushes that did leak out, Rob *is* trying quite hard, which I found quite a shame because he would potentially have been a good Prendick had he actually been allowed to deliver a performance." Stanley suspects that Morrow saw that the production was doomed. "The first few days were a relentless nightmare; nothing was going right," he says. "And it was also plain that Val was going to carry the day and [that] none of us had any chance of countermanding him. Rob was still a lightweight in terms of his box-office value, as were Fairuza Balk [and] myself. We were all basically little people."

With Stanley having left *The Island*, closely followed by Morrow, New Line needed not only to find a new director but a new leading man. Filling the former vacancy was veteran film-maker John Frankenheimer (*The Manchurian Candidate*), who agreed to step in at short notice — as he had previously done on *The Birdman of Alcatraz* and *The Train* — on the proviso that he would be allowed to alter the story. "I wasn't really excited about doing it," he told *Cinescape* at the time. "I did it because I liked the idea of working with Marlon Brando. And I thought it could represent a very commercial movie for me, which I need at this point in my career." Morrow's role, meanwhile, would be filled by British actor David Thewlis, whose startling turn in Mike Leigh's *Naked* had led to a number of higher profile roles in such studio films as *Dragonheart*. "The irony is that Thewlis was one of the people on my wish-list right from the start," Stanley reveals, "but whom they would never have let me have [because] they didn't want the lead guy to be British."

No sooner had production begun again, with Frankenheimer now calling the shots, than Kilmer clashed with the replacement director. "I don't like Val Kilmer, I don't like his work ethic, and I don't want to be associated with him ever again," Frankenheimer told *Entertainment Weekly* soon after shooting wrapped. It must have been a relief to Frankenheimer that Kilmer's part had been reduced to a supporting role. "If they'd had to put up with Val in every shot of every day, they'd have had a real [problem]," Stanley suggests. Nevertheless, Thewlis found him easy to work with. "I actually like Val," he told *Cinescape*. "I know he gets a lot of bad press, but I like him a lot. Sometimes [people] can want a little bit of control and want [their] own way... and not have an idea in their head. The fact is that Val wants the control, but he has some great ideas."

Kilmer, for his part, says that his reputation for being difficult was borne out of his insistence on perfectionism. "If people want to try and trash me, that's fine," the actor told *Midweek*. "I have no interest in getting caught up in mudslinging contests. I'm only interested in the work and I'm sorry if some people find that a difficult concept to live by. I'm not easy to work with if the work is going badly," he added, "but in the end the film is better, my performance is better, and the audience gets their money's worth. I don't care if I finish last in the Mr Popularity competition." The actor also shrugs off bad press as an occupational hazard. "Every actor has to put up with it," he added. "It's part of the price we pay for being celebrities and the fact that it's image and not art which drives the market for movies. If [the press] find a way to smear you in print, they'll do it and there's nothing you can do about it except wait for the shitstorm to roll over. My job is to give the best performance as an actor that I can and I've always fought for art over garbage."

If Kilmer felt that he had become a sort of all-purpose whipping-boy for the press, Stanley found himself in a similar situation with the producers, becoming the victim of a number of malicious rumours — among them that he was planning to return to Queensland and burn down the set, the result of an ill-advised but casual joke made to a crewmember. "I started getting weird phone calls from New Line's legal department and my agent," Stanley says. "They'd suddenly become terribly afraid that I would attack the cast or the main compound or whatever, which quite offended me because, of course, I would never do anything which could be construed as malicious towards my cast and crew. [But] even though I was getting telephone calls in Sydney — very rudely — at three and four in the morning [from people] on American time, I couldn't convince them that the prefix for the number at which they were calling me was thousands of miles away from where the shoot was going on."

Other equally scurrilous stories began to spread, including one told to Brando — who had yet to arrive in Australia — that Stanley had gone crazy on the set, assaulted a member of the crew and even punched his girlfriend, Kate. "Of course, Brando's immediate response was to phone

Kate and say, 'Is this true?'" Stanley says. "She said, 'No, of course not!' So he knew [even] before he arrived that everyone was lying to him." Feeling that he had become the scapegoat — "an all-purpose boogeyman" — for the production's myriad problems, Stanley understandably felt the need to set the record straight, particularly with Brando, for whom he had the deepest respect. "Although I had left peacefully at the time, as a result of the huge amount of disinformation that had started pouring out I eventually turned around and decided to go back up to Queensland," he explains. "I had been heavily warned by everyone that if I came anywhere near the set I'd be sued for trying to disrupt the shooting, so it became obvious that if I did go, I'd have to do it incognito. I believe there were even people watching the airports to see if I was on any of the flights, and there were security guards in unmarked cards showing up outside places they thought I would go. One actress reported that there was a security guard waiting in her driveway in a car with the lights off because he'd received some tip-off that I was going to show up there."

Stanley skirted the security set up by New Line and eventually found Brando, who had, by this time, had his own clashes with the wayward Kilmer. Angry at his co-star's misbehaviour, in particular his frequent non-appearances on set, Brando had arranged for his trailer to be moved away from Kilmer's and had, according to *Entertainment Weekly*, told the younger actor, "Your problem is, you confuse the size of your talent with the size of your paycheck." Perhaps unsurprisingly, Stanley found Brando sympathetic to his plight. "I put my case [to him]: that I would never have harmed anyone [and that] any stories about me trying to threaten or harm the cast or Val were just wish-fulfilment. [Brando] very sweetly offered to pay me off," he says, touched by the recollection, "you know, he offered me a chunk of money, which I, of course, refused."

Once Stanley was happy that he had cleared his name with Brando, he decided to take a break from the increasingly insane world in which he found himself, heading into a section of unbroken rainforest with a close female friend. "[We] lived out in the woods for a few weeks with food, coconuts and mangoes on the trees, good sunlight and fresh water," he says. "I was given a couple of dingo pups to look after by some feral, and kind of went native for a while. We pretty much forgot about the world and refused to have anything more to do with the shoot." Then, after a couple of weeks in the forest, the feral film-maker was surprised to find a group of former *Dr. Moreau* crewmembers who, having been fired by Frankenheimer, were camped just downriver, ready to exact their revenge. One of the campers was Lewis, who had the distinction of having been fired *twice* from the production. "Lewis had started as a carpenter working on Moreau's house," Stanley recalls, "and he'd been fired for standing round thinking too much, which tells his story! He then got re-hired as a driver." Unfortunately, he adds, when "the shit hit the fan" and everyone was trying to leave the mess behind, Lewis was caught trying to help Fairuza Balk to escape. "She ran away with him," he says, "but they only got as far as Sydney [before] they caught her and put her on a plane back to Queensland, and fired Lewis for the second time."

Thus it was that with the aid of other former *Dr. Moreau* crewmembers, each with a grudge against the production, a cunning plan was hatched around the campfire. One of the actors on the film had managed to appropriate one of the beast-man costumes, the 'melting dogman', from Stan Winston's workshop, on the pretext that it was for a prank at the hotel. Now, it was decided, Stanley would attempt to get himself re-hired on the production as an extra playing one of the 'beast-people'. Having already procured the costume, Stanley would not have to report to make-up or wardrobe, and would naturally be familiar enough with the movie to know what he was required to do in order to keep up the ingenious deception. Although Stanley chooses not to go on record confirming the specifics of the ruse, one of the prank's alleged participants explains, "He would black himself out and put on the bulldog face and hands, sit in his car until all the extras were called, then just go on with the rest of the beast people."

Now that Stanley had found a way to observe at close hand Frankenheimer's efforts to complete the film, he found the veteran's directorial approach very different to his own. "They were making it up as they went along," he says succinctly. "Everyone was desperate. The most commonly spoken line on the shoot was, 'I don't know.' As in, 'What are we shooting today?' 'I don't know.' 'What time is Val arriving?' 'I don't know.' 'Is Brando coming today?' 'I don't know.' There was so much disunity within the basic shoot," Stanley adds, "that a lot of the Australians among the crew — even some of the ADs [assistant directors] — actually knew I was there, but my presence inside the compound was kept secret from the Americans. So, despite what New Line and Frankenheimer [said later] — that they knew I was there and that it was all a joke — they actually had no idea at all."

There were close calls, however. One night, Stanley was spotted talking to fellow beast-person, Ron Perlman, who, having sworn never again to be filmed in prosthetic make-up after four years as Linda Hamilton's co-star in *Beauty and the Beast*, had agreed to do it once more for Stanley, a director he very much admired. "He'd consented to play the Sayer of the Law, just because the part was so loaded to start off with," Stanley says proudly. Now Perlman was angry, because during four series of *Beauty and the Beast*, he was only asked to put on the make-up *once* without it being shot, whereas on *Dr. Moreau*, he was filmed only once for every five times he got made up. "The rest of the time," Stanley says, "he'd put it all on, come to the set and stand around, with no lines and nothing to do, go home again and take it off without doing anything. This went on for weeks.

"The particular night I got spotted," he recalls, "I was talking to Ron when word came on set that Val had decided he couldn't come again. He'd thrown another number, so shooting was cancelled for the night. This was typical for the whole shoot," he adds. "Every time Val would throw a tantrum, the strong line that Frankenheimer took with him was that he'd close down shooting, which to me was incredible because you'd be standing there with Ron, Temeura Morrison, Marco Hofschneider, Fairuza Balk, David Thewlis and Marlon Brando, and they'd close down shooting because of Val. They had so many good people there, and a good crew, you'd imagine they'd be able to shoot *something*. Anyway, at that moment, Ron, who was trying to learn his lines, said, 'God, what's the point of learning this then?' and made a big gesture of tearing up the script and throwing it down. It drew people's attention, [and it] was the last time I came on, because after that rumours start to fly that I was actually there… " So was Stanley, in effect, present more often than Kilmer, the film's supposed star? "Probably not," he says with a smile, "but when they were shooting on the boats, I was having a fairly good time sitting on the beach with binoculars, watching them floundering around in the distance!"

As word filtered back to the US and Britain about the increasingly bizarre nature of events occurring in Australia on *The Island of Dr. Moreau* shoot, Stanley made the difficult decision not to go to the press with his story. "At the time, an agreement was struck with New Line whereby, if anyone asked what had happened, we would just shrug and say 'creative differences' and let it go. I actually kept my end of the bargain, [but when] Mike De Luca or New Line started saying, 'We should have had a stronger director,' or, 'Stanley's rushes didn't cut together,' I felt moved to try and actually set the record straight in some way." Nevertheless, Stanley feels that what happened really *was* his fault, because he should have been in control of the circumstances. But how could he hope to control those circumstances without the backing of the studio making the film? "I blame the system," he says wryly. "The *auteur* theory has always been largely hype, but it was rammed down my throat when I was growing up [and it] gave me a lot of wrong ideas about the power of the individual. With *Dr. Moreau*, the company was always much more in charge than I [was].

"As soon as it goes over a certain budgetary level, you're in the hands of the company. As much as anything else — the bad weather, the flu epidemic, the car crash I had on the morning of the first day, Val and everything else — I think that the budget did a lot of the damage. When it hit $35 million, my position started to become untenable [because] unless you're Steven Spielberg or James Cameron, they're not going to say 'yes' to you. They're going to say, 'It has to be this way, kid — the waist-high field of marijuana plants has to go, the animal sex has to go, you can't have the female lead cooked and eaten.'" Stanley feels it might have been prudent to attempt to raise money for a lower-budget version of the story, "but I was always kind of stuck because of the eighty creatures, the tropical location, and so on." He does believe, however, that a great deal of money could have been saved in the areas of make-up and special effects. "Unfortunately," he jokes, "by the end everyone was just running off with bundles of money under each arm — including myself!"

The demise of Stanley's vision of *The Island of Dr. Moreau* as "a really slick, epic, voodoo gothic horror movie on a grand scale", has left the film-maker with a number of regrets, the most painful of which is that the potential to create a truly unique genre movie — with the added bonus of a great performance from Brando — has been lost forever. Nevertheless, he points out, "one must never forget that [*The Island of Doctor Moreau*] is actually a very fine novel by H. G. Wells, and it's been filmed twice before, which means that I was attempting another remake. So, right from the start I was taking something which was somebody else's and which I didn't own. I had never at any point owned the rights, which were passed down for a long time from AIP to Orion, then ended up in New Line's hands. I was there basically to do my version of it, [but] they then removed me from it [and] ended up with something very akin to the [1977] AIP. The only thing they got from me is my cast.

"Where it all becomes a real tragedy," he adds, "is that Val didn't mean to do what he did. If someone says, 'Oh, we'll move everything from your sight that troubles you, sir,' then one automatically behaves that way. One can't really fault the guy for being a bit of an asshole." ("He's not an asshole," Fairuza Balk told *The Face*. "He never did the things they said he did.") Stanley now believes that Kilmer was simply doing what thousands of stars before him have done — exercising his right to behave like a star. "I believe that [he] was just trying to demonstrate who the top dog was, to show how much power he had and make the cast jump through a couple of hoops, so they'd behave in future. What he didn't realise was that by getting rid of me, he also gave the company the chance to finally turn it into the movie that they really wanted to [make]."

Certainly, Frankenheimer grasped the opportunity to make the film *he* wanted to make, as he admitted to *Cinescape*. "I didn't like the horror film aspect of it or the spoof aspect of it, [so] I did change the script quite a bit." Indeed, comparing Stanley's original draft to Frankenheimer's shooting script is as futile and frustrating as trying to find more than a passing resemblance to Wells's novel. The word which occurs most frequently in the shooting draft is 'OMITTED' — it is, in fact, the very first word of the screenplay. "They changed everything that was any good," Stanley says, "starting with the main character. [He] originally had the same name as the character in the Wells novel, which I felt strongly about because everyone always changes Prendick's name, because it's such a silly name — you know, you can't have a lead called Prendick. [But] I thought, well, people in real life have silly names, so I'd rather have him called Prendick and make him precious about it, and have everyone else make fun of him. They call him 'Prawn-dick' for most of the way in the original draft and generally treat him quite badly. Of course, as soon as I was gone, they changed his name to Douglas, which they thought was more manly."

Frankenheimer also changed Prendick's profession, removing reference to his work as a human rights lawyer for the United Nations, a conceit Stanley had invented because he felt that a character whose life was devoted to defending the civil rights of oppressed peoples would have a field day with Moreau. "Then, after Moreau dies, he is ironically cast in the role of lawgiver and has to sort things out for the beast people. In the original draft," Stanley says, "it was going to turn into a kind of piss-take on Yugoslavia or Somalia, where the man from the UN did extremely badly and succeeded in messing things up even worse for the people he was trying to protect." All of this was lost in Frankenheimer's version of the script, revised with the assistance of TV movie writer Ron Hutchinson (*Fatherland*, *Against the Wall*) and uncredited contributions from Walon Green (*The Wild Bunch*). "So although Thewlis is a very fine actor, he's playing a very conventional character called Douglas who is just a heroic castaway."

Stanley had also taken a leaf out of William Golding's *Lord of the Flies*, setting the story at a time when a limited nuclear exchange has broken out in the rest of the world, an intriguing premise which was not part of the original novel but which provided the cornerstone of Stanley's update. "So even when Prendick reaches the island, there's an issue as to whether there's an outside world left. The beast-people [become] like the cradle of civilisation, and were potentially what was going to come next in the evolution of the species. And of course," he adds, "Moreau was diligently working on a replacement species for Man."

Frankenheimer made other significant changes. The problem, Thewlis suggested, was that "people didn't really know what kind of film they wanted to make. It was such a mixture of styles... The original script Richard wanted to make was more spoofy, and then I think it became an action-horror film." Says Stanley, "It [was] blanded out, changed, and basically watered down. Thewlis's character is now the clearcut good guy with no negative qualities, and Moreau is more of a textbook bad guy than he was meant to be, either in the Wells novel or in my draft. On top of that, ironically, the extremes of unpleasantness are gone, [so that] even though they've got more obvious bad guys, all the genuinely unpleasant stuff that happened in the script has gone, including the graphic demises of almost all the cast. I was heading towards a much tougher third act, which just isn't there at all in any respect. I mean," he adds, "nobody gets cooked and eaten!"

What is arguably most surprising about the final cut of the film is the number of apparently critical elements of the Wells story missing in Frankenheimer's version, the best examples of which are the sidelining of the 'Saying of the Law' — perhaps the most memorable part of the novel — and the complete omission of the infamous 'House of Pain', no longer even mentioned in the shooting script. This, Stanley suggests, is like attempting an adaptation of George Orwell's *1984* but leaving out Room 101. "He's dropped so many things which you would have thought no one could ever have dropped; things that were part of the Wells novel and which I think are some of the strongest things in the story." Frankenheimer, understandably, is disinclined to agree: "What we made, I think, is a moral fable that asks, 'What goes wrong when you just let scientists go unchecked?'"

For most of those close to the production, the more pertinent question was, "What goes wrong when you just let actors go unchecked?" Even Brando, no stranger to Hollywood's more outlandish excesses — having played supporting roles in *Superman* and *Apocalypse Now* — recognised during shooting that the film was probably beyond salvation. As Thewlis told *Cinescape*, "Marlon described the film at one point as trying to do a crossword puzzle while plunging down an elevator shaft. Then he qualified that and said, 'It can be done, it just takes a lot of concentration.' That was pretty accurate." After the film opened in September 1996, struggling to a $40 million world-wide box-office take, Thewlis was more forthcoming, admitting to *Premiere* that making *The Island of Dr. Moreau* was "a terrible time. I went to rushes because I didn't know what was happening. Richard Stanley is the only one who has gone public. I would be sued." Reviews were withering, led by *Variety* who described the film as "an embarrassment for all concerned."

Stanley likens the making of his first feature, *Hardware*, to a child delivered by forceps, its skull slightly crushed in the course of pulling it out so that it ends up deformed or brain damaged. "It was mine," he says of his début, "but it was kind of dumb and mad, though still very active," he says, enjoying the analogy. "I guess *Dr. Moreau* was more like a bucket job, in that it came straight out of the womb and into the shredder." ■

Afterword

In some ways, *The Greatest Sci-Fi Movies Never Made* is a tragedy. It's a melancholy examination of that which will never come to pass...

My own job is to peer into the future of film, and there is no sadder task than watching projects with great potential unravel before my eyes. For whatever reason, the stars do not align and, despite the prayers of film lovers, the Movie Gods choose not to let it be.

The Movie Gods gave us a great David Webb Peoples script called *Soldier*, a brave dip into the realm of *Blade Runner*. And what do these unjust beings do? Give the script to Paul Anderson... *Why?* And how did that project come to pass whilst Ridley Scott's *I Am Legend* fell apart?

Two great sci-fi films that never were didn't make it into this book — perhaps they'll appear in a second volume — two that I feel are the *crème de la* crop. Sure, I weep for the dearly departed amongst these pages, but these two films could have changed the course of the science fiction film.

The first: *Time Machine 2*. What? Oh yes, it is true. Before George Pal made *Doc Savage: The Man of Bronze*. Before Ray Harryhausen made *The Golden Voyage of Sinbad*. Well, there was *Time Machine 2*.

I was set up at the Dallas Fantasy Fair in Dallas, Texas, in the summer of 1993, when Ray Harryhausen came into my booth. We talked for about three hours, and at one point he came to the original one-sheet for George Pal's *The Time Machine*. I began fawning over the film, when Ray suddenly said, "You know, George and I were going to do a sequel to *The Time Machine?*"

My jaw dropped. A sequel to *The Time Machine?* Really? Ray went on to tell me that George and he had thrown concepts back and forth with one another. That Ray was going to do stop motion and creature designs, based around a story that Pal and he were working on. I was incredibly excited by the news... ahhhh, a sequel given life by Ray Harryhausen and George Pal... Imagine... Then reality hit me. This project didn't exist. It isn't on my shelf at home. What happened?

Ray became rather solemn. With the then-current space programme and the hubbub over computers, the executives at MGM decided that the Time Machine itself would need to be more... modern. More electronicky. George lost heart in the project, and it fell by the wayside, occupying the same place as Harryhausen's *Sinbad on Mars* project; a rumour prior to his *Clash of the Titans*.

Moving on to *the* greatest sci-fi film that never was, we find a movie that could have radically changed cinema history: *John Carter of Mars*.

Prior to Walt Disney's *Snow White and the Seven Dwarfs*, Bob Clampett (famed animator) was working with John Coleman Burroughs (famed Tarzan and John Carter cover artist) on an animated feature. The wondrous tests came out as something akin to a moving oil painting.

Imagine if in 1936, before *Snow White*, the first animated feature film was *John Carter of Mars*. If instead of a fairy tale, we had been given a science fiction fantasy. To this day we have never seen a feature adaptation of this, my favourite Edgar Rice Burroughs work.

However, financing fell through... the investors lost faith, doubting that an audience could stand to watch a feature length animated film. And the project vanished into the mists of time.

Now you have reached the end. What can we take from reading about the failures and the what-might-have-beens?

For one, I look at every fantastic genre project that I have on my shelves and think, "Thank God!" You see folks, it takes a great deal of effort to make even *Plan 9 from Outer Space*. Edward D. Wood Jr managed to get his idea from paper to screen... no matter the end results. And now we can plop it in our VCR, or our DVD, or even go to our local alternatively cool movie theatre. And it will last in your memory and mine...

There is a bit of magic to the unmade. The purity of hopes and dreams. We can make believe that the studios fully financed it. That the greatest cast was in fact assembled. That it would have changed the very fabric of our fandom had it been made.

Great stories though, find a way of coming to the screen. Perhaps you, reading this book, will take a look at one of these projects and make it your life's ambition to see it come to pass. Well, I can dream.

Harry Knowles
Austin, July 2001

AUTHOR'S ACKNOWLEDGEMENTS

It may be hard to believe, since you're holding the book in your hands, that *The Greatest Sci-Fi Movies Never Made* very nearly befell the fate of the films detailed among its pages. Indeed, it spent almost as long in the publishing equivalent of 'development hell' as *The Tourist*.

Originally pitched in 1995, the book was rejected by several companies over the course of the next few years, before being enthusiastically received by 'Another Publisher'. After a year in a holding pattern, during which time I continued to conduct interviews, engage in research, and actually started writing the book, it was finally rejected on the grounds that... well, I never did find out what the grounds were. Suffice it to say that when it was re-pitched to Titan, they liked the idea so much they insisted I begin it immediately, and promised to publish it within three months. So you see, some stories of development hell have a happy ending.

Immense thanks are therefore due to David Barraclough, Adam Newell and anyone else behind the scenes at Titan who gave the book a shot (and a decent advance); to my agent Chelsey Fox (for negotiating the advance); my accountant Michael Barrs (for hiding most of the advance in an offshore account); to my bankers John and Heather (for extending my overdraft until I was paid the advance), and to the IRS (for appreciating that the advance really wasn't that big when you came to think of it). Thanks also to Julia Delmas, Angus Spottiswoode and Dane McMaster for replacing my negligence with diligence; to Dan Persons at *Cinefantastique*, Graham Humphreys, Paul Simpson and everyone else who granted or gave reproduction permission; to my wife Zahida — who definitely gave me reproduction permission, hence children Harry and Jenna — for putting up with yet another book project; to David Willing, Gordon and everyone else at my second home, Picture Production Company; and to the fine baristas at Starbucks and Costa Coffee, my third and fourth homes respectively. Finally, thanks to Chris Hewitt at Fish, Liz, Mike, Jane, Jackie, Pelham, Christina Rubtsova, the Beautiful Southmartins and everyone else I've either forgotten here, or neglected for the last two years — I promise I'm taking the next six months off!

I would also like to thank H. R. Giger and Harry Knowles for their kind contributions, and all of the individuals I interviewed during the six-year development of this book, whether I wound up quoting them or not: Neal Adams, Paul Anderson, Richard Anderson, Darren Aronofsky, Rick Baker, Rick Berman, Chris Bryant, Chris Cunningham (né Halls), Sylvain Despretz, Dexter Fletcher, Chris Foss, Neil Gaiman, Rudy Gaines, Brian Gibson, Terry Gilliam, Rick Heinrichs, Lance Henriksen, Peter Hewitt, Philip Kaufman, Karey Kirkpatrick, Patricia Knop, Tani Kunitake, John Logan, David Lynch, William Malone, Renée Missel, Alan Moore, Stephen Norrington, Clair Noto, Craig Penn, Dan Petrie Jr, Mark Protosevich, Kevin Smith, Richard Stanley, Patrick Stewart, Mark Stetson, Wesley Strick, Miles Teves, Tom Topor, Vincent Ward and Tim Zaccheo. Without you all, this book would have contained much that is apocryphal, or at least wildly inaccurate. May you never suffer in development hell.

INDEX OF QUOTATIONS

Note: Quotes given in the text in present tense (eg 'says Adams'; 'Adams recalls'), are taken from an author interview (AI). All available information on the sources is given. Any omissions will be corrected in future editions where possible.

DESTINATION: DEVELOPMENT HELL

Page 8: "Has reached a..." From *The Stars My Destination* by Alfred Bester. **p9** "Of all brutes..."; "EDUCATION: NONE..."; "After thirty years ..." ibid. **p10** "When I found..." William Gibson, quoted in flypapers of 'SF Masterworks' edition of *The Stars My Destination* by Alfred Bester. "[It] is, after..." Neil Gaiman, ibid. "A dazzling, dizzying..." James Lovegrove, ibid. "one of the..." Thomas M. Disch, ibid. "on everybody's list..." Robert Silverberg, ibid. "the greatest single..." Samuel Delany, ibid. "only a few..." Joe Haldeman, ibid. **p11** "You can't always..." and all other Neal Adams quotes, AI. **p13** "a couple of..." and all other Paul Anderson quotes from 'Destination Known' by Mo Ryan, *Cinescape*, March 1995. **p14** "*The Stars My Destination...*" Jeremy Bolt, quoted in *Talking Pictures* by Graham Jones and Lucy Johnson. "By this point..." and all other Rudy Gaines quotes, AI. **p16** "He recoiled in terror..." from *The Stars My Destination* by Alfred Bester.

A DIFFICULT CHILDHOOD

Page 18 "It's inevitable that..." and all other Philip DeGuere quotes from 'A New Beginning for Childhood's End' by James H. Burns, *Starlog*, January 1981. "the proverbial good..."; "of mythic grandeur"; "the reasons for believing..."; "the impact (and perhaps even lack of impact..." Stanley Kubrick, quoted in *The Lost Worlds of 2001* by Arthur C. Clarke. "[Kubrick] wanted to make a movie..." Arthur C. Clarke, ibid. **p20** "What I did was..." and all other Neal Adams quotations, AI.

WHERE NO-ONE HAS GONE BEFORE

Page 24 "I'm sure the..." and all other Philip Kaufman quotes, AI. "God was a..." Jon Povill, quoted in *The Making of the Trek Films* edited by Edward Gross. "[Ellison's] story did..."; p25 "What is actually..." James Van Hise, quoted in *Enterprise Incidents*, issue unknown. "It involved going..."; "*I'm* to know..."; p26 "So *I* said..." Harlan Ellison, quoted in *Danse Macabre* by Stephen King. "They were preoccupied..." Leonard Nimoy, from *I Am Spock*. "My partner and..." and all other Chris Bryant quotes, AI. p28 "Roddenberry got in..." Alan Dean Foster, quoted in *The Making of the Trek Films* edited by Edward Gross. "I wanted to..."; "Michael had one..." Harold Livingston, ibid. "Eisner slammed his..." Robert Goodwin, ibid. "The fans have..." Michael Eisner, ibid. p30 "Gene was a..." Harold Livingston, ibid. p31 "More than anything..." Jeffrey Katzenberg, ibid. "enhanced the script..." Harold Livingston, ibid. "On a scale..." Jeffrey Katzenberg, ibid. "It was a..." Michael Eisner, ibid. p33 "Suppose you trained..." Michael Minor, ibid. "My personal objection..." Samuel Peepes, ibid. "Neither the Jack..." Robert Sallin, ibid. "I looked at..." Nicholas Meyer, ibid. p34 "It is, in all candour..." Robert Sallin, ibid. "It would have..."; p35 "A proposal was..."; "That led us..." Harve Bennett, ibid. "But the depiction..." Leonard Nimoy, quoted in *I Am Spock*. p36 "I had a..." Daniel Petrie, AI. "On the surface..."; "It was a..."; "I told him ..." Leonard Nimoy, quoted in *I Am Spock*. "I'm a Trekkie..." Eddie Murphy, quoted in *The Making of the Trek Films* edited by Edward Gross. p37 "So much of..." Harve Bennett, ibid. "I still think..." Nicholas Meyer, ibid. p38 "I took the..." William Shatner, quoted in *Captain's Log: William Shatner's Personal Account of the Making of Star Trek V: The Final Frontier* as told by Lisabeth Shatner. "As originally conceived..." David Loughery, quoted in *The Making of the Trek Films* edited by Edward Gross. p39 "I was sure..." William Shatner, quoted in *Captain's Log: William Shatner's Personal Account of the Making of Star Trek V: The Final Frontier* as told by Lisabeth Shatner. "Are they going..." George Takei, quoted in *Warped Factors: A Neurotic's Guide to the Universe* by Walter Koenig. "It's a great..." Ralph Winter, quoted in *The Making of the Trek Films* edited by Edward Gross. "We were really..." David Loughery, ibid. p40 "not stunt guys..."; "In this loneliest ..." Walter Koenig, quoted in *Warped Factors: A Neurotic's Guide to the Universe*. p42 "I was asked..." Rick Berman, quoted in *The Making of the Trek Films* edited by Edward Gross. "There was basically..."; "It basically becomes..." Maurice Hurley, ibid. p43 "Their whole thing..."; "Part of me..." Ronald D Moore, quoted in *The Making of Star Trek: First Contact* by Lou Anders. p44 "Cochrane is unconscious..." Brannon Braga, ibid. "Picard basically did..." Ronald D. Moore, ibid. "We tried in..." Brannon Braga, ibid. "We went, 'Duh!..." Ronald D Moore, ibid. p45 "I can tell..."; "Rick had said..." Michael Piller, quoted in 'Star Trek: Insurrection' by Anna L. Kaplan, *Cinefantastique*, January 1999. p46 "By the time..." Rick Berman, ibid. "The idea of..."; "When Rick said..."; "We tried to ..." Michael Piller, ibid. p47 "I went in..." and all other John Logan quotes, AI.

CLOSE, BUT NO CIGAR-SHAPED OBJECT

Page 48 "I might have..." Steven Spielberg, quoted in *Steven Spielberg: A Biography* by Joseph McBride. "Nobody expects one..." Steven Spielberg, quoted in *Steven Spielberg: The Unauthorised Biography* by John Baxter. p49 "eventually got called..." and all other John Sayles quotes from *Sayles on Sayles* by Gavin Smith. p50 "The assignment was..." Rick Baker, quoted in 'How E.T. Found His Smile' by Christopher Meeks, *Cinefantastique*, November-December 1982. "It was so..." Rick Baker, AI. "I knew [it]..." Rick Baker, quoted in 'How E.T. Found His Smile' by Christopher Meeks, *Cinefantastique*, November-December 1982. p51 "I got this..." Rick Baker, AI. "One of the..." Rick Baker, quoted in 'How E.T. Found His Smile' by Christopher Meeks, *Cinefantastique*, November-December 1982. p52 "I asked Melissa..." Steven Spielberg, quoted in *Steven Spielberg: A Biography* by Joseph McBride. "the idea of ..." Melissa Mathison, quoted in ibid. "I was working..."; "[Then] he walks..." Rick Baker, quoted in 'How E.T. Found His Smile' by Christopher Meeks, *Cinefantastique*, November-December 1982. p53 "I said, 'Well..." Rick Baker, AI. "I told him..." Rick Baker, quoted in 'How E.T. Found His Smile' by Christopher Meeks, *Cinefantastique*, November-December 1982. "When we went..." Kathleen Kennedy, ibid. "I was very..."; "Steven fell back..." Rick Baker, ibid. "Steven took all..." Rick Baker, AI. p54 "tried to make..." Carlo Rambaldi, quoted in 'Creating a Creature', *Time*, 31 May 1982. "If Spielberg and..." Rick Baker, quoted in 'How E.T. Found His Smile' by Christopher Meeks, *Cinefantastique*, November-December 1982. "We had a..." John Veitch, quoted in *Steven Spielberg: A Biography* by Joseph McBride. "a wimpy Walt..." quoted in ibid. "although Steven had..." Frank Price, ibid. "Steven had no..." Sid Sheinberg, ibid. p55 "I think that..." John Veitch, ibid. "comedy about antics..." quoted in *Motion Picture Product Digest*, 2 December 1981. p56 "asked this incredible..."; "I got a..." Stephen King, quoted in *Steven Spielberg: The Unauthorised Biography* by John Baxter. "*not really directing...*" quoted in 'Those Noisy Spirits Never Rest' by Jeff Silverman, *Los Angeles Herald-Examiner*, 5 June 1981. "spans all aspects..." Tobe Hooper, ibid. "When I came..." David Giler, quoted in *Steven Spielberg: A Biography* by Joseph McBride. p57 "My enthusiasm for..." Steven Spielberg, quoted in the *Los Angeles Times*, 24 May 1982. p58 "would do nothing..." Steven Spielberg, quoted in *Steven Spielberg: A Biography* by Joseph McBride. "extensively detailed her..."; p59 "some similar references..." Sol Rosenthal, quoted in 'E.T. Scripter Awarded 5% of Merchandising" by David Robb, *Daily Variety*, 1 March 1989. "as Ms Mathison..." Bruce Ramer, quoted in 'Credit on Creation of E.T.' (letter to the editor), *Daily Variety*, 6 March 1989. "I hadn't looked..." Rick Baker, quoted in 'How E.T. Found His Smile' by Christopher Meeks, *Cinefantastique*, November-December 1982. "We talked about..."; "It was a..." Rick Baker, AI. "I would have..." Rick Baker, quoted in 'How E.T. Found His Smile' by Christopher Meeks, *Cinefantastique*, November-December 1982.

THE TOURIST TRAP

Page 60 "I think a..." and all other Franc Roddam quotes, from '*The Tourist*' by Fred Szebin, *Cinefantastique*, August 1994. "There was a..."; "If you put..." Clair Noto, AI. **p61** "When the film..." Clair Noto, quoted in '*The Tourist*' by Fred Szebin, *Cinefantastique*, August 1994. "He had read..." Clair Noto, AI. **p62** "I wanted her..." Clair Noto, quoted in '*The Tourist*' by Fred Szebin, *Cinefantastique*, August 1994. **p63** "I think maybe..." Clair Noto, AI. "I had optioned..." and all other Renée Missel quotes, AI. "I got to LA..." and all other Brian Gibson quotes, AI. **p64** "He was working..."; "I got a..."; "incredibly supportive..."; **p65** "It was passed..."; **p66** "You really don't..."; **p67** "I had a meeting..."; Clair Noto, AI. **p68** "There are certain..." Clair Noto, quoted in '*The Tourist*' by Fred Szebin, *Cinefantastique*, August 1994. **p69** "Brian Gibson was..." and all other Patricia Knop quotes, AI. "I was commissioned..." H. R. Giger, quoted in *H. R. Giger's Film Design.* **p70** "I had mentioned..."; "but I was..." Clair Noto, quoted in '*The Tourist*' by Fred Szebin, *Cinefantastique*, August 1994. **p73** "I delivered what..." and all other Tom Topor quotes, AI. "[Renée] didn't want..."; **p75** "Every time somebody..." Clair Noto, quoted in '*The Tourist*' by Fred Szebin, *Cinefantastique*, August 1994. "What constantly amazed..."; "I had worked..."; **p76** "Universal said, 'We..."; "Now it's a..." Clair Noto, AI. **p79** "*The Tourist* has always..." Clair Noto, quoted in '*The Tourist*' by Fred Szebin, *Cinefantastique*, August 1994. "The update is ..." Clair Noto, AI.

PROFITS OF DUNE

Page 80 "A lot of..." Frank Herbert, quoted in *Eye.* **p81** "I didn't set..."; **p82** "He took a..." Frank Herbert, quoted in *The Making of Dune* by Ed Naha. "*Dune* is much..." Alejandro Jodorowsky, quoted in 'Versions of Arrakis You'll Never See' by Paul M. Sammon, Stephen Jones, Frederic Albert Levy, *Cinefantastique*, September 1984. "Jodorowsky was absolutely..." Chris Foss, ibid. **p83** "It was a..." Chris Foss, quoted in 'Hold On, You'll Like This...' *Skeleton Crew*, August 1990. "an American painter..."; "Bob Venosa telephoned..." and all other Giger quotes, from *H. R. Giger's Film Design.* **p84** "The producer and..." Chris Foss, quoted in 'Versions of Arrakis You'll Never See' by Paul M. Sammon, Stephen Jones, Frederic Albert Levy, *Cinefantastique*, September 1984. "Basically it was..." Dan O'Bannon, ibid. "Dan was equally..." Chris Foss, quoted in 'Hold On, You'll Like This...' *Skeleton Crew*, August 1990. "Alejandro Jodorowsky spent..." Frank Herbert, quoted in *The Making of Dune* by Ed Naha. **p85** "Being an ardent..." Alejandro Jodrowsky, quoted in 'Versions of Arrakis You'll Never See' by Paul M. Sammon, Stephen Jones, Frederic Albert Levy, *Cinefantastique*, September 1984. "I had a special..."; "I don't know..." Dino De Laurentiis, quoted in *The Making of Dune* by Ed Naha. **p86** "The *Dune* adaptation..."; "I took what..." Rudolph Wurlitzer, quoted in 'Versions of Arrakis You'll Never See' by Paul M. Sammon, Stephen Jones, Frederic Albert Levy, *Cinefantastique*, September 1984. **p87** "After seven months..." Ridley Scott, quoted in *Ridley Scott: The Making of his Movies* by Paul M. Sammon. "I found it..." Frank Herbert, quoted in *The Making of Dune* by Ed Naha. "I didn't like..." David Lynch, AI. "It took David..." Raffaella De Laurentiis, quoted in 'Versions of Arrakis You'll Never See' by Paul M. Sammon, Stephen Jones, Frederic Albert Levy, *Cinefantastique*, September 1984. "The *Dune* that..." Chris Foss, quoted in 'Hold On, You'll Like This...' *Skeleton Crew*, August 1990.

TWIN FREAKS

Page 88 "It might be..." David Lynch, quoted in *Inner Views: Filmmakers in Conversation* by David Breskin. "Ronnie was like..." and all other Dexter Fletcher quotes, AI. **p90** "I hope my..." David Lynch, quoted in *The Elephant Man: The Book of the Film* by Joy Kuhn. "When we shot..." David Lynch, quoted in *Inner Views: Filmmakers in Conversation* by David Breskin. **p91** "I met Michael..." David Lynch, AI. "It's not a..."; "No, no, no..." David Lynch, quoted in *Inner Views: Filmmakers in Conversation* by David Breskin. "deliriously happy..." Michael J. Anderson, quoted in the *New York Daily News*, April 1991. "After so many..." David Lynch, quoted in 'Lynch's *Fire Walk* Stirs a Mixture of Passions at Cannes' by Kenneth Turan, *Los Angeles Times*, 18 May 1992. **p92** "a long time"; "If I had gotten..."; "Nothing ever happened..." David Lynch, AI. "an out-and-out ..." David Lynch, quoted in *Inner Views: Filmmakers in Conversation* by David Breskin. "David is somewhat..." Mark Frost, quoted in 'Mark Frost' by Phillipa Bloom, *Empire*, August 1993. **p93** "I thought of..." David Lynch, quoted in *Inner Views: Filmmakers in Conversation* by David Breskin. "right after *Blue Velvet*"; "I almost was..."; "It hasn't really..." David Lynch, AI.

ALIENATED

Page 94 "I hoped that..." and all other Vincent Ward quotes given in the present tense, AI. "They felt there..." Walter Hill, quoted in *Starlog*, issue unknown. "The producers I..."; **p95** "[Walter Hill] showed..." Dan O'Bannon, quoted in 'Dan O'Bannon on *Alien*' by Dave Schow, *Cinefantastique* Vol 8 No1, circa 1979. "I stepped into..." Ridley Scott, quoted in *Ridley Scott: The Making of his Movies* by Paul M. Sammon. "We talked to..." Sigourney Weaver, quoted in the *Boston Herald*, 23 November 1997. **p96** "People have suggested..." Sylvain Despretz, AI. "Fox basically said...;'" and all other James Cameron quotes, from 'Loving the Alien' by Philip Nutman, *Skeleton Crew*, August 1990. **P97** "they were arguing ..."; "I expected this..." and all other William Gibson quotes, from 'William Gibson's "Neuroaliens"' by Sheldon Teitelbaum, *Cinefantastique*, June 1992. **p99** "We got the..." David Giler, quoted in 'Development Hell' by Sheldon Teitelbaum, *Cinefantastique*, June 1992. "At the start..."; **p100** "When *Aliens* came..." Sigourney Weaver, quoted in 'Dream Weaver' by David

Hughes, *Alien³ Movie Special*, September 1992. "The basic problem..."; "When I met..." Eric Red, quoted in 'Development Hell' by Sheldon Teitelbaum, *Cinefantastique*, June 1992. "It was a..." David Giler, ibid. **p101** "I specifically worked..." Renny Harlin, ibid. "They put together..." Sigourney Weaver, quoted in 'Dream Weaver' by David Hughes, *Alien³ Movie Special*, September 1992. "She is the ..." Joe Roth quoted in 'Bald Ambition' by Douglas Perry, *Cinescape Insider* Vol.3 No.9. "We started work..."; **p102** "came in with..." Sigourney Weaver, quoted in 'Dream Weaver' by David Hughes, *Alien³ Movie Special*, September 1992. "We were supposedly.." John Fasano, quoted in 'Development Hell' by Sheldon Teitelbaum, *Cinefantastique*, June 1992. "At that point..." David Twohy quoted in 'Bald Ambition' by Douglas Perry, *Cinescape Insider* Vol.3 No.9. **p103** "Vincent came to..." H. R. Giger, quoted in 'The Giger Sanction' by Stewart Jamieson, *Alien³ Movie Special*, October 1992. "We couldn't figure..." David Giler, quoted in 'Development Hell' by Sheldon Teitelbaum, *Cinefantastique*, June 1992. **p104** "I wrote a..." Vincent Ward, quoted in 'Alien³' by Patrick Hobby, *Cinefantastique*, June 1992. "He said, 'Well...'" Sigourney Weaver, quoted in 'Dream Weaver' by David Hughes, *Alien³ Movie Special*, September 1992. **p105** "It was a..." H. R. Giger, quoted in 'The Giger Sanction' by Stewart Jamieson, *Alien³ Movie Special*, October 1992. "Ferguson's quite a..."; "It's a difficult..."; "They snuck this..." David Giler, quoted in 'Development Hell' by Sheldon Teitelbaum, *Cinefantastique*, June 1992. **p106** "a complete rewrite..." Rex Pickett, ibid. **p107** "We were about..."; "We previewed it..."; "[It] just never ..."; "The change to..."; **p108** "Everybody did a..." David Fincher, quoted in *Alien The Special Effects*, Don Shay and Bill Norton. **p109** "The comic was..." and all other Peter Briggs quotes, from letters to the website *Coming Attractions*. **p111** "It's science fiction..." David Giler, quoted in "The Fate of Ripley and Alien 4" by Sheldon Teitelbaum, *Cinefantastique*, June 1992. "Some of us..." and all other Joss Whedon quotes, from 'In His Own Write' by Edward Gross, *Cinescape*, March 1995. "I'd heard they..." Sigourney Weaver, quoted in *The Boston Herald*, 23 November 1997. **p112** "I have never..." Sigourney Weaver, quoted in an interview with *TV Guide Online*, circa 2001. **p113** "I sort of..." Sigourney Weaver, quoted in 'Alien Resurrection' by Edward Gross, *Cinescape*, December 1995.

LIGHTS, CAMERON, NO "ACTION!"

Page 114 "There is no..." Stan Lee, quoted in announcement to the press, circa 1991. **p115** "I wanted to..." James Cameron, quoted in *James Cameron: An Unauthorised Biography* by Marc Shapiro. "I basically learned..." James Cameron, ibid. **p116** "I was crazy..." Menahem Golan, quoted in 'Tangled Web' by John Horn, *Premiere*, September 1998. "The world's best-selling ..." publicity material, quoted in ibid. "brilliant"; "What Jim managed..." Stan Lee, quoted in 'Tangled Web' by John Horn, *Premiere*, September 1998. **p118** "I'm doing the..."; "I think the..."; "One of the..." James Cameron, quoted in 'Truth or Dare' by Iain Blair, *Platinum*, February 1995. **p119** "It's a tangled..." Sam Perlmutter, quoted in 'Tangled Web' by John Horn, *Premiere*, September 1998. "It's a great..." Tom Rothman, ibid. **p120** "the shame of..." Robert Schwarz, ibid. "Jim's a big fan..." Rae Sanchine, ibid. "For years now..." Stan Lee, quoted in 'Spidey Swings into Action', *Dreamwatch*, April 1999. "This is a..." John Calley, ibid. "Here's where I..." James Cameron, quoted in *Premiere*, November 1998. **p121** "I went in..." David Fincher, quoted in 'Spider-Man', *Cinescape*, January/February 2001. "I would have..." James Cameron, quoted in 'Ape Crusaders' by Benjamin Svetkey, *Entertainment Weekly*, 27 April 2001. "I have a..." James Cameron, quoted in *James Cameron: An Unauthorised Biography* by Marc Shapiro. "There's a very..." James Cameron, quoted in 'Truth or Dare' by Iain Blair, *Platinum*, February 1995. **p122** "[Cameron] is not..." Rae Sanchini, quoted in 'Tangled Web' by John Horn, *Premiere*, September 1998. **p123** "We're developing a..." James Cameron, quoted in *Titanic and the Making of James Cameron* by Paula Parisi. "*Avatar*, I am..."; "I want to..." James Cameron, quoted in *James Cameron: An Unauthorised Biography* by Marc Shapiro.

LEGEND OF THE FALL

Page 124 "Vampires were passé..."; **p125** "weird Robinson Crusoe..." from *I Am Legend* by Richard Matheson. "I think the..." Stephen King, quoted in flypapers of *I Am Legend* by Richard Matheson. "A long time..." Brian Lumley, ibid. "the most clever..." Dean R. Koontz, ibid. **p126** "it was so..." Richard Matheson, quoted on *movieforum.com*. "The first one" and all other Mark Protosevich quotes, AI. **p129** "There was a..." Ridley Scott, quoted in 'The Talented Mr Ridley' by Martyn Palmer, *SFX*, Christmas 2000. "When Ridley gets..." and all other John Logan quotes, AI. **p131** "People are always..." Ridley Scott, quoted in 'The Talented Mr Ridley' by Martyn Palmer, *SFX*, Christmas 2000. **p132** "The idea was..." and all other Tani Kunitake quotes, AI. "Everything had stopped..."; "He's a director..."; **p133** "There is actually..." Sylvain Despretz, AI. "There were some..." Sylvain Despretz, quoted in 'Design for Life' by Stewart Jamieson, *SFX*, February 2000. **p134** "God knows I...'" Ridley Scott, quoted in *Ridley Scott: The Making of his Movies* by Paul M. Sammon. "Alec gave me..." and all other Miles Teves quotes, AI. **p135** "They wanted us..." and all other Tim Zaccheo quotes, AI. "We wrote a..." Craig Penn, AI. "For the longest..."; **p137** "People were picking..."; "There was always..."; **p139** "In the climate..." Sylvain Despretz, AI. **p140** "If Ridley could..." Sylvain Despretz, quoted in 'Design for Life' by Stewart Jamieson, *SFX*, February 2000. "the most rewarding..." Sylvain Despretz, AI. **p141** "I had several..." Arnold Schwarzenegger, quoted in 'On *6th Day*, He Rested' by Amy Wallace, *Los Angeles Times*, 10 October 2000. "When we heard..."; **p143** "I heard rumours..." Sylvain Despretz, AI.

WHO WATCHES THE WATCHMEN?

Page 144 "Frankly, I didn't..." Alan Moore, quoted in an interview by Danny Graydon for *Amazon.co.uk*, January 2001. **p145** "the *War and Peac...*" Terry Gilliam, quoted in *Gilliam on Gilliam* edited by Ian Christie. "I can see..." Alan Moore, quoted in an interview by Danny Graydon for *Amazon.co.uk*, January 2001. "A lot of..." Dave Gibbons, quoted in *Artists on Comic Art* by Mark Salisbury. **p146** "You get people..." Alan Moore, quoted in an interview by Danny Graydon for *Amazon.co.uk*, January 2001. "We felt constantly..." Sam Hamm, quoted in 'Caped Fears' by Ken Tucker, *Entertainment Weekly*, 16 June 2000. "Dismal cyberpunk is..."; "I will come..."; **p147** "The joke going..." Sam Hamm, quoted in 'Caped Fears' by Ken Tucker, *Entertainment Weekly*, 16 June 2000. "Joel told me..." Terry Gilliam, quoted in *Gilliam on Gilliam* edited by Ian Christie. "[Hamm] had made..."; "It's really dense..." Terry Gilliam, quoted in *Dark Knights and Holy Fools* by Bob McCabe. **p148** "It was such..." Terry Gilliam, quoted in *Gilliam on Gilliam* edited by Ian Christie. "[Gilliam] asked me..." Alan Moore, quoted in an interview by Danny Graydon for *Amazon.co.uk*, January 2001. "If you follow..." Alan Moore, quoted in 'An Idea Straight from Hell' by Dan Vebber, *Film Threat*, October 1995. **p149** "Alan was very..." Sam Hamm, quoted in 'Spotlight on Sam Hamm' by Andy Mangels, *Starburst*, issue unknown. "At the time..." Alan Moore, quoted in an interview by Danny Graydon for *Amazon.co.uk*, January 2001. "I think I..." and all other Darren Aronofsky quotes, AI. **p150** "There's so much..." Sam Hamm, quoted in an interview with *Coming Attractions*. **p151** "It was most..." Dave Gibbons, quoted in 'Caped Fears' by Ken Tucker, *Entertainment Weekly*, 16 June 2000. "In a way..." Terry Gilliam, quoted in 'Terry Gilliam's Ten Movies They Wouldn't Let Me Make', uncredited, *Neon*, March 1997. "It reminds me..." Kevin Smith, quoted in 'Caped Fears' by Ken Tucker, *Entertainment Weekly*, 16 June 2000.

THE FANTASTIC JOURNEY

Page 152 "I want a..." Bernd Eichinger, quoted in '*The Fantastic* Forsaken' by Steve Daly, *Entertainment Weekly*, 30 September 1994. **p154** "I thought, a month..." Alex Hyde-White, ibid. "The people at..."; "We busted our..." Oley Sassone, ibid. "I feel very..." Stan Lee, ibid. "both delight and", and all other James Legeros quotes, from *Fantastic Four* review, *rec.arts.movies.reviews* **p155** "Everyone involved with..." and all other Michael France quotes, from 'To Die Four' by Edward Gross, *Cinescape*, January 1996. **p157** "We had budgetary..." Chris Columbus, quoted in 'To Die Four' by Edward Gross, *Cinescape*, January 1996. "In retrospect, it..." and all other Rudy Gaines quotes, AI. "The Fantastic Four are generally..." Sam Hamm, quoted in 'Fantastic Four', uncredited, *Cinescape*. March/April 2001. "It's probably the..." Avi Arad, quoted in 'Looking Marvelous' by Gillian Flynn, *Entertainment Weekly*, 6 June 2000. **p158** "I worked really..." Raja Gosnell, quoted in 'Comedy Director Primes for *Fantastic* Journey' by Claudia Eller, *Los Angeles Times*, 1 August 2000. "We expect and..." Tom Rothman, ibid. "It's in the..." Raja Gosnell, quoted in 'Fantastic Four', uncredited, *Cinescape*, March/April 2001. "Bringing this one..." Chris Columbus, quoted in 'Peyton Reed to Reed Richards: '*Bring It On!*'' by Stax, *IGN FilmForce.com*, 26 April 2001. "more comedic, not..." Raja Gosnell, quoted in 'Fantastic Director Signed', uncredited, *Dreamwatch*, June 2001. "He has just..." Avi Arad, quoted in 'The Fantastic Four', uncredited, *SFX*, June 2001.

THE SILVER SCREEN

Page 160 "There was a..." and all other Rudy Gaines quotes, AI. **p161** "We were both..." and all other Erik Fleming quotes, from 'F/X Herald: Silver Surfer' by Rob Worley, *Comics2Film.com*, 31 March 2001.

THE DEATH OF SUPERMAN LIVES

Page 172 "Who is Warner..." Kevin Smith, quoted in 'Religious bigotry. Bucking the system. Silent Bob. Scripting Superman. Quitting movies. And now whipping up a Catholic controversy with *Dogma*. So, Kevin Smith, sultan of slackerdom, do you want to *talk* about it?' by Bob McCabe, *Empire*, January 2000. **p173** "I think based..."; "He knows this..." Jonathan Lemkin, quoted in 'Super Duper' by Edward Gross, *Cinescape*, September/October 1997. **p174** "write a great..." Jonathan Lemkin, quoted in 'Cape Fear' by Rebecca Ascher-Walsh, *Entertainment Weekly*, 29 May 1998. "Let's face it..."; "How do you..."; "[Superman] demands fantasy"; "stepping-off point,"; "[Superman] literally dies..."; **p175** "and some of ..." Jonathan Lemkin, quoted in 'Super Duper' by Edward Gross, *Cinescape*, September/October 1997. "I said I..." Kevin Smith, quoted in 'Cape Fear' by Rebecca Ascher-Walsh, *Entertainment Weekly*, 29 May 1998. "There's certain rules..."; **p176** "Here are all of the ingredients..." Kevin Smith, quoted in interview with *aint-it-cool-news.com*, circa 1998. "I was quoted..." Kevin Smith, quoted in 'Mr Smith goes to Hollywood' by Mark Salisbury, *Premiere* (UK edition), December 1997. **p177** "I really, really..." Robert Rodriguez, quoted in 'I, Spy' by J. Rentilly, *Cinescape*, March/April 2001. "At the time..." Kevin Smith, quoted in 'Faith Dealer' by Shari Roman, *Fade In*, Vol V No.4. **p178** "the one genre..." Nicolas Cage, quoted in *Premiere*, June 1997. "I think Nic..." Kevin Smith, quoted in "Mr Smith goes to Hollywood" by Mark Salisbury, *Premiere* (UK edition), December 1997. **p179** "The studio was..." Kevin Smith, quoted in 'Religious bigotry [etc]' by Bob McCabe, *Empire*, January 2000. "What are they..." Kevin Smith, quoted in 'Mr Smith goes to Hollywood' by Mark Salisbury, *Premiere* (UK edition), December 1997. "under the impression..." Kevin Smith, quoted in 'Cape Fear' by Rebecca Ascher-Walsh, *Entertainment Weekly*, 29 May 1998. "As soon as Tim..." and all other Wesley Strick quotes, AI. **p181** "Tim first spoke..." and all other Rick Heinrichs quotes, AI. "The phase we..."; "His take on..." Sylvain Despretz, AI. "a freak, but..." Nicolas Cage, quoted in *Premiere*, June 1997. "The types of..." Sylvain Despretz, quoted in 'Design for Life' by Stewart Jamieson, *SFX*, February 2000. **p182** "They were trying..."; "Peters was basically..."; "This was how..."; "He got really..."; **p183** "It was just..."; "I still have a sketch..." Sylvain Despretz, AI. "It's not like..." Lorenzo di Bonaventura, quoted in 'Cape Fear' by Rebecca Ascher-Walsh, *Entertainment Weekly*, 29 May 1998. **p184** "We didn't have..." Bob Daly, ibid. "We know we're..." Lorenzo Di Bonaventura, ibid. **p185** "Out of commitment..." quoted on *supermanlives.com*. "I 'made' the..." Tim Burton, quoted in 'Tim Burton Hollers About *Hollow*'s R Rating' by Stephen Schaefer, *Mr. Showbiz*, circa 1999. "We have a mandate..." Lorenzo Di Bonaventura, quoted in 'Cape Fear' by Rebecca Ascher-Walsh, *Entertainment Weekly*, 29 May 1998. **P186** "We are now..." Jon Peters, quoted on *Cinescape Online*, circa 1999. "Attanasio will sift..." quoted in 'Attanasio's 2 Scripts for WB to Net $3.4 mil' by Zorianna Kit, *Hollywood Reporter Online*, 19 April 2001. "If they stick..." Kevin Smith, quoted in interview with *aint-it-cool-news.com*, circa 1998. "Working on *Superman*..." Kevin Smith, quoted in 'Religious bigotry [etc]' by Bob McCabe, *Empire*, January 2000. "have contributed creative..." Lorenzo Di Bonaventura, quoted in 'Cape Fear' by Rebecca Ascher-Walsh, *Entertainment Weekly*, 29 May 1998. **p187** "At the time..." Sylvain Despretz, quoted in 'Design for Life' by Stewart Jamieson, *SFX*, February 2000. "Superman is popular..." Lorenzo Di Bonaventura, quoted in "Cape Fear" by Rebecca Ascher-Walsh, *Entertainment Weekly*, 29 May 1998.

THE SIX MILLION DOLLAR MOVIE

Page 188 "Getting the job..." Kevin Smith, quoted in 'Mr Smith goes to Hollywood' by Mark Salisbury, *Premiere* (UK edition), December 1997. **p189** "Many, many kids..." and all other Lee Majors quotes, from an interview with Paul Simpson. "I believed there..." and all other Richard Anderson quotes given in the present tense, from an interview with Paul Simpson. **p190** "The first one..." and all other Lindsay Wagner quotes, from an interview with Paul Simpson. **p192** "Jim Jacks, the..." Kevin Smith, quoted in an interview with *aint-it-cool-news.com*'s Elston Gunn, circa 1998. "It took me..." Kevin Smith, quoted in 'Mr Smith goes to Hollywood' by Mark Salisbury, *Premiere* (UK edition), December 1997. **p193** "It's actually not..." Kevin Smith, quoted in an radio interview with WHTG-FM, 6 October 1996. "Universal was in..." Kevin Smith, quoted in 'Mr Smith goes to Hollywood' by Mark Salisbury, *Premiere* (UK edition), December 1997. **p194** "And I said..." Kevin Smith, quoted in an interview with *aint-it-cool-news.com*'s Elston Gunn, circa 1998. "I hesitate saying..." Richard Anderson, quoted in 'Up to Speed' by Paul Simpson, *Dreamwatch*, February 1999. **p195** "That was the..." Kevin Smith, quoted in an radio interview with WHTG-FM, 6 October 1996. "They're making it..." Kevin Smith, quoted in an interview with *aint-it-cool-news.com*'s Elston Gunn, circa 1998. "There's this billion-dollar-man..." Bobby Farrelly, quoted in 'Lost in Space', uncredited, *Entertainment Weekly*, 16 October 1998.

DO PANIC!

Page 196 "[Like] trying to..." Douglas Adams, quoted in 'Douglas Adams' by Nicholas Wroe, *The Guardian*, 15 May 2001. **p197** "We seemed to..."; **p198** "thank heaven, abortive"; "It was like..."; "One is told..."; **p199** "and when you've ..."; "I didn't want..."; "And that began..."; **p200** "The material just..." Douglas Adams, quoted in *Don't Panic — Douglas Adams & The Hitchhiker's Guide to the Galaxy* by Neil Gaiman. "It really didn't..."; "fell between two..."; "the worst script..."; "rather distressing..."; "I think it really..."; **p201** "We had a..."; "Suddenly, somebody..."; "In the end..."; "He's a very interesting..."; **p202** "When I was making..."; "Nevertheless..."; "Somebody said..."; Douglas Adams, quoted in *The Onion*, April 1998. **p203** "favourite choice..." Jay Roach, quoted on Teletext, circa January 2000. "A terribly disjointed..." Stax, quoted in 'The Stax Report: Script Review of *The Hitchhiker's Guide to the Galaxy*' by 'Stax,' *ign.com*, 30 May 2000. **p204** "a version of..."; "I finished and..."; "Arthur may not..."; "I think that..." Douglas Adams, quoted on *slashdot.org*, 21 June 2000. "Jay loves it" Douglas Adams, quoted on *douglasadams.com* "The studios see..." Douglas Adams, quoted in *The Onion*, April 1998. **p205** "It's quirky and..."; "unless there's an..."; "The budget was..." Jay Roach, quoted in 'Jay Roach Denies Departing *Guide*' by Stax, *ign.com*, 19 March 2001. "a tragedy for..."; "It's all a ..." Jay Roach, quoted in 'Roach talks "Austin" and "Hitchhiker"' *Popcorn.co.uk*, 6 June 2001. "All I know..." Douglas Adams, quoted in *The Onion*, April 1998.

THUNDERBIRDS AREN'T GO

Page 206 "We really have..."; unnamed producer, quoted by Gerry Anderson in 'The Anderson Tapes' by Stephen O'Brien, *SFX*, November 2000. "I was approached..." Gerry Anderson, ibid. "My heart goes..."; **p209** "Interscope called me..." Karey Kirkpatrick, AI. "Movie executives really..." Karey Kirkpatrick, quoted in 'Thunderbirds Are Go!' by M. J. Simpson, *SFX*, April 1998. "I kept my tabs..." and all other Peter Hewitt quotes, AI. "Pete [Hewitt] and..."; "There are some..." Karey Kirkpatrick, quoted in 'Thunderbirds Are Go!' by M. J. Simpson, *SFX*, April 1998. **p211** "That whole Moon..."; "It was an..."; "The story was"; **p213** "There was another..." Karey Kirkpatrick, AI. "The charm of..."; "everything in *Thunderbirds*..." Karey Kirkpatrick, quoted in 'Thunderbirds Are Go!' by M. J. Simpson, *SFX*, April 1998. **p214** "I knew quite..." Gerry Anderson, quoted in 'The Anderson Tapes' by Stephen O'Brien, *SFX*, November 2000. "I was really..." Karey Kirkpatrick, AI. **p215** "absolute rubbish"; "If you look..." Sylvia Anderson, quoted in 'The Lady Varnishes' by Nick Setchfield, *SFX*,

May 2001. "It's a very difficult..." Gerry Anderson, quoted in 'The Anderson Tapes' by Stephen O'Brien, *SFX*, November 2000. "We did some..." Karey Kirkpatrick, AI. "She's fun..." Sylvia Anderson, quoted in 'The Lady Varnishes' by Nick Setchfield, *SFX*, May 2001. "Somebody like her..." Gerry Anderson, quoted in 'The Anderson Tapes' by Stepehn O'Brien, *SFX*, November 2000. "inching toward committing..." quoted in 'Inside Moves' by Benedict Carver and Chris Petrikin, *Daily Variety*, 19 January 1998. **p216** "That would be..."; "I met the..." Sylvia Anderson, quoted in 'The Lady Varnishes' by Nick Setchfield, *SFX*, May 2001. **p217** "The way I.."; "I thought this..."; **p218** "Working Title were..." Karey Kirkpatrick, AI. "I think they're..." Karey Kirkpatrick, quoted in 'Thunderbirds Are Go!' by M J Simpson, *SFX*, April 1998. **p219** "More expensive projects..." quoted in 'Working, U Working for Canal Funds' by Adam Dawtrey, *Daily Variety*, 29 March 1999. "We don't make..." Eric Fellner, quoted in 'Working Title, Hit Factory' by Colin Kennedy, *Empire*, June 2001. "We've learned along..." Tim Bevan, ibid. "At the present..." Tim Bevan, letter to the author dated April 2001. "they may well..." Gerry Anderson, quoted in 'The Anderson Tapes' by Stephen O'Brien, *SFX*, November 2000.

LOST IN SPACE

Page 220 "It just started..." William Malone, quoted in 'The Black Hole: How *Supernova* Plunged MGM and a Crew of Directors into an Abyss' by John Horn, *Premiere*, February 2000. **P221** "I had this..." William Malone, AI. "It was capable..." William Malone, quoted in *H. R. Giger's Film Design* by H. R. Giger. "[Malone] had written..." H. R. Giger, ibid. "[Giger] was going..." William Malone, AI. "Amidst the hordes..."; "Among the things..." William Malone, quoted in *H. R. Giger's Film Design* by H. R. Giger. **p222** "a much simplified..."; "If the film..." H. R. Giger, ibid. "There was a..." William Malone, AI. "Bill Malone is..." and all other Daniel Chuba quotes, from 'Supernova' by Dale Kutzera, *Cinefantastique*, February 2000. **p223** "centered on Jack..." from 'ER in Space' by Hugh Davies, *Dreamwatch*, March 1997. **p224** "It was kind of unusual..." Walter Hill, quoted in 'Supernova' by Dale Kutzera, *Cinefantastique*, F ebruary 2000. "spaceship gets an..."; "The way they..." Walter Hill, quoted in MGM press materials. **p225** "I showed up..." and all other Patrick Tatopoulos quotes, from 'Supernova' by Anthony C. Ferrante, *Fangoria*, date unknown. "He called me..." Sylvain Despretz, AI. **p226** "Walter's vision for..." David Campbell Wilson, quoted in 'The Black Hole: How *Supernova* Plunged MGM and a Crew of Directors into an Abyss' by John Horn, *Premiere*, February 2000. "I'm told a lot..." and all other Jack Sholder quotes, from 'Supernova' by Anthony C. Ferrante, *Fangoria*, date unknown. "I hope that..." Francis Ford Coppola, quoted in 'The Black Hole: How *Supernova* Plunged MGM and a Crew of Directors into an Abyss' by John Horn, *Premiere*, February 2000. **p227** "a frustrating jumble..." quoted in review of *Supernova* by Doug Brod, *Entertainment Weekly*, 28 January 2000. "We delivered our..." Bob Hoffman, quoted in 'The Black Hole: How *Supernova* Plunged MGM and a Crew of Directors into an Abyss' by John Horn, *Premiere*, February 2000.

ISLAND OF LOST SOULS

Page 228 "I look about me..." from *The Island of Doctor Moreau* by H. G. Wells. "He really put me..." and all other Richard Stanley quotes, AI. **p230** "childish and impossible" Joel Schumacher, quoted in 'Psycho Kilmer' by Rebecca Ascher-Walsh, *Entertainment Weekly*, 31 May 1996. "lines written for..." anonymous source, AI. **p231** "I didn't give..." Michael De Luca, quoted in 'Psycho Kilmer' by Rebecca Ascher-Walsh, *Entertainment Weekly*, 31 May 1996. **p232** "I wasn't really..." John Frankenheimer, quoted in 'The Beast Within' by Mo Ryan, *Cinescape*, August 1996. "I don't like..." John Frankenheimer, quoted in 'Psycho Kilmer' by Rebecca Ascher-Walsh, *Entertainment Weekly*, 31 May 1996. "I actually like..." David Thewlis, quoted in 'The Beast Within' by Mo Ryan, *Cinescape*, August 1996. **P233** "If people want..." Val Kilmer, quoted in 'Oh, Really Sad, Man...' by Jan Janssen, *Midweek*, 14 November 1996. **p234** "Your problem is..." Marlon Brando, quoted in 'Psycho Kilmer' by Rebecca Ascher-Walsh, *Entertainment Weekly*, 31 May 1996. **p235** "He would black ..." anonymous source, AI. **p238** "He's not an ..." Fairuza Balk, quoted in 'Fairuza Balk' by Charles Gant, *The Face*, November 1996. "I didn't like..." John Frankenheimer, quoted in 'The Beast Within' by Mo Ryan, *Cinescape*, August 1996. **P239** "people didn't really..." David Thewlis, ibid. **p240** "What we made..." John Frankenheimer, ibid. "Marlon described the..." David Thewlis, ibid. "a terrible time..." David Thewlis, quoted in 'David Thewlis' by Katherine Wheeler, *Premiere* UK edition, October 1998. **p241** "an embarrassment for all concerned." from 'Few Delights in Unearthly Island' by Todd McCarthy, *Variety*, 26 August-1 September 1996.

SELECTED BIBLIOGRAPHY

Adams, Douglas *The Hitchhiker's Guide to the Galaxy*. London: Pan Books, 1979.

Anders, Lou *The Making of Star Trek: First Contact*. London: Titan Books, 1996.

Baxter, John *Steven Spielberg: The Unauthorised Biography*. London: HarperCollins, 1996.

Bester, Alfred *The Stars My Destination*, 'SF Masterworks' Edition. London: Millennium, 1999.

Breskin, David *Inner Views: Filmmakers in Conversation*, expanded edition. New York: Da Capo Press, 1997

Clarke, Arthur C. *Childhood's End*. New York: Ballantine Books, 1987.

Eisner, Michael *Work in Progress*. New York: Random House, 1998.

Elley, Derek *Variety Movie Guide 1999*. London: Boxtree, 1999.

Ellison, Harlan *Harlan Ellison's The City on the Edge of Forever*. Clarkston, GA: White Wolf Publishing, 1996.

Engel, Joel *Gene Roddenberry: The Myth and the Man Behind Star Trek*. New York: Hyperion, 1994.

Gaiman, Neil *Don't Panic — Douglas Adams & The Hitchhiker's Guide to the Galaxy*. London: Titan Books, 1993.

Giger, H. R. *H. R. Giger's Film Design*. London: Titan Books, 1996.

Gilliam, Terry and Ian Christie (editor) *Gilliam on Gilliam*. London: Faber and Faber, 1999.

Gross, Edward *The Making of the Trek Films* (1995 Edition). New York: Image Publishing, 1995.

Heard, Christopher *Dreaming Aloud: The Life and Films of James Cameron*. New York: Doubleday, 1997.

Herbert, Frank *Dune*. New York: Doubleday, 1965.

Herbert, Frank *Eye*. New York: Berkley, 1985.

Jones, Graham and Lucy Johnson *Talking Pictures*. London: BFI Publishing, 1997.

Jurgens, Dan et al *The Death of Superman*. New York: DC Comics, 1993.

King, Stephen *Danse Macabre*. New York: Everest House, 1981.

Koenig, Walter *Warped Factors: A Neurotic's Guide to the Universe*. Dallas, TX: Taylor Publishing, 1997.

Kuhn, Joy *The Elephant Man: The Book of the Film*. London: Virgin Books, 1981.

Lewis, John E. and Penny Stempel *Cult TV: The Essential Critical Guide*. London: Pavilion Books, 1997.

Matheson, Richard *I Am Legend*. New York: Tor, 1995.

McBride, Joseph *Steven Spielberg: A Biography*. London: Faber and Faber, 1997.

McCabe, Bob *Dark Knights and Holy Fools*. New York: Universe Publishing, 1999.

Moore, Alan and Dave Gibbons *Watchmen*. New York: DC Comics, 1987.

Naha, Ed *The Making of Dune*. New York: Berkley, 1984.

Nimoy, Leonard *I Am Spock*. London: Century, 1995.

Pirani, Adam *The Complete Gerry Anderson Episode Guide*. London: Titan Books, 1989.

Ross, Jonathan *For One Week Only: David Lynch* (documentary). Channel 4, 1990.

Salisbury, Mark *Artists on Comic Art*. London: Titan Books, 2000.

Sammon, Paul M. *Ridley Scott: The Making of his Movies*. London: Orion Books, 1999.

Sayles, John and Gavin Smith (editor) *Sayles on Sayles*. London: Faber and Faber, 1998

Shapiro, Marc *James Cameron: An Unauthorized Biography*. Los Angeles: Renaissance Books, 2000.

Shatner, Lisabeth *Captain's Log: William Shatner's Personal Account of the Making of Star Trek V: The Final Frontier as Told by Lisabeth Shatner*. New York: Simon and Schuster, 1989.

Shatner, William with Chris Kreski *Star Trek Movie Memories*. London: HarperCollins Publishers, 1994.

Shay, Don and Bill Norton *Alien: The Special Effects*. London: Titan Books, 1997.

Stradley, Randy and Phill Norwood *Aliens vs. Predator*. London: Titan Books, 1991.

Index